RESEARCH IN INTERNATIONAL BUSINESS AND FINANCE

Volume 7 • 1989

THE MODERN INTERNATIONAL ENVIRONMENT

RESEARCH IN INTERNATIONAL BUSINESS AND FINANCE

A Research Annual

THE MODERN INTERNATIONAL ENVIRONMENT

Editor: H. PETER GRAY
Department of Economics and
School of Management
Rensselaer Polytechnic Institute

VOLUME 7 • 1989

JAI PRESS INC.

Greenwich, Connecticut *London, England*

55 Old Post Road, No. 2
Greenwich, Connecticut 06836

JAI Press Ltd.
3 Henrietta Street
London WC2E 8LU
England

ISBN: 0-89232-906-8

Manufactured in the United States of America

CONTENTS

LIST OF CONTRIBUTORS vii

INTRODUCTION ix

PART I. BACKGROUND

A QUESTION OF DEPARTED TRANQUILITY?
H. Peter Gray 3

PART II. THE INTERNATIONAL FINANCIAL SYSTEM

THE MACROECONOMIC SAFETY NET:
DOES IT NEED TO BE IMPROVED?
Hyman P. Minsky 17

A MODEST SET OF PROPOSALS
FOR RESOLVING THE
INTERNATIONAL DEBT PROBLEM
Paul Davidson 29

POOLING FOREIGN ASSETS AND LIABILITIES
OF LATIN AMERICAN DEBTORS
TO SOLVE THEIR DEBT CRISIS:
ESTIMATES OF CAPITAL FLIGHT AND
ALTERNATIVE POLICY MECHANISMS
David Felix and Juana Sanchez 43

PART III. EVOLVING PATTERNS OF TRADE

THE CHANGING ROLE OF
MULTINATIONAL CORPORATIONS IN
U.S. INTERNATIONAL TRADE
F. Steb Hipple 65

INTRA-INDUSTRY TRADE PATTERNS:
A TEST OF THE VARIETY HYPOTHESIS
Kay A. Smith 81

MARKET SHARE EFFECTS OF THE
LOMÉ CONVENTION AND THE GSP
Demetri P. Tsanacas 129

TRADE POLICY OPTIONS IN
THE DESIGN OF DEVELOPMENT
STRATEGIES
George N. Yannopoulos 209

PART IV. INTERNATIONAL TRADE NEGOTIATIONS

THE ROLE OF DEBT AND THE
MACROECONOMY IN THE URUGUAY
ROUND: THE CASE OF LATIN AMERICA
Julio Nogués 227

RAMIE: THE OPENING AND CONTROLLING
OF A LOOPHOLE IN THE MULTIFIBRE
ARRANGEMENT
Brenda A. Brockman 243

LIST OF CONTRIBUTORS

Brenda A. Brockman	Staff U.S. Congress
Paul Davidson	Department of Economics University of Tennessee
David Felix	Department of Economics Washington University
H. Peter Gray	Department of Economics and School of Management Rensselaer Polytechnic Institute
F. Steb Hipple	Bureau of Business and Economics Research East Tennessee State University
Julio Nogués	The World Bank
Juana Sanchez	Department of Economics University of Missouri at Rolla
Kay A. Smith	U.S. Department of Energy Energy Information Administration Office of Energy Markets
Demetri P. Tsanacas	Department of Economics Ferrum College
George N. Yannopoulos	Department of Economics University of Reading

INTRODUCTION

This book is concerned with the rapidly evolving and changing economic environment in which international commercial and financial transactions take place. In such a world, it behoves the businessperson to be much better informed about world events than is necessary in a stable and tranquil system.

The heightened interdependence of national economies and, particularly, the integration of national financial markets inevitably exposes businesspeople to the risk of greater instability. No longer can any business executive calmly neglect or ignore events overseas: Foreign events can affect markets in different continents almost simultaneously. True, the financial press now inundates us with information but the information is but loosely-related, if at all, and the businessperson may end up more confused than informed. The need for awareness grows as interdependence makes events in relatively unknown areas capable of making waves in the developed economies of North America, East Asia, and Europe.

At the political level, there is inadequate attention given to the obvious implications of the abject poverty which the Debt Crisis has brought on in Latin American countries. These implications may be long-run and political pressures are notoriously short-run but the developed world neglects such poverty at its peril: Extreme political systems thrive in economic despair. There is a lack of economic cooperation at the highest levels among leaders of the major nations. Despite annual economic summit meetings, each leader pays lip service to the potentially much greater economic ills caused by a failure of the smooth functioning of the global economy and then uses the summit as an opportunity to push his/her country's own narrow best interests as well as promoting a little political capital domestically. In Spring 1987, *The New York Times* referred to the economic summits as *charades* and, while the idea is a good one, in principle, it has brought forth very little in terms of mutual cooperation for the benefit of the global economy.

It is necessary to distinguish among sources of change. The most obvious kind is the steady development of the global economy which results from new technology and economic growth. Here, the major concern must be with the rapidity of change and whether or not change falls within the ability of the national economies to adapt to the new conditions without severe social strain. The spread of technology to the developing countries, largely under the auspices of multinational corporations, has imposed serious pressures on labor markets in the industrialized countries. The rapid growth of the newly industrializing countries under the impetus of export-led growth has also raised the required rate of change in the industrialized world. Because the rate of change achievable in those countries has not been adequate, protectionist forces have developed and now threaten the relatively free trade regime which marked the 1950s and the early 1960s. The second type of disruption stems from severe shocks or disturbances imposed on the global economy. Here the oil-price shocks of 1974 and 1979 are the most obvious examples but no one should neglect the many other sizeable shocks that have occurred (not least the two enlargements of the European Community in the mid-1970s and the mid-1980s). These shocks cause functions to shift and impose severe reallocation (adjustment) on the individual national economies. Any adjustment will benefit some sectors and depress others. If the shock is international in its implications, one may expect real exchange rates to change as well. In contrast, there is the problem of increased variability within a more-or-less unchanging global system. The most straightforward example of this kind of even is the increased instability of financial markets which is attributable, to no small degree, to the increase in financial integration which has taken place. Much of this increase can be attributed to new, improved communications and data-generating technologies; these forces have been reinforced by the development of new theories of finance and new financial instruments. Here, it is necessary to note the practice of exploiting the benefits of global portfolios. The global meltdown of equity markets on October 19, 1987 and its repercussions are the classic example of this kind of change. The Third World debt crisis is another instance of severe shock deriving from increasing financial integration and international lending. Here, the argument can be made that a major contributing feature was that the banks did not know enough about the balance-sheet positions of their borrowers.

Any change in the global environment will impinge upon the activities of individual corporations. There is little that can be done except to react to the change in conditions. Information is valuable and judgment invaluable. To the extent that the origin of the change is domestic, businesspeople may be well-informed. But it is probable true to say that nearly all of the major shocks that have afflicted the global economy have come about as a result of economic/political upheaval in the Third World and as a result of change in international (i.e., *between* nations) interfaces. Such changes are felt in economies that may already be adjusting to politically-inspired internal change and it is not always clear that the political process takes into account the needed, ongoing adjustment when instituting new arrangements. The original Treaty of Rome did allow for the elimination of tariff barriers among the original six members of the European Community to be introduced gradually, but some politically-inspired economic moves have been tailored more to domestic political needs than to any concern for global economic dynamics. Such neglect is, of course, quite permissible in a tranquil world in which shocks and major changes come infrequently and in which individual economies have not lost their innate ability to adjust (so-called "economic sclerosis" has not set in). Recently, nations have been instituting changes without considering the needs of the global economy. Of these, the largest and most damaging is the extravagant deficit of the U.S. government. While such a policy might have been irresponsible in a small country, it is potentially catastrophic in the key-currency nation.

What the world faces for the foreseeable future is a world in which rapid change, crisis, and shocks may be expected to impinge on the economies of the industrialized world with increasing severity. This is a huge subject and no research annual can hope to do justice to the whole problem (even if its authors were wise enough). However, the book does address, in detail, some of the major problems which will afflict the business environment to be faced in the industrialized countries.

Gray's introductory essay looks at this whole question of turbulence or tranquility in greater depth. The ability of industrialized economies to adapt to change, evolutionary or dislocative, is emphasized because it implies the degree to which political resistance to change may be expected. Unfortunately, this ability is neglected by most mainstream economics which fails to consider the process of adjustment in an overweening emphasis on general equilibrium.

Part II concerns itself with the health of the international financial system. Minsky is, of course, the authority *par excellence* on financial instabilityy and his essay is concerned with the underlying theoretical mechanism. The thought-provoking essays of Davidson, and Felix and Sanchez are more applied: Both essays suggest policies which might be taken to remedy the financial fragility which exists.

Part III addresses the evolution of patterns of international trade in response to changes in conditions. Hipple is concerned with the role of multinational corporations and finds a somewhat surprising reduction in the importance of intra-firm trade according to the most recent survey of multinational corporate behavior. Smith offers an empirical analysis of the pattern of development of international trade in manufactures among the industrialized nations, and Tsanacas an empirical analysis of the effect of bloc formation on the patterns of global trade flows. Finally, Yannopoulos looks anew at the role of trade strategies for developing economies.

Part IV addresses changes in the pattern of trade in response to the new initiative for multilateral agreement on lower global barriers to trade—the so-called Uruguay Round—as well as a fascinating study of how the best-laid plans of government negotiators must fail before the ingenuity of people. Nogués considers the interaction between the debt crisis and Latin American concerns in the trade negotiations and Brockman provides an empirical study of the importance of ramie as a means of circumventing the Multifibre Agreement (MFA) and the response to the success of producers of goods which the MFA failed to countenance.

All of the phenomena covered here impose strains on the global economy. They all force adjustment on national economies and provide the grounds for a steady change in the relatively value of national currencies. The danger to be avoided, at all costs, is a breakdown in the global trading and financial systems. The Third World debt problem, coupled with the huge indebtedness of the key-currency nation, present the possibility of financial crisis. Rapid changes in the patterns of trade (brought about through changes in financial markets or in goods markets) can become sources of friction among sectors and, by extension, among nations, and the global cooperation is neglected in efforts to placate local constituencies. Moreover, there exists the unknown interaction between the robustness of the financial system and the prospects of global recession and trade frictions. The Uruguay Round is seen as a positive step although its achievements will lie in the future. Whether or not the negotiations will produce anything which warrants concern by any corporation not in the Fortune 500 or its non-American equivalent may depend more on the developments in the financial markets and on the degree of adjustment imposed by trade between the developing and newly-industrializing countries, on the one hand, and the established industrialized economies, on the other.

Nothing suggests that there is any immediate prospect of a return to a calm evolutionary global economy. There are simply too many sources of rapid change. The future may hold the prospect when each major corporation will require the services of at least one international economist whose responsibility will be to report directly to the CEO the implications of actual and possible world events for the corporate interests. It is for this economist and for scholarly researchers in the area of international economic change and evolution, that this book is compiled.

H. Peter Gray
Editor

PART I

BACKGROUND

A QUESTION OF DEPARTED TRANQUILITY?

H. Peter Gray

This short essay addresses the possibility that the world economy can no longer be relied on to behave in a tranquil manner. If the global economy is to be in a continuous state of flux or turbulence as it responds to first one and then another shock or instance of market instability, national economies cannot be shielded from the turbulence: Analyses that rely on some set of dominating self-centering mechanisms will serve no relevant purpose, and management practices that depend on some accepted estimates of risk and probability distributions will not provide a good basis for corporate decision making. Corporate managers will need to face the fact that there will be signals sent by the marketplace, which may have little positive informational value and which may be misleading (Gowdy and Yesilada 1988). Turbulence obviously has serious implications for economic analysis and policy formulation but, because of the narrower focus, it has even more serious implications for the conduct of individual businesses. Sauvant (1986) suggests that the accessibility of information and the ability to analyze the data very quickly has enabled the multinational corporations to survive without serious damage in a world in which rates of exchange have been extremely volatile. Smaller firms with less sophisticated access to data and which engage in international trade must,

Research in International Business and Finance, vol. 7, pages 3-14.

ISBN: 0-89232-906-8

then, ensure that they have a safe (hedged) position in foreign exchange at all times.

It is necessary to define the two major terms to be used. *Tranquil* describes a world in which individual markets are stable and events do not disrupt markets so hugely or so frequently that there need be any fear of economic instability caused by individual shocks and responses or by interaction between them. Under such circumstances, firms need not operate in a continuous damage-control mode. Another way of describing the state of tranquility is that the natural behavior of actors in the economy, coupled with intelligent government policy, will assure the economy of the avoidance of any serious widespread recession and/or of violent swings in the prosperity of individual industries. These descriptions of tranquility are in the spirit of Robinson (1956, pp. 59, 66):

> In order to separate long-run from short-run influences, it is a useful device to imagine an economy developing in conditions of tranquillity, and to postulate that the expectations about the future, held at any moment, are in fact being fulfilled. This yields results equivalent to assuming correct foresight, without raising any metaphysical problems about free will and predestination.

In consequence, the dangers from sudden economic change and that political forces will be unleashed to disturb and distort the economy, are small. Davidson (1982-1983) has termed analyses of such states of affairs as assuming *ergodicity* and illustrated the dangers underlying such an assumption. Davidson's doubts about analyses that assume ergodicity are set in an evolutionary rather than in an explicity turbulent context but the distinction is one of degree: Too rapid an evolution can cause dislocation which is the major characteristic of turbulence. A state of "turbulence" involves the existence of shocks of varying kinds that either shift functional relationships and cause serious problems of adjustment to new conditions, or engender sufficient price variability in important markets to the degree that the world can be flung into recession or, if the markets are financial, into the early stages of a financial panic (Kindleberger 1978, Chapter 2) by their volatility. Such shocks (disturbances) or market volatility can have their source either in national markets or in the international interfaces among national markets. What matters is the magnitude of the shock (or in a sequence of lesser shocks, their mutually-reinforcing, cumulative mass) and the frequency of such shocks. If shocks come frequently, there exists the possibility that the economic system may not have absorbed the first shock when a second shock arrives resulting in the greater part of its stabilizing power having been used up. There is also the question of how quickly a national or global economy can restore its innate capacity for neutralizing shocks. Clearly the concept of turbulence involves not only shocks and bouts of market instability which exceed any innate capacity on the part of the affected economy to neutralize or to adapt to such disturbances without serious social costs but also an inherent notion of the ability of the economy—global or national—to respond to distruptions. In Leijonhufvud's (1973) terms, the question is the degree to which the homeostatic mechanisms of the economy are fully operative. In any event, the arrival of shocks in rapid succession suggest that no corporate enterprise will be able to operate in an optimization mode in a setting in which it cannot distinguish between price signals resulting from competitor's actions and those resulting from external forces (Heiner 1983).

If the shock has its origin in a particular country, then the degree to which it will be transmitted to other economies will depend upon the degree of integration of the several national markets concerned. It is easy, because of the high degree of integration of national capital markets, to conceive of a collapse or near-collapse of a financial system in one industrialized country having immediate and damaging repercussions on the solvency of financial institutions in other industrialized countries. Thus, the capacity for global harm from a state of turbulence depends directly upon the degree of economic integration among national economies (i.e., upon the efficiency of the transmission mechanism).

A purely Smithian analysis relies upon the stability of the system in the face of individual isolated acts by economic units. Of course, Adam Smith left only a very small role for government in the economy and did not conceive of huge private or public economic units making individual decisions of a magnitude capable of causing disruption. Neither did Smith countenance the existence of highly unstable markets over a range which allowed them to throw other markets into turmoil. Nowadays, governments are deeply involved in assuring stability in their own economies and what matters is that their behavior not cause disruption by accident. The way in which that is most likely to occur on a global scale is through the incompatibility of national economic goals and desires and through governments paying almost complete attention to the goals and needs of the domestic, national economy without any consideration of the interdependence of the global economy. Even if national policies were monolithic and inflexible, the likelihood of trauma in a world of many equal-sized nations would be small. But, for better or for worse, the world currently has a key-currency nation in North America that has strained or come close to straining its borrowing limits, a large bloc of aging economies in the European Economic Community, a dynamic group of countries in East Asia, and a group of would-be industrialized countries in the Third World. If the concept of international turbulence is temporarily defined here to derive only from disturbances in the international interface and the existence of major shocks originating within a single economy is ignored, then any possible longlasting departure from tranquility depends directly on: (1) a high probability of sudden and major shifts in functional relationships in the world economy; (2) instability in important global markets under certain conditions;

or (3) the possibility of a lack of compatibility among the goals and policy actions of national economies, which ultimately induces a crisis: all of these effects considered in light of the innate ability of the system to respond to the sources of turbulence. The potential for *global turbulence* deriving from such phenomena depends on the degrees to which the phenomena are transmitted internationally or whether their impact is compounded by the automatic or deliberate responses in the affected national economies, and the possibility that the phenomena actually trigger further shocks in another category. These possible sources of global turbulence can be examined in sequence.

The major thesis of this essay can be described another way: In seeking for national and private goals, firms and governments can take actions that push the global economy into a position which requires that changes occur so rapidly as to outpace the global ability to adjust. It then becomes possible that seeking gain enhances the potential for instability in key markets. Bryant (1987) has juxtaposed the gains in (allocative) efficiency derived from greater international financial integration with the costs measured in terms of greater exposure to the possibility of international financial instability or crisis. In the terms used in Gray and Gray (1982), it behoves the world to pay attention to the need for "stability efficiency" defined as the ability of the international financial system to withstand some shock without inducing financial crisis and this benefit should be explicitly considered in juxtaposition to gains in allocative efficiency. Note that the greater the tendency for turbulence in the world economy and the greater the efficiency of any transmission mechanisms, the greater is the need for stability-efficiency measures at the cost of allocative efficiency. Some might argue that proponents of laissez-faire downplay the need for stability-efficiency considerations in the enthusiasm of their fervor for economic growth and allocative efficiency. Certainly, much of the global fragility could be attributed to a reluctance on the part of office-holders to impose restraints on the freedom of economic activity.

It may be useful to distinguish here between macro- and microeconomic measures to promote stability efficiency. The concerns faced by Minsky in his paper (this volume, pp. 17-27) are essentially microeconomic: They deal with the ability of financial institutions to maneuver around the regulations imposed by the regulatory authorities so that the process of providing stability efficiency (through regulation of the key members of the sector) is a dynamic game of catch-up and advance. Microeconomic concerns also involve the question of the capital adequacy of the major international banks (Committee on Banking Regulations and Supervisory Practice 1987) as well as the capacity of and allocation of responsibility among the lenders of last resort. In addition, macroeconomic forces can aggravate the fragility of the financial system. Here the huge indebtedness of the key-currency nation that the Reagan administration has overseen in a queer mixture of ideology and *insouciance,* is paramount. Table 1 provides an indication of the magnitude of the problem:

Table 1. The International Net Worth of the United States, 1982-1987[a]
($ billions)

	1983	*1984*	*1985*	*1986*	*1987 (est.)*
International net worth at end of preceding year	137.0	89.6	3.6	-111.9	-263.6
Current account balance	-67.0	-112.5	-122.1	-144.3	-144.3[c]
Adjustments[b]	+19.6	+26.5	+6.6	-5.4	none
INW at end of year	89.6	3.6	-111.9	-263.6	-407.9

Notes: [a]Includes the U.S. gold stock valued at $42.22 per troy ounce. This valuation results in an underestimate of U.S. international net worth of roughly $100 billion for all end-of-year data. (Gold holdings are valued officially at $11.1 billion.)

[b]Includes the effect of price changes for assets or liabilities and of exchange rate changes.

[c]Based on a quotation attributed to Ambassador Clayton Yeutter, cited in *The Financial Times* (September 2, 1987). This may be conservative as the trade balance had deteriorated in the first eight months of 1987 and tourism expenditures abroad were reported to have increased sharply over 1986.

Source: *Survey of Current Business* (June 1987), pp. 39-40, 54-55.

Table 2. Outstanding Financial Assets of Foreigners in U.S. Financial Markets, December 31, 1986 (billions of U.S. $)

Foreign Official Assets	240.8
Foreign Private Assets	881.4
U.S. Treasury securities	96.0
Corporate and other bonds	142.1
Corporate stocks	167.4
Liabilities of nonbank concerns	26.7
Liabilities of banks	449.2

Source: Survey of Current Business (June 1987), p. 39.

The international net worth of the United States has declined by an estimated $540 billion in the five years ending in 1987. Finally, there is the macro-micro dimension that turns on the microeconomic consequences of the macroeconomic phenomena: Table 2 shows how the financing of the decrease in the international net worth of the United States has resulted in large amounts of short-term liabilities on the part of the U.S. financial system being owed to foreigners (as of the end of 1986). In other words, the withdrawal of these assets can be made far more quickly than the U.S. economy could ever expect to achieve a surplus on current account to pay off the liabilities. The prerequisites for crisis, and possibly panic, in foreign exchange markets and the possibility of substantial volatility of exchange rates are both present.

The three possible sources of turbulence (shocks, volatility, and goal incompatibility) can be examined in sequence.

1. Prior to 1971, the world economy was shielded from turbulence by the international financial system known as the Bretton Woods system whereby the United States was the absorber of all shocks. Because the world had a super stability-efficiency system in place (the willingness of the United States to act as the *n*th country that counterbalanced the net desires of all *n*-1 countries) such shocks as occurred were effectively neutralized. But the ability of the United States to play this role was gradually eroded with the passage of time (Gray 1979, pp. 604-608) and was hastened by the balance-of-payments strains induced by the surge of direct foreign investment by multinational corporations in the early 1960s, by the accompanying transfer of technology, and by the inflationary strains brought about by the Vietnam War. On August 15, 1971, President Nixon was forced to terminate the role of the United States as the super-stabilizer: The capacity to play that role had been exhausted by an unwillingness to safeguard that capacity. Since then the shocks and instabilities have come quickly and have had major impacts on the global economic and financial systems. Beginning before the breakdown of the Bretton Woods system, the major shocks were:

1966 The unemployment rate of adult white males in the United States hit 0.6% as the war economy competed with the demands for consumer goods and classic demand-pull inflation set in.

1971 The United States balance-of-payments deteriorated to the point that the United States could no longer sustain fixed rates of exchange with other countries. In August, President Nixon announced that the United States would no longer sell gold at $35 per Troy ounce. The Bretton Woods era was terminated.

1971 The dollar was devalued in December in terms of the Smithsonian Agreement.

1973 The dollar was set free to float as the devaluation was unable to stem the American balance-of-payments deficit.

1973 Agricultural prices rose worldwide and food prices increased in urban America.

1974 The first oil-price shock increased the wholesale price of oil by 300%. This, together with the increase in food prices and the inflationary psychology inherited from the Vietnam war, set in motion a cost-push and wage-push inflation in the United States and worldwide. The effect of the oil-shock was less severe in countries whose currencies were appreciating against the dollar (Gray 1981).

1978 Inflation eased as the industrialized economies slowly adjusted to the higher prices for oil, but U.S. inflation outspaced Japan and West Germany.

1979 The Shah fled Iran in January and the second oil-price shock took place. Inflation was renewed.

1979 A potential international financial crisis caused the Federal Reserve System to impose a credit crunch and forced nominal and real rates of interest to historic levels. The nominal prime rate rose from 11.9% in August to 14.4% in October and 15.3% in December. The inflation-adjusted or real rate (defined as prime less the percentage change in the consumer price index) rose from 2.45% in January to 2.95% in November.

1980 The nominal prime rate peaked in April at 19.8%. Inflation did not keep up with the increase in the prime and the real rate increased to just over 5%.

1982 Mexico was unable to service international debts and the Third World debt crisis erupted as developing debtor nations could not service debt as the industrialized world slid into deep recession with high nominal and real rates of interest on dollar-denominated securities.

1981 The real rate climbed to 10.43% with a nominal prime rate of 20.03 in June. By December, the real rate had declned to 7.95%.

1982 The U.S. unemployment rate peaked in December at 10.8%. The Reagan administration instituted large cuts in personal income taxes. The real rate of interest hit 9.8% in May as inflationary rates fell more sharply than nominal interest rates.

1983 Federal budget deficit in the United States hit $195.4 billion. Agricultural prices declined steeply and world oil prices broke, ultimately causing regional weaknesses in U.S. financial instutitions. In March, the annual percentage change in the CPI had declined to 3.6% but the nominal rate remained at 10.5% so that the real rate was quite high for the macroeconomic conditions.

1985 The dollar peaked in foreign exchange markets at 260 yen in January. In September, the Reagan administration was forced to abandon its cherished belief in the efficacy of free foreign exchange markets and agreed with other industrialized nations to intervene to weaken the dollar. By October, the dollar had fallen to 215 yen and by more than 20 yen between September and October alone.

1986 The weakening of the dollar continued but little progress was made in eradictating either the federal fiscal deficit ($220.7 billion in fiscal 1986) or the current deficit ($141 billion in calendar 1986). Portugal and Spain joined the European Community and were embraced by the Community's Common Agricultural Policy: This changeover was delayed on serious U.S. representation in the face of the loss of important markets for exports of grains.

1987 As a result of U.S. initiatives, the dollar weakened rapidly after September: From 147 yen in September to 128 yen in December. The current account deficit remained largely unaffected although some beginning of the erosion of the current deficit was perceived in early 1988.

All of these events indicate that there can be no automatic reliance on tranquility: The days of *pax economica Americana* are over. Shocks are no longer unusual events, if indeed—other than in the immediate postwar years—they ever were. The fundamental question is whether there will be shocks of comparable magnitude and frequency in the future, that is: Is turbulence now an inevitable feature of the world economy?

If disturbances are likely to have their triggers mainly in goods markets and in national policies concerning the allocation of production among nations and sectors, then financial shocks may be expected to be more likely to have their basic triggers in the next two possibilities.

2. Instability in markets that is capable of triggering a serious economic malaise requires that the commodity traded must be crucial to the smooth operation of the world economy and/or that it be capable of generating

instability in important financial markets. Oil is just such a commodity and the embargo on oil shipments by the Arab members of OPEC in 1973 revealed the price-inelasticity of the demand for oil and the market power that OPEC had at its disposal. In 1979, after the flight of the Shah, it was market forces that created a speculative bubble which pushed market prices up well ahead of OPEC prices. It was this process that engendered the price of $40 per barrel and the attempts of OPEC to maintain that entirely unrealistic price probably contributed to its downfall. In the 1970s, the sophistication and interlinkages of financial markets allowed the immediate shock impacts of the oil-price shocks to be tempered as the Euro-currency markets allowed the transfer of funds from surplus to deficit units to be effected smoothly. Unfortunately, the system worked too well and the intermediaries either had inadequate information or neglected the balance sheets of borrowers and the Third World debt crisis was launched (Guttentag and Herring 1986). The system of transfer worked so smoothly that deficit nations were not allowed to institute adjustment to the new conditions until crisis broke around their heads. Now the sophistication and interlinkages of financial markets may be a potential cause of volatility in the foreign exchange markets (see Tables 1 and 2). Such a possibility must be a key concern because of its potential for causing widespread insolvency in both financial and nonfinancial corporations. (Minsky [this volume, pp. 17-27] argues that concern over the possibility of financial instability or panic is a post-Keynesian concept and is neglected by mainstream thinking [see also Kindleberger 1978, Chapter 1].)

3. The possibility of incompatible targets on the part of the nations of the world is endemic in the sense that nearly all industrialized nations seek a surplus on current account and the reality of the situation precludes such a goal (global current balances must sum to zero). This constraint is weakened by any nation willing to run a current deficit as part of a development plan but the Third World debt crisis has eliminated most Latin American states from playing this (their traditional) role in the 1980s. This possibility of seriously incompatible targets, if developed to a serious degree, opens up the prospect of violent shifts in commercial policy by nations threatened with a sizeable current deficit (Sinai 1988) with a consequent loss of global economic efficiency. The problem in the late 1980s is that one nation has been temporarily willing to oblige the other nations of the world by running huge current deficits. During the time that the U.S. behavior eliminated any serious incompatibility, the world economy functioned quite well with the United States enjoying relatively high rates of economic growth and with Japan and West Germany, in particular, enjoying substantial trade surpluses and much lower rates of unemployment than would have existed in the absence of the U.S. current deficits. However, the balance sheet has caught up with the flow equilibrium and the United States cannot continue to incur foreign liquid debts at a rate in excess of roughly

$130 billion per annum without endangering the stability of the U.S. financial system (and, in this way, the world financial system). It is important to recognize that the United States financed its current deficits, as is possible for a key-currency nation, by allowing relatively high rates of interest to attract foreign saving into liquid domestic financial instruments. The liabilities to foreigners are liabilities of American financial institutions and in financial markets and are more liquid than would have occurred had the United States borrowed foreign exchange by means of bank loans and debt issuance in foreign markets. The United States suffers from "maturity mismatch" as well as from negative international net worth.

The fact that the world has endured some turbulence does not point inevitably to continued turbulence in the future, but there are strong indications that the probability of turbulence for the foreseeable future is high. There are two sources of further turbulence: (1) the aftereffects of the incomplete adjustment to the shocks which have been experienced to this time; and (2) the change in the international environment that now contributes to a greater likelihood of shocks and market instabiity in the future.

The world has built some tensions into its economic system that are unlikely to be unravelled without some turbulent changes and socially-costly economic adjustment. The foremost problem is the huge liquid indebtedness of the key-currency nation. The world's financial system is fragile and susceptible to large movements of funds internationally so that crisis may be forever dominating the thinking of central banks and they may be induced to take quite sharp action to avoid the possibility of panic. Sharp action coupled with an inflexibility in national economies imposes the dislocation that constitutes turbulence. The sharp increase in the U.S. rate structure in 1979 was just such a response and this event, in turn, played a major part in triggering the Third World debt crisis. Until, the U.S. financial system has reduced its liabilities to foreigners, the U.S. financial system presents the biggest single challenge. Here the problem lies in the will of American politicians to force increases in revenues (taxes) on a seemingly unwilling American electorate that is not sufficiently sophisticated to recognize how close to the brink of financial collapse, the current U.S. deficits are driving the system. But there is another problem which must be seen as residing mainly in Japan and West Germany (the two largest international creditors): If the United States is to reduce the liabilities to foreigners of its financial system, the United States must run current surpluses on international account: It must save vis-à-vis foreigners. This requires, because the world is a closed economy, some other nations to run current deficits and to reduce their international net worths. This will be a difficult problem for politicians in Japan and West Germany that must adjust their economies not only from a large current surplus to balance but beyond balance to a deficit.

The likelihood of disturbances and instances of market instability, in a world that is highly-integrated, cannot be neglected. The integration of global economies and financial markets continues to grow in the presence of the data-transmission and data-processing innovations which are far from exhausted. For anyone to suggest that the international political system is quiescent is heroic. The future world supply of oil is another potential source of turbulence. The diminution of North Sea oil production is likely to take place in the mid-1990s and this could give rise to a reemergence of a powerful OPEC cartel. Finally, in what must be an incomplete list, is the ongoing revolutionary set of breakthroughs in data processing and transmission, which according to Sauvant (1986) shows every sign of completely changing the way in which goods are produced and the patterns of international trade.

It is not beyond the realm of possibility that the world economy could regain tranquility. Such an eventuality would require that the governments of the major economic powers undertake some substantial measures to promote stability-efficiency (i.e., to increase the ability of the global economy to withstand shocks). Proposals have already been made to reduce the degree of integration of world financial markets by imposing a transactions tax in foreign-exchange markets (Tobin 1978). Although Tobin does not make the point, such a tax would be better if limited to wholesale transactions in excess, say, of $250 million. Similarly, the Bank for International Settlements has sponsored measures to make regulations on the amount of bank capital required of major international banks internationally consistent *and* higher. But such measures need to go beyond single issues and will require a commitment on the part of the political leaders of the major economic powers that they will put the needs of the global economy before that of their own national economies. The political leaders will have to become spokesperson for the global economy in national constitutencies: The democrative system and politicians' overwhelming goal of being reelected suggest that this sort of commitment is unlikely.

Finally, it is necessary to make the point that a system of fixed exchange rates, a new Bretton Woods era of some kind or other, requires tranquility and does not generate tranquility in the absence of a strong key-currency nation. At present, the United States is unable to play that role because of its indebtedness and current deficits. Neither is there any likelihood of a combination of Germany, Japan, and the United States being able to play that role. The role of the key-currency nation is to act as an *n*th nation that will offset the combined desires of the other *n*-1 nations in the global economy: This requires large resources and a capacity for self-discipline that the United States does not currently have and that would be difficult to instill into a combination of sovereign democracies (Gray and Gray 1988/89).

REFERENCES

Bryant, R.C. (1987). *International Financial Intermediation.* Washington, D.C.: The Brookings Institution.

Committee on Banking Regulations and Supervisory Practices. (1987). "Proposals for International Convergence of Capital Measurement and Capital Standards." Bank for International Settlements Consultative Paper (December).

Davidson, P. (1982-1983). "Rational Expectations: A Fallacious Foundation for Studying Crucial Decision-Making Processes." *Journal of Post Keynesian Economies* 5 (Winter): 182-198.

Gowdy, J.M. and A. Yesilada (1988). "Decisionmaking under Conditions of Turbulence and Uncertainty: The Case opf the Kinked Demand Curve." Paper presented at the Fourteenth Annual Meetings of the Eastern Economic Association (March).

Gray, H.P. (1979). *International Trade, Investment and Payments.* Boston: Houghton Mifflin.

———— (1981). "Oil-Push Inflation: A Broader View," *Banca Nazionale del Lavoro Quarterly Review* (March). 49-67.

Gray, H.P. and J.M. Gray (1981). "The Multinational Bank: A Financial MNC?" *Journal of Banking and Finance* 5 (March): 33-63.

———— (1988/89). "The International Accounts in a Flow-of-Funds Format." *Journal of Post Keynesian Economy* 11(Winter):241-260.

Guttentag, J.M. and R.J. Herring (1986). "Disaster Myopia in International Banking." *Princeton Essays in International Finance* No. 164 (September).

Heiner, R. (1983). "The Origin of Predictable Behavior." *American Economic Review* 73 (September): 560-585.

Kindleberger, C.P. (1978). *Manias, Panics and Crashes,* New York: Basic Books.

Leijonhufvud, A. (1973). "Effective Demand Failures." *Swedish Journal of Economics* (Spring): 27-43.

Robinson, J. (1956). *The Accumulation of Capital.* London: Allen and Unwin.

Sauvant. K.P. (1986). *International Transactions in Services: The Politics of Transborder Data Flows.* Boulder, CO: Westview Press.

Sinai, A. (1988). "The Crash of '87 and the Economy of '88." *Challenge* 31 (January/February): 11-21.

Survey of Current Business (June 1987).

Tobin, J. (1978). "A Proposal for International Monetary Reform." *Eastern Economic Journal* 4 (October-December): 153-159.

PART II

THE INTERNATIONAL FINANCIAL SYSTEM

THE MACROECONOMIC SAFETY NET:
DOES IT NEED TO BE IMPROVED?

Hyman P. Minsky

INTRODUCTION

Although every economist pays lip service to Heraclitus' remark that "Nothing endures but change" or as Shelley put it "Man's yesterday may ne'er be like his morrow," economic regulators and intervenors, and the economists who examine regulation and intervention, almost always assume that the behavior of economic units will not change to take advantage of opportunities for profit or gain created by regulations and interventions. In truth behavior does adapt. Such changed behavior will affect the efficacy of the in-place system of regulation and intervention: The impact of adaptation will generally be adverse.

In time the ability to achieve an original set of objectives by means of an unchanged inherited set of regulations and interventions diminishes. As a result the situation that the structure of regulations and interventions was created to correct is likely to reappear, perhaps in a new guise. Thus a macroeconomic safety net, whose main purpose is to prevent serious recessions or depressions, is likely to be effective for a run of years and then lose its effectiveness; constant

Research in International Business and Finance, vol. 7, pages 17-27.

ISBN: 0-89232-906-8

vigilance and revision of the mechanisms of the safety net are the prices of continued success.

Adaptation and evolution that undermines the efficacy of any unchanging set of regulations and interventions are especially evident in financial markets. No one knowledgeble about how money markets and banking organizations have changed will deny that the effect of central bank operations (monetary policy actions) on the behavior of the economy are much different in 1988 than they were in 1958 or 1948. An era of evolution in response to market opportunities has combined with technical changes in communication, data processing, and capacity to compute to throw into doubt many of the precepts that have guided monetary and fiscal policy and analysis over the past fifty years (Minsky 1982).

It is much too much to expect that banking and financial regulations and interventions that were put in place more than fifty years ago in an effort to contain instability do not need to be reviewed. As Henry Simons (1948, p. 172) noted:

> Banking is a pervasive phenomenon, not something to be dealt with merely by legislation directed at what we call banks. The experience with the control of note issue is likely to be repeated in the future: many expedients for controlling similar practices may prove ineffective and disappointing because of the reappearance of prohibited practices in new and unprohibited forms. It seems impossible to predict what forms the evasion might take or to see how particular prohibitions might be made more than nominally effective.

Whenever innovations in regulation and intervention take place, the behavior of units changes. This can be interpreted as a learning process, in which it takes time for units to discover their best behavior in the new environment. Much of what transpires that attenuates the effectiveness of regulations and interventions occurs because units learn, but regulators and intervenors do not. This model of smart agents and stupid regulators has some descriptive value for the current issues of de- and re-regulation in financial markets. It also indicates that the macroeconomic safety nets need to have the ability to adapt built into their structure.

For macroeconomic regulation and intervention to be successful it needs to be grounded in an understanding of:

1. the principles that guide the behavior of units,
2. how the instability that regulation and intervention is to contain is brought into being,
3. how regulations and interventions create opportunities for gain, and
4. how changed behavior affects the efficacy of the regulatory intervention regime.

The authorities who regulate and intervene need to be aware that economic evolution is in part an adaptation to regulation and intervention.

THE PRIORS

Priors, or theoretical presuppositions, underlie every argument on economic policy and the role of economic institutions in determining system behavior. All too often in economic argumentation the priors are an unspoken assumption of the validity of the Smithian view that if economic units pursue their own ends they are guided, as if by an invisible hand, to generate a result that is a social optimum. What follows is not in this tradition. The prior is the financial version of Post Keynesian economics. This theory argues that the endogenous processes of the economy will from time to time generate conditions conducive to financial crises and deep depressions. Whereas, within the Smithian tradition, intervention and regulation can only cause mischief, within the financial instability version of Post Keynesian economics apt intervention is constructive (for a statement of the financial version of post-Keynesian economics, see Minsky 1975, 1986).

THE COMPONENTS OF THE DOMESTIC MACROECONOMIC SAFETY NET

The macroeconomic safety net consists of measures that will override the endogenous dynamics of the economy whenever those dynamics threaten to generate unacceptable values of specified variables; the macroeconomic safety net is simply another term for stabilization policy. If the regulations and interventions have been built into relations determining system behavior, such as the spending programs and taxes of government, they may be characterized as rules and be considered automatic. On the other hand, the regulatory and intervention system may require some authority or agency to draw inferences from system behavior and respond; in this case there is an authority (the Federal Reserve Board, the Congress) that has discretionary powers.

An appreciation of economic evolution leads to the view that the authorities need to understand the import of changes in the institutional structures and to react to novel situations. This means that economic policy cannot be reduced to a set of invariant rules. The authorities must interpret what happens and, therefore, they must possess the power to discriminate.

Monetary and fiscal policies are the macroeconomic interventions and regulations in an advanced capitalist economy. Although the power of trade unions and the structure of industries affect the efficacy of monetary and fiscal policies, the rules and institutional arrangements that determine these structures will not be considered here as part of the macroeconomic safety net.

Stripped to the bare bones, the macroeconomic safety net aims to prevent a disasterous drop in one or both of

1. the total of business profits or
2. the market price of capital and financial assets in the unit of account (for a rationalization of the use of profits as the policy objective, see Minsky 1986a).

Note that if (1) occurs then in a capitalist country with a small government, (2) is sure to happen.

To sustain business profits, fiscal policy—i.e., government taxing and spending—needs to be so arranged that profit-sustaining deficits quickly appear whenever private investment tends to fall. To the extent that the budget automatically generates a deficit when income declines, profits are automatically stabilized. But if the automatic deficit is insufficient to sustain profits then, in the environment that has ruled since World War II, Congress and the administration are expected to quickly take discretionary actions that will achieve a sufficient deficit to sustain profits.

The link between monetary policy and profits is not as direct as that of fiscal policy. Nevertheless, the rules of contracyclical monetary policy aim to achieve aggregate demand objectives which can be translated into efforts to sustain profits. The impact of monetary policy has typically been strongest and most straightforward on construction, a component of investment and, therefore, a determinant of profits.

In addition to the safety net under aggregate profits, a financial safety net, which consists of the central bank and other governmental endorsing and insuring agencies acting as lenders of last resort, prevents a massive fall in asset values relative to current output prices. This lender of last-resort function reflects a subtextual view that the relative price level of capital assets and current output is the principal determinant of major swings in investment and, therefore, in profits and the ratio of actual to full employment.

An era of turbulence began in 1966, when the credit crunch signalled the end of the tranquil era that had ruled from the end of World War II, and has continued until now. During these now more than twenty years, the two components of the macroeconomic safety net—the stabilization of profits and lender of last-resort interventions—working in tandem have succeeded and are still succeeding in containing and reversing threatened financial crises and depressions. The question of improving the macroeconomic safety net implicitly reflects fears that synchronized interventions that were successful in the past will not be successful in the future.

In retrospect, it is clear that the robust financial structure, which was the essential element that made the tranquil performance of the economy during the first 20 years after World War II possible, was being undermined during this period by changes in the composition of the assets and liabilities of businesses, households, banks, and other financial institutions that were almost unnoticed as they were taking place. It is now clear that a period of effective profit stabilization through deficits and asset price stabilization through lender of last-resort interventions leads to institutional and usage changes that adversely affect the effectiveness of like interventions in the future.

THE MACROECONOMIC THEORY OF PROFITS

Any economy that is investing or which has a state apparatus will have the equivalent of profits, in that the output of consumer goods has to be distributed to those who produce consumer goods and those who produce investment goods or serve the state. Prices as a rationing device will not only cover costs but they will also carry profits. However, profits are of special importance in a capitalist economy, because the proximate owners and operators of the capital assets of the economy have, as a rule, borrowed money to obtain control of assets. This borrowing means that the operators are under contract to pay money to the lenders.

If heroic assumptions are made it can be shown that profits equal investment. As investment is an activity that is based on conjectures of what the future will bring, it can be asserted that investment causes profits. As saving equals investment after the event some have inferred that investment is somehow self-financed. Fanciful theories have been advanced that prices are determined by the need for funds by firms to finance investment and that investing firms have the market power to assure the adequacy of their mark-ups. However, even if industries are competitive, the effect of investment demand on price will generate profits.

The arithmetic result that the sum of the mark-ups of consumer and investment prices over labor costs equals investment (in the simplest Kalecki model) reflects how demand is financed and not an exercise of market power. (The emphasis on profits as determined by the structure of demand is due to Kalecki [1971]; see also Levy and Levy [1983].)

Gross profits in the first instance are earned by firms. The liability structure of firms determines the way such profits are distributed. The first function of profits in a well-behaved capitalist economy is to validate the liability structure, to enable businesses to meet the payment commitments to banks, suppliers, and bond holders that are detailed in the liability structure. Further, the value of capital assets collected in a firm depends on the profits earned by the firm. Such capital assets were brought in the past, and the flow of profits either validates or repudiates investment decisions made in the past. If validation is the general result then the state of what Keynes called animal spirits will be favorable to investment. In a capitalist economy, where investment is based upon the views of businessmen and bankers about the course of particular profits, the maintenance of the aggregate level of profits is the first prerequisite for the maintenance of investment.

If we recognize that profits arise from the simple fact that the workers who produce investment goods have to "eat," then any source of demand for "food" that is not the result of wages earned in the production of "food" will lead to profits. If government is introduced into the economy, and if it is assumed that income from government employment leads to the same demand for consumer goods as income from employment in producing investment and consumption goods then, after allowing for taxes, profits equal the sum of investment and the government deficit.

The critical role of profits is that they simultaneously validate the past, enable current commitments to be fulfilled, and provide both the incentives and the psychology that favor investment decisions.

There is always a question as to what stabilization policy really stabilizes. In a capitalist economy, where banks create money in exchange for business debts, positions in capital assets are financed by complex liability structures, and investment is based on profit expectations, stabilization policy will be effective as it prevents a collapse of profits. A capitalist economy in which government is big, in the sense that it spends and collects taxes on a large scale, is a system that has an in-place mechanism for sustaining profits in the event that private investment fails.

One question about the revision of the safety net that arises is whether the repeated use of the profit-stabilizing effect of government deficits can somehow or other erode the efficacy of this mechanism. In particular, over the six years of recession and recovery since 1981 U.S. government deficits have become structural rather than contracyclical. Has this, so to speak, spent the ammunition that might be needed in the next recession?

A second question that arises is whether operators in financial markets have learned that in big government capitalism, profits in the aggregate are stabilized against any significant downside movement. As they learn this, they can be expected to draw three conclusions:

1. Equity prices can be higher than if there was significant downside risk for aggregate profits.
2. The liability structure of a representative firm can carry more debt than had hitherto been deemed prudent.
3. Portfolio owners can use debt to finance their asset holdings.

Given that the protection of aggregate profits is not inconsistent with wide swings in sectoral profits, the vulnerability of the aggregate value of equity shares and financial instruments may evolve so that the protection to asset values provided by the stabilization of gross profits is eroded. The greater leverage that is put in place because of the confidence in stability undermines stability. This leverage effect is an example of how stability can affect behavior so that the stability of the economy is compromised: Stability can become destabilizing.

THE ROLE OF CENTRAL BANKING

In an economy such as ours, which is characterized by systems of borrowing and lending, it is possible to borrow on short-term to carry assets which yield a long stream of returns. Market rates are often such that it pays to borrow short to carry long positions. Whenever this is done, a need to refinance current debts is built into the financial structure: This need to refinance is a constitutional flaw in the financial structure.

The replacement of maturing debt by new debt is a normal financial activity. In such a structure of financial relations it is normal that during any short period some units will fail to roll over debt. When this happens, the unit is forced to sell assets. This is called "The making of position by selling out the position."

If this happens as an isolated event, in an otherwise tranquil situation, no great harm is done. If this becomes systemic or general then the price level of those capital and financial assets that are sold in the making of position can fall to the disaster level, where for broad classes of units, the value of liabilities far exceeds the market's valuation of assets.

Central banks, deposit-insuring organizations, and Treasury interventions into financial markets are all designed to prevent the need for a significant weight of units to make position by selling out position: Their primary function is to act as a lender of last resort. (The primacy of the lender of last-resort interventions is demonstrated in Giordano 1987). Between 1929 and 1933, the Dow-Jones fell from the neighborhood of 400 to the neighborhood of 40. By 1933, it was obvious that the lender of last-resort safety net in place in 1929 had failed. If the prices of equity shares are a reflection of the market valuation of the underlying real capital of the community, especially when large changes in relative prices of shares and current output take place, then the collapse of the Dow-Jones during the great contraction implies that the price level of capital assets fell to a small fraction of their prosperity level.

Over this period, the price level of capital assets fell much more than the price level of current output, including investment output. This meant that it did not pay to order investment output. As a result, investment output collapsed and, as government was small, gross profits fell. By 1933, gross profits were a small fraction of their 1929 level.

The market value of capital assets at any time reflects the flow of profits as well as the impact of the need to make position by selling out position, whenever the need to do so arises. The initial impulse that led to the great depression might have been the result of the need to sell assets to acquire cash in a highly-fragile financial structure where the most fragile elements were outside of the protection of the Federal Reserve. The depth and the length of the depression reflected the collapse of business profits that followed.

It is worth noting that today's in-place big government makes it virtually impossible for profits to collapse to the extent that they collapsed in the 1930s. As a result of the stabilization of profits due to government, the failure of the lender of last resort to sustain asset values may not have the long lasting effect on asset values such as occurred in the past. The existence of big government means that the lender of last-resort intervention need not be as prompt and as complete as would be necessary if government were smaller: Asset prices can fall and debt repudiation can be allowed to proceed somewhat further than would be wise in the absence of the structural feature, big government.

A critical element in the initial collapse of the stock market in 1929 was the existence of a low-margin equity market: It was possible to finance positions in securities that were listed on the New York Stock Exchange with as little as a 10% ownership interest. The funds for the financing of these positions came from customer accounts and borrowings by brokerage houses from banks; in many cases, New York banks acted as brokers and the accounts were for the account of others. By the traditons and procedures of the Federal Reserve system, in 1929, the Federal Reserve had no responsibility for maintaining the value of stock exchange-linked assets in the portfolios of member and nonmember banks. In fact, we could expect that the Federal Reserve would have been severely criticized if it had taken losses on account of any intervention to protect the value of either stock exchange assets or the bank loans based upon stock exchange collateral. (The Federal Reserve intervened on October 19 and 20, 1987 to maintain orderly conditions in the Stock Market [see *The Wall Street Journal* 1987].)

THE INTERNATIONAL DIMENSION

The new dimension that the design of a macroeconomic safety net has to take into account is the emergence of Japan and West Germany as major independent financial centers. The great international trade deficits of the United States since the late 1970s has resulted in the accumulation of vast amounts of international dollar liquidity by the rest of the world, and most particularly by the countries with great export surpluses. This means that the two pillars of the macroeconomic safety net have to be reconsidered in the light of the new international asset and liability structures and the way in which profits created by investment and the government deficit in one country show up as profits in another country by way of the balance of trade. (This section draws heavily on Minsky [1986b].)

The Concept of Fiscal Independence

A concept that clearly identifies the role a country need play in the international financial world if the structure is to be at all stable is that of fiscal independence. Fiscal independence can be measured by the stock of internationally-acceptable assets that the country owns and the flows of property income. When a country has a large stock of international assets and when it has a large property income from abroad then it is fiscally independent. A country that is fiscally independent needs to be a source of international funds to the debtor countries either by running a deficit on current account or by taking long-term equity and debt positions in foreign countries. In either situation, it needs to be a net supplier of liquidity.

In the present world economy, there are three countries that have serious fiscal independence, the United States, Japan, and West Germany (which may be a surrogate for the Common Market). The stop-go experience of Britain over the postwar period illustrates what happens to a country that acts as if it were fiscally independent when, in truth, it is not. The experience of France under Mitterand is another example of how a country with little or no fiscal independence is constrained in its behavior.

At present, the international financial structure is at risk because the two countries with newly-earned fiscal independence, Japan and West Germany, seem to be incapable of either making the changes in their domestic income distribution and productive regimes that would enable them to be the net importer that their financial position requires or adopting an international investing posture which supplies funds on a large scale to the highly-indebted poorer countries.

A problem that the redesign of the macroeconomic safety net may have to face is whether a regime with a number of countries that have fiscal independence is compatable with the wide swings in exchange rates among the principal currencies that have taken place since the Bretton Woods system broke down. Although the Bretton Woods system was ostensibly a multinational system it was, in fact, a dollar system. A regime of relatively restrained rates, which requires adjustments by countries with appreciating as well as those with depreciating currencies, may be preferable to what we now have.

Beggar My Neighbor Economic Policies

Linked with the concept of fiscal independence is the idea that if a country with fiscal independence runs a persistent trade surplus then it is achieving its domestic prosperity by making its trading partners worse off. If a country persisted in such policies then its trading partners had the duty to their own to impose restrictions upon trade. In the days when the concept of beggar my neighbor had more currency than it now has, a chronic export surplus would have been the result in a regime of fixed exchanges of an undervalued currency.

Today export surpluses are likely to result from insufficiently expansive fiscal policies or an income distribution that leads to excessively high savings ratios. The need for international cooperation may be evident, but if the arguments center around income distribution, which may take the form of propositions that wages are too high or too low in one country or another, then there are no precedents for how cooperation is to be achieved.

THE CURRENT "CRISES"

Within the United States the continued effectiveness of deposit insurance for the thrifts, even though the FSLIC is bankrupt and many institutions are open that have little or even a negative net worth, shows that deposit insurance is not now, and never was, proper insurance. Deposit insurance is viable because it pledges the full faith and credit of the Federal Government. One can of course argue that deposit insurance was mismanaged, in that little or no room was made for depositor surveillance or for coinsurance. Of course we should correct the evident flaws for the next time, but in the current crisis there is no alternative but for the Federal Government to accept that it has to refinance the savings and banking insurance institutions.

The situation with the Latin American loans in the portfolios of banks is similar to that of the thrifts. The loans will have to be either funded or written off. If funded, the banks might very well have to make interest rate concessions and quite likely they will sell out their position taking losses against earnings; the recent transference of funds to loan loss reserves by the giant banks can be viewed as a first step to the selling out of the position. (Perhaps we will see securities with these Latin loans as the corpus of the collateral in the near future.) Given that the Federal Government, through its deficits, will be able to maintain the aggregate of profits (measured in dollars) available to business and therefore to validate bank assets, the likely worst-case scenario from the Latin debt crisis for domestic credits in the United States is that a drag on bank profits may make banks more conservative. Of course, channels for the financing of Latin American expansion will be closed unless securitization fills the gap.

CONCLUSION

On the whole the macroeconomic safety net, in the limited sense in which I have defined the idea, has functioned well enough for the domestic economies of the main advanced economies: The evidence for this assertion is that we have not had anything approximating a deep and long depression in the era of big government and activist central banking. The grim cases such as the Midlands in Britain and the slums in the United States are the result of structural problems, compounded by the inadequacy of aggregate demand due to the constraints that follow from the international capital market. The wide swings in exchange rates, which have imparted a stop-go to the patterns of international trade, have created industrial slums in the countries that are victims of beggar my neighbor policies.

The truth of the matter is that the aggregate safety net due to big government and activist central banking has been able to function well enough over the postwar period with a wide variety of economic structures. However, past success is no guarantee of future success. The new era, in which the dominance of the United States is, to say the least, attenuated, may well see the current regime of multinationalism that gives free reign to beggar my neighbor policies, replaced by coprosperity areas. Historically, when multinational trading and financial patterns are deemed constraining, bilateralism and regionalism gain acceptance. This may be a wave of the proximate future.

The safety net that worked so well in the turbulent 1970s and so far in the 1980s was based on the unquestioned fiscal independence of the United States. Of course, this fiscal independence was used to support income and employment in the United States, but this domestic emphasis was not inconsistent with the promotion of international expansion and, given the fiscal independence of the United States, it was not inconsistent with free international trade and finance. The recent developments in finance, the wastrel fiscal policy that has promoted prosperity by a national binge of living off of capital, and the new world financial order of shared fiscal independence means that the inherited macroeconomic safety net may be insufficient. A likely result of the failure or even the continuing insufficiency of global aggregate demand maintenance will be structural changes that move the world away from the multinationalism that has ruled since World War II.

REFERENCES

Giordano, R.M. (December 1987). *The Federal Reserve's Response to the Stock Market Crash.* Financial Market Perspectives. New York: Goldman Sachs.

Kalecki, M. (1971). *Selected Essays in the Dynamics of the Capitalist Economy 1933-1970.* Cambridge: Cambridge Unviersity Press.

Levy, S.J. and D.A. Levy. (1983). *Profits and the Future of American Society.* New York: Harper & Row.

Minsky, H.P. (1975). *John Maynard Keynes.* New York: Columbia University Press.

______ (1982). "Central Banking and Money Market Changes." Pp. 162-178 in H.P. Minsky (ed.), *Can "It" Happen Again?* Armonk, N.Y.: M.E. Sharpe.

______ (1986a). *Stabilizing an Unstable Economy.* New Haven, CT: Yale University Press.

______ (1986b). *Global Consequences of Financial Deregulation.* Vol. 2, No. 1: *The Marcus Wallenberg Papers on International Finance.* Washington, D.C.: International Law Institute and School of Foreign Service, Georgetown University.

Simons, H. (1948). "Rules Versus Authorities in Monetary Policy." Pp. 160-183 in H. Simons (ed.), *Economic Policy for a Free Society.* Chicago, IL: University of Chicago Press.

The Wall Street Journal. (1987). "Terrible Tuesday: How the Stock Market Almost Disintegrated A Day After the Crash." (November 20).

A MODEST SET OF PROPOSALS FOR RESOLVING THE INTERNATIONAL DEBT PROBLEM

Paul Davidson

The specter of two international debt problems haunts the free world—one is associated with the liabilities of the Less Developed Countries (LDCs) of Latin America, the other involves the obligations of the world's largest debtor, the United States. These two debt situations are, in one sense, unrelated in that they developed at different times and for different reasons. The Latin American debts of both oil-producing and oil-consuming LDCs are essentially the result of the oil price explosions of the 1970s; while the United States debt is due primarily to the Reagan recovery from the Great Recession of 1979-1982.

But in a more fundamental sense, these twin debt situations are inextricably tied together in that (a) they threaten the very viability of the international financial community and (b) their resolution will require innovative and unorthodox policies.

The United States Debt. Between 1982 and 1986, the Reagan Government administered the largest peacetime dose of "Keynesian" deficit spending in history in order to promote an economic recovery from the worst recession

Research in International Business and Finance, vol. 7, pages 29-42.

ISBN: 0-89232-906-8

in half a century. Some of the resulting increased demand for goods spilled over into a demand for foreign goods and services thereby stimulating additional employment and prosperity in foreign lands. As a result of the economic recovery since 1982, U.S. purchases of imports have soared relative to exports causing significant annual deficits in payments balances between the United States and its trading partners.

Conservatives see this deficit as indicative of Americans consuming beyond their means; and, they add, with a tone of moral righteousness, that Americans are not saving enough—they are using foreign savings to finance a sinful splurge of wanton consumption.[1]

Germany, Japan, South Korea, and other nations have been beneficiaries of this increased U.S. demand for their products. They, however, did not reciprocate by stimulating their own domestic economies. If they had, their resultant higher income would have set up a backflow of orders for U.S. goods, which would have helped redress the imbalance between U.S. imports and exports that has developed since 1982. Instead, these nations enjoyed export-induced economic growth, in contrast to the United States where economic growth, between 1982 and 1986, was primarily due to the deficit spending—tax reduction policies of the Reagan administration.

As a direct result of the Reagan administration's expansionist policies, the U.S. government debt doubled from $1 trillion in 1981 to $2 trillion by 1986, while the U.S. balance of export goods and services vis-à-vis imports dropped from an annual export surplus of $6 billion in 1981 to an annual value of imports over exports (a deficit) of $148 billion in 1986. To finance this huge deficit, U.S. residents have had to either borrow and/or to sell assets to foreigners in order to obtain the necessary foreign funds to meet import purchase commitments. The Japanese and Germans have been only too happy to oblige. In the four-year period between 1982 and 1986, United States moved from being the world's major creditor nation to become the globe's largest debtor.

The Latin Debt. The fundamental fact that must be faced is that most of the international debt of Latin American nations is, or will be, in default. The repayment of the debt is not possible in the foreseeable future—and given the magic of compound interest, even the paying of interest on the existing debt will be in default—or already is, as in the case of Brazil, unless additional credits are provided by the banks. It should be obvious that conventional modes of thinking about international debt and the resulting policy recommendations for solving the debt problem have been faulty. Conservative, conventional analysis has not been to resolve or even ameliorate the international debt situation. Instead, this debt is a ticking time bomb that could cause devastation to the international monetary system. There is an urgent need for innovative policies which (a) will permanently remove the threat of default—and the ensuing ramifications on the balance sheets and banking systems of major creditor nations, and (b) will prevent future recurrences of these problems.

In this paper, the conventional solution recommended to all debtors as well as why these suggestions do not provide a healthy resolution is discussed in the first section. I then analyze why trade deficit nations are often incorrectly accused of "living beyond their means." The third section applies this "means" test argument directly to the case of LDCs. Then a proposal is presented that will prevent future recurrences of this international debt problem. The paper concludes with an analysis of alternative methods to remove the threat of default of the already existing debt.

THE ORTHODOX SOLUTION

It is an economic truism that if a nation is importing more than it is exporting, other nations must be exporting more than they are importing. The former nation is running an international payments deficit while the latter are in surplus. Conservative conventional economic "wisdom" teaches that the deficit nation is "living beyond its means" and *must* take drastic action to reduce spending on imports. The deficit nation is, therefore, required to "tighten its belt" and adopt some form of deflationary policy. Surplus nations are not required to make any adjustments on their own initiative.

Thus conservative economists tell the United States and the Latin American nations that they must either increase taxes to reduce consumer spending and/or reduce the level of government services provided to their citizens. That such a policy would further aggravate the depressionary tendencies in these nations, and create widespread unemployment and economic hardship, does not disturb these economists. This barbaric policy of creating income loss, unemployment, and increased poverty is "the *necessary* price that must be paid" for the nation's prodigal ways!

If government policymakers find this belt-tightening politically unacceptable, then an alternative (or a supplemental) policy would be to permit (encourage?) a decline in the exchange rate so that the "impersonal" foreign exchange market will reduce the nation's standard of living by making imports more expensive. With lower real income, residents will buy less! Moreover, our orthordox economist will rhapsodize (with a smile on his face), that this decline in the value of the currency will make the nation's industries "more competitive" in both overseas markets and at home. Our conservative economic expert does not explain that this policy of encouraging a falling dollar (or peso, or cruzado, as the case may be) will, if successful, merely export the deficit nation's unemployment to foreign workers whose bosses will find their companies suddenly becoming less competitive.

A third alternative, namely the introduction of "protective tariffs"—such as undertaken by the Reagan administration against the Japanese microchip industry on April 17, 1987—will not be recommended by conservative economists because tariffs "interfere" with free markets. Yet, tariffs will have an effect similar to the recommended fall in the exchange rate in that it will reduce imports and make the deficit nation's industries more "competitive" in the domestic market. Protective tariffs merely export the debtor nation's unemployment to the surplus nation's industries. The ultimate effect of either tariffs or a lower exchange rate is to reduce the standard of living of *both* deficit and surplus nations. The debtor nation's living standard falls because its people must pay a higher price for the goods they use; the "surplus" nation's standard declines as it suffers from increasing unemployment as its export market in the debtor countries shrinks.

Whenever a debtor nation follows the economic dogma of conservative economists, the resulting policy will, at best, divert some demand from the creditor nation's industries to the debtor nation's industries. From a global standpoint, there will be no improvement in the world's economy as unemployment and idle capacity is shifted from one nation to another as the exchange rate declines. Global employment will fall and more entrepreneurs will fail if a tighter fiscal or monetary policy is instituted to help reduce the payments deficit.

Moreover, if exchange rate decline or tariffs policies are aggressively pursued, then, as the history of the Great Depression demonstrates, the former surplus nations will not stand idly by when their industries lose foreign markets; instead, they will retaliate with like policies in an attempt to re-export the unemployment of others. The resulting trade wars can only make *all* nations worse off!

ARE DEFICIT NATIONS LIVING BEYOND THEIR MEANS?

When orthodox economists state that a deficit nation is living beyond its means, the implicit "means" test being employed is the annual income earned by selling goods and services to foreigners. Employing this specific means test implies, *by definition,* that anytime a nation runs a "trade deficit" it must be living beyond its means!

The fallacy in this "living beyond one's means" argument involves a belief that a nation's means is the *actual export income* it earns. A nation's "means" is not its actual export earnings; rather it is the income the nation would have earned if it operated with the full employment of all its resources. Using this full employment concept of "means," is it true that the United States (or even most LDCs) really is living beyond its means?

In both 1985 and 1986 the U.S. trade deficit was equal to approximately 3% of the nation's GNP. In these years, approximately 7% of our labor force and 20% of our productive capacity was idle. If the United States had put its unemployed and idle capacity to work, the United States could have produced a GNP which was at least 5% larger than it was in 1985 and 1986. Thus, had foreigners used their surplus income earned from exports to buy additional goods "produced in the U.S.A.," America clearly had the resources to meet this foreign demand. The problem, therefore, is not that the United States did not have the means (resources) to earn more income; rather that the United States did not have the opportunity to earn more because nations such as Germany and Japan refused *to live up to their means!*

WHAT ABOUT THE LDCs?

LDCs appear to be particularly susceptible to developing trade deficits and resulting international payments problems. There are only two reasons why any LDC will have a persistent international deficit: Either (a) the resources of the LDC are fully employed but the LDC faces very unfavorable terms of international trade, or (b) the LDC suffers from unemployment because there is a lack of effective international demand for all the LDC can produce.

If the problem is an insufficient international effective demand for the things a nation produces, the solution—as Keynes stated a half century ago—is to increase demand for the products of the nation's industry, not, as the conservatives would have it, to reduce demand. A civilized solution to a payments deficit of a nation that had significant unemployed resources, therefore, would be to develop international policies that encourage additional foreign purchases of the products of the deficit nation in order to give it the opportunity to earn more!

Only if the debtor LDC is already at full employment, can it be said that the nation is living beyond its means (its full employment income) and hence restrictive demand management may be, in some sense, justifiable. But even in this case, the problem, from a global prospective, is that this fully employed "poor" nation is poor and cannot earn enough to buy all it needs because the international market value of its output is so low.

This poor nation is analogous to a working-poor family within a nation such as the United States. A family that is still in poverty, although it is working to its capacity, can not support itself on the market value of the labor services that it sells. To ask the fully-employed poor to tighten their belt because they are low-income earners is simply an uncivilized attitude. It does not make good political, or economic, sense to require "belt tightening" for either the working-poor families within a country or the family of working-poor nations in the global community.

Moreover, belt-tightening by deficit nations cannot be in the self-interest of the surplus nations for it means less export demand for the industries of these rich nations. To foster deflatonary policies on the deficit countries will merely unleash global recessionary economic forces making both creditor and debtor nations economically worse off.

A MODEST PROPOSAL FOR AVOIDING FUTURE DEBT CRISES

If we are to create a truly civilized international system, then it must be recognized that the surplus creditor nations have a responsibility to initiate policies to correct trade imbalances. If these nations will actively pursue expansionist policies to prevent themselves from running persistent trade surpluses, they will eliminate global recessionary forces that can only harm debtor and creditor nations alike. Moreover, the payments surplus that the creditor nation can earn provides the wherewithal for painlessly engaging in such a corrective adjustment. Unlike the debtor nation, the creditor nations always have the ability to pay for any necessary adjustment that must occur—they can always buy more imports and/or give grants to LDCs to pay for the foreigners' import demands. Just because they are earning high incomes, creditor nations have a greater global responsibility to perpetuate global prosperity.

When surplus nations build up and hoard international reserves and foreigners debts—as the Japanese and Germans have been doing in recent years—this excessive demand for international liquidity not only depresses global economic activity but it also creates a future set of commitments by debtor nations to pay interest and principal which are not likely to be met by the borrowers, except in the most optimstic of all future circumstances. If the best case scenario does not work out, as the current plight of the Latin American nations and their bankers demonstrate, the contractual debt servicing requirements can create devastation not only for the debtor but also for the creditor nations' banking system. Hence, there is both the obligation and the responsibility, in their own self-interest, for creditor nations to initiate adjustments—within an expansionary global economic context, to avoid persistent export-income earning surpluses. And if a troubled international debt situation already exists, as it does in Latin America today, the creditors must, at all costs, avoid either calling in the loan or cutting off further credits!

In a civilized international community, creditor nations should be required to initiate actions to recycle their export surpluses through either directly increasing import purchases (as long as idle resources exist in foreign nations) or by giving foreign grants and aid as the United States did for almost a quarter of a century after World War II (via the Marshall Plan and foreign aid) to prevent an international debt crisis from building up. This would allow deficit countries to either earn sufficient income or to obtain liquid funds (without committing exorbitant quantities of future exports to service a debt) to purchase the products of the surplus nation's industry, thereby maintaining a full employment prosperity in the surplus nation while improving the economic lot of deficit nations in general, and in the case of grants, the LDCs in particular.

In 1943, at the Bretton Woods Conference to plan the post-war international monetary system, Keynes proposed a scheme which would have required nations that run persistent export surpluses to spend—or give away—these earnings, Keynes's farsighted proposed scheme was not adopted. Had it, or some variant of it, been adopted, the civilized approach suggested above would have already been in place and the international debt crisis of the 1980s, which threatens the free world economy, would have never occurred.

AVOIDING DEFAULT OF THE EXISTING DEBT

Keynes once noted that when a man owes his banker £5 it is the man's problem but when he owes the banker £5000 it is the bank's problem. The major Latin American debtors together are equivalent to the £5000 debtor in Keynes's analogy. The outstanding Latin American debt is truly the international bankers' problem.

When Mexico defaulted on its international debt payments in August 1982, many bankers and other financial advisors were surprised.[2] Had the Mexican default been permitted to remain, the Western world would have suffered through an international banking crisis as the outstanding international loans were written down on the balance sheets of major banks. Emergency measures for rolling over and stretching out the debt were instituted with the organization and cooperation of the Federal Reserve and other central bankers. These arrangements preserved the net worth of the lending banks by converting a potentially huge capital loss into an actual income gain, while reducing the initial cash drain on the debtor. The hope—and it was only a hope—was that this accounting sleight-of-hand would buy sufficient time for the debtor nation to develop a trade surplus which would grow sufficiently (as a result of inflating dollar values?) to permit the debtor to continue to meet stretched-out debt service obligations. Similar arrangements were then pursued with other Third World debtors.

With the decrease in the global rate of inflation experienced since 1982, and the deterioration of the terms of trade for primary producers, any reasonable hope for such muddling through on the Third World debt problem should have disappeared. When the next major recession hits the United States, if not before, all the Latin American (and other Third World) debtors will find their dollar export earnings insufficient to service their debts and provide for economic growth. If the overhanding debt problem has not been remedied before, the global financial collapse is very possible.

In the September 5, 1986 issue of the *New York Times,* reporter Flora Lewis noted that government and business leaders recognize that "the issues of trade, debt, and currency exchange rates are intertwined." The world is on a course leading to an economic crisis, yet according to reporter Lewis, "nobody wants to speak out and be accused of setting off a panic . . . the most sober judgment is that the best thing that can be done now is to buy more time for adjustments to head off a crash." Lewis warns that "decision makers are not going to take sensible measures until they are forced to by crisis."

In February 1987, Brazil's default on approximately half of its debt service payments obligations to the major banks had brought the world close to the brink of such a financial crisis. The Brazilian default taken by itself can, in the short-run, be absorbed at a significant but bearable cost by the banking community. Citibank's decision to write down the value of its $14 billion portfolio of developing country loans by about 20% as the result of the Brazilian default, folowed by similar actions by most of the remaining U.S. banks, resulted in the U.S. banking industry posting a record loss[3] of more than $10 billion in the second quarter of 1987.

Any further large reduction in the book value of their international loan portfolio could seriously jeopardize the net worth of the major international banks. The pressure is, therefore, on the bankers to induce the Brazilians to resume all their debt-servicing payments, before the other debtors voluntarily choose, or are forced by poor net export earnings, to follow Brazil's lead. Any Argentinean default—with a Mexican crisis not far behind (especially if oil prices decline or interest rates rise) is certainly possible in the near future. The international banking system could not stand a cumulative default of the debts of the Latin American nations. Vigorous, innovative, positive action to head off the possibility of a cumulative Latin American default must be taken immediately.

Both the debtors and creditors have a common interest in resolving the debt problem while there is time—and without the emergency of a potential crescendo of bank failures. To paraphrase a founding father of the United States, if the debtor nations and the creditor banks do not all hang together, they will certainly all hang separately!

Because the debt cannot be repaid in the foreseeable future, then the value of the loan portfolio must ultimately be written off. Will the world wait for a global default crisis before writing down these assets to their "true" (near zero) worth and therefore jeopardize the viability of the banks and the ability of countries to get credit for the necessary financing of increased foreign trade? Or do we devise some amicable scheme which removes these contractual liabilities from the backs of the debtor nations while saving face (and the net worth) of the creditor banks and avoid putting the global economy through the wringer of a major depression and decline in trade?

Why Not Try to Muddle Through?

The first question one might raise is: Why not wait, a crisis may not occur? Some have argued (e.g., Professor Martin Feldstein) that the Baker plan, which encourages a form of quasi-Ponzi financing in that debtors will be provided with additional loans equal to a significant portion of their annual interest payments, will buy sufficient time to muddle through. Although this Baker finance scheme would *increase* the Latin American debt through the rest of this century, given sufficiently optimistic forecasts of economic growth in these nations (and no adverse change in the terms of trade), their dollar-denominated debt-income ratios would fall over time. Consequently, *if* a constant proportion of the projected rate of growth in income is committed to servicing the debt, then by the turn of the century, the debtors might begin to amortize the debt.

For example, in an article in the June 27, 1987 issue of *The Economist,* Professor Feldstein projects that by 1998 Brazil will be able to amortize 1/2 of 1% of its accumulated debt. This "optimistic" forecast is not based on any facts. It results from the mathematical outcome of assuming that the annual debt service payments will grow geometrically at 3.5% per annum while Brazil's needs for external credit grows arithmetically at $4 billion per year into the indefinite future. Similar thinking and hopeful projections underlay the "solution" adopted in 1982. The past five years have not borne out similar earlier projections (wishes) that the debtors will be able to increase their annual debt-serving payments geometrically while keeping their financial requirements to, at most, some arithmetic progression. There is no reason to believe that a renewal of this course in 1987 will be any more successful.

Some conservative economists might argue that if a crisis did occur, such an outcome would be desirable. For those who believe in a free market philosophy of survival of the fittest, the death of some banks is a necessary Darwinistic requirement to promote efficiency in banking. The bankers who made, from hindsight, "bad loans" would be punished by the "invisible hand." The remaining bankers, if any, would avoid such bad loans in the future. Of course, a banking collapse would involve the mortality of some of the free world's mightiest financial institutions as their net worth disappeared, while the debtor nation's cannot go bankrupt.[4]

If a banking crisis does occur, however, it will be systematic to the banking industry and not episodic to individual bankers who have made mistakes. A systemic crisis can bring the whole financial system down. Any cumulative Latin American debt default could just about wipe out the international banking industry just as an earlier biological crisis removed the dinosaurs from the face of the earth leaving only their small reptile cousins to carry on. Man could survive and even thrive without the presence of dinosaurs. Economic man, as we know him, cannot survive without a viable international banking community.

We cannot permit the private sector international banking system to crash merely to "improve its efficiency." To do so, would be equivalent to optimizing the position of the deck chairs on the Titanic as it experiences its unfortunate encounter with an iceberg!

When it is recognized that an international debt crisis is not in anyone's interest, the only question is how to remedy the problem. Two basic ways are:

1. Debt for equity swaps, or
2. Debt foregiveness.

Debt-equity Swaps

Under a typical debt-equity swap, the banks would sell, in secondary markets, whatever portion of their Third World loan portfolio they wish. The nonbank entities who purchase these debt obligations could then present these obligations to the central bank of the debtor nation in exchange for domestic currency (at the going rate of exchange) equal to the face amount of the loan. This currency would then be used to buy either existing equity securities and/or new issues of either private sector firms or denationalized enterprises.

The net effect of such a debt for equity swap would be that the debtor country would never have to amortize the existing obligations. Foreign investors, however, would expect to obtain a perpetual stream of dividends.[5] The debtor nation would, therefore, be accepting the obligation to pay dividends in perpetuity equal to the dollar value at the current obligation for interest payments.

This relief from amortization, however, may be more imaginary than real. Using the Feldstein projection for Brazil as an illustration, it becomes obvious that even in this best-case scenario the Latin American debt is likely to continue to rise until the end of this century. Accordingly, no significant permanent amortization of the total external Latin American debt can be expected in the foreseeable future. Aggregate external-debt amortization by the Latin American countries is consequently irrelevant—except perhaps in the long run when we will be dead!

In return for the release from an irrelevant contractual amortization obligation, the debtor nations would, in essence, implicitly be agreeing to a perpetual drain of income to foreign investors—unless the enterprises fail to earn any profits and management did not bleed the enterprise by repatriating funds even if profits could not sustain such payments.

The debtor nations recognize that following a debt-for-equity swap of any major magnitude, future international bank loans would be all but impossible to obtain under reasonable credit terms. No prudent banker would make reasonable commercial loans to a debtor who was unable to pay back an earlier loan and who essentially forced the banker to take (directly or indirectly) an equity position in lieu of debt repayment. Once burned by this international debtor, the prudent banker, if he could survive the loss in net worth, would not make additional loans without significant guarantees from his government and central banker. Accordingly, a debt-for-equity swap should not be a very attractive alternative for the debtor nations vis-à-vis the current situation where, because the outstanding debt is the bankers' problem, debtor nations find they can negotiate further credits (and even Ponzi finance their debt service payments) merely by promising to pay in the distant future.

Neither would the bankers really benefit under a typical debt-equity scheme. The bankers would have to accept a capital loss, based on the secondary market's evaluation of the outstanding debt, in exchange for liquefying an otherwise unproductive loan obligation. The severity of the impact of the resulting loss on the banks' net worth would depend on how deeply the secondary market discounted the outstanding debt obligation.[6]

To avoid this bookkeeping loss from damaging net worth, Citibank and some other major bankers want a debt-equity swap where, for some time, the bank would *buy and hold* equity investments for their own portfolios. This would permit the bankers to exchange (at face value) nonperforming loans for equity securities valued (at least initially) at the same dollar value. Hence the bankers could, in principle, avoid accounting for the capital loss (or at least postpone it for a significant length of time). Hopefully, the bankers could sell these equities in the distant future at less of a loss than the secondary market's current discount of Latin American debt.

In sum them, the typical debt-for-equity swap would recognize the weakened net worth position of the bankers without offering any real benefits for the debtor nations vis-à-vis the current situation. The Citibank swap variant, where the banker directly swaps debt for equity to hold, merely avoids the current accounting recognition (until some indefinite future date) of the capital loss due to debtor default.

The bankers may prefer the smaller, but actual, loss involved in restoring their liquidity via a typical debt-equity swap compared to the potential catastrophic loss of a financial crisis. Hence, they would be willing to negotiate a swap arrangement. Moreover, with the Citibank swap variant, the bankers can avoid any capital loss on their current financial statements even though they remain locked in to some very large illiquid equity investments. In sum, a debt-for-equity swap is preferable to a cumulative debtor-default crisis. Moreover, it will force the bankers to choose between accepting a market loss of their loan portfolio in return for a restoration of some liquidity, or avoiding accounting for the market loss by holding illiquid equity securities instead of nonperforming loans.

The debtor nations, in essence, gain nothing from any swap arrangement since they are unlikely to amortize the existing debt obligations in the foreseeable future anyway. With a swap arrangement, they implicitly accept the need for a *perpetual* income outflow to foreign investors.

For the global trading community, any solution which does not restore the full liquidity of the international banks and simultaneously relieve the burden of perpetual income-repatriation payments from the backs of the Latin American nations is likely to hold back global economic expansion and prosperity. Thus, in my view, debt-for-equity swapping is far from the most desirable permanent remedy for the existing external debt problem, especially when compared to a policy based on debt foregiveness.

Debt Forgiveness

Double-entry bookkeeping is the way to keep score in the game of "economics." Unfortunately, the rules for keeping score can adversely affect how the game is played—and no where is that more obvious than in the question of how we can extricate the international bankers from scoring such large capital losses on their financial statement scoreboard when they are no longer able to play the game! For it is a fundamental requirement of the entrepreneurial economy in which we live that the production and international trading of economic goods necessarily requires a viable, vigorous international banking system that is able to provide "reall bills" as quickly as entrepreneurs can increase global production and trade.

Under conventional accounting practices, the existing international debt situation will not permit either a vigorous international banking system to persist or the LDC debtor nations to show marked economic improvement. It is of little value to retrace history to see who is to blame for arriving at this situation and to "punish" them. The purpose of policy should be to remedy the situation in the most productive way possible, not to assess and attribute blame.

What is required is some creative accounting which lifts the yoke of the inevitable nonperforming international loans from necks of the bankers *and* simultaneously reduces the obligations of LDCs to what their export earnings can afford. A sufficient portion of the export earnings of these Latin American debtor nations must be free to buy enough imports to sustain a rate of economic growth which exceeds their population growth.

Debt foregiveness is the obvious solution.[7] It permits the debtor countries to more fully use their export earnings to increase economic growth and raise the consumption standard of their people. Unfortunately, the managers of the major banks are legally unable to provide such forgiveness for it would jeopardize the net worth of their enterprises and thereby make the managers legally liable for the resulting damages to the stockholders. Hence, no matter how obvious it is to the bankers that the current situation is intolerable and debt forgiveness is inevitable, they cannot publicly admit it. Consequently, the responsibility falls on the major central bankers to provide the foresight, leadership, and the creative accounting practices to readily resolve the problem without any real costs to the global economy.

A modest proposal to remedy the situation at no real costs to the global economy is for the central bankers, in cooperation with government leaders of the various nations which regulate the creditor banks, to stand willing to accept loans in exchange for stock in the central bank. This would relieve the bankers of any threat of capital loss, while providing them with earning assets. The central bank would, in turn, sell these loan securities to its government in exchange for government bonds. The government would, in turn, negotiate a forgiveness ratio with each debtor nation.

In essence, this proposal would provide that the developed nations would be cooperating in a sort of Marshall Plan where the government grants (forgiveness) are used to retire a portion of the debtor countries' external debts and free up their export earnings for more productive purposes than debt service payments. One would desire, in line with the argument devleoped earlier in this paper, that those nations that have amassed large foreign reserves as a result of persistent current account surpluses in recent years be especially generous in their forgiveness ratios.

What amount of international debt the central banks should stand willing to purchase from the international bankers (and at what penalty if any), and what forgiveness ratio each country should try to negotiate is beyond the scope of this paper. What would be required is some International Conference of Creditor and Debtor Nations—away from the eyes of the media (similar to Bretton Woods)—where these aspects could be thrashed out and negotiated in a spirit of achieving a cooperative global remedy for what otherwise might be the worst global financial crisis of the twentieth century.

NOTES

1. The statistics do not support such a supposition. Between 1982 and 1986, U.S consumption rose 17.9%, while U.S. gross domestic investment rose 45.1%.

2. Most bankers believed that oil prices would continue to rise—perhaps reaching $100 per barrel by the end of the century. (Hence, the Mexican loans were thought to be well secured by Mexico's large oil reserves.) This belief in an anual rate of increase in crude oil prices was rationalized by orthodox economists who predicted, using the Hotelling model of market pricing for optimally allocating a depleting resource over time, that the price of oil would continue to rise geometrically. When oil prices peaked in 1980, the Mexican loans were in trouble.

3. The industry's previous worst performance was during the Great Depression—when for all of 1934, the loss was $600 million—equivalent to about $4 billion in 1987 dollars.

4. In the case of a debtor default crisis, the debtor nations may find it impossible, in the short-run, to obtain any additional credit. Accordingly, it would be in their best interest to preserve their international reserves in a form (of gold or other assets) whose market value would not be completely wiped out in the ensuing banking system collapse. Hence, if debtor nations expect to default, they may try to build up their gold reserves.

5. If the dividend stream is not to be perpetual, then foreign investors will want the debtor nation to pay full compensation at some future date in order to repurchase the equity position.

6. According to the July 18, 1987 issue of *The Economist,* the secondary market evaluates the face value of the Latin American debt as follows: Brazil 58% of face value, Argentina 48%, Mexico 53%, Venezuela 68%, Chile 67%, Bolivia 10%, Peru 10%, Ecuador 42%, and Columbia 82%.

7. The major argument against international debt forgiveness is that it will merely encourage "profligate" governments to again build up huge debts that could not be repaid, thereby recreating the problem. If, however, the previously suggested proposal is adopted, such future debt buildups would be more difficult, if not impossible.

POOLING FOREIGN ASSETS AND LIABILITIES OF LATIN AMERICAN DEBTORS TO SOLVE THEIR DEBT CRISIS:

ESTIMATES OF CAPITAL FLIGHT AND ALTERNATIVE POOLING MECHANISMS

David Felix and Juana Sanchez

A specter haunts the Latin American debt crisis: capital flight. A protean specter, it assumes different shapes, fearsome or benign, according to the eye of the beholder. For some, it is the fatal leakage that drains the IMF adjustment program of any likelihood of success.[1] For others, the accumulating stock of unrecorded private foreign assets means that the Latin American debt burden has been grossly overestimated. Pooling foreign assets and liabilities in textbook trade theory fashion—that is, Country A transacting with Countries B, C, . . . N, without regard for which agents in Country A are transacting—considerably lowers the net foreign indebtedness of many of the Latin American debtors. All that is needed is an effective real-life pooling mechanism.

At a less aggregated level, perverse pooling mechanisms already function well. Recent advances in financial globalization have greatly reduced the

Research in International Business and Finance, vol. 7, pages 43-61.

ISBN: 0-89232-906-8

transaction costs of capital flight, enabling the Latin American wealthy to optimize their portfolios much more efficiently than in past financial crises. U.S. international banks, who shifted after 1981 from soliciting Latin American loans to providing discrete IPB—International Private Banking—channels to facilitate capital flight, have offset half or more of their Latin American loans with clandestine Latin American deposits.[2] Unfortunately, these magnificent advances in financial market efficiency come with a kicker. They are inflicting heavy damage on many debtor economies and, as we shall elaborate later, are also harming the creditor economies.

Spectrality has two other aspects: (1) ghostly allusions by debtor and creditor officialdom to the capital flight phenomenon and (2) shadowy data on its dimensions. Latin American ministers petition for additional "adjustment" loan packages and the petitioned creditor agencies, such as the IMF and the World Bank, treat capital flight as an embarrassing family ghost. In their documentary interchanges, bureaucratic circumlocutions muffle its clanking presence, and it is typically exorcised with perfunctory incantations about interest and exchange rate corrections.[3] The discretion keeps crucial dimensions of the stocks of private foreign assets of the various debtor countries shrouded in obscurity. Estimates of the outflow can be made with at least rough confidence, although not without some disagreement among the experts about the appropriate estimating formula. However, not much is available—at least to nosy academics—about the location, compositon, and yields of the various stocks.

This paper has two objectives: To provide updated estimates of the capital outflow phenomenon, and to assess alternative asset and debt pooling mechanisms. The first part gives estimates of annual capital outflow for the period, 1971-1985, and of the cumulated value of foreign assets for six major Latin American debtors: Argentina, Brazil, Chile, Mexico, Peru, and Venezuela. The outflow estimates are compared to debt increments and foreign asset estimates with foreign debts. The second part regresses annual capital flows on various explanatory variables using single country and pooled data sets. The objective is to test whether the flows reflect mainly interest and exchange rate arbitraging or deeper causal factors. The paper concludes by discussing alternatives to the current crisis containment strategy, including a more direct pooling mechanism, initially put forth in 1985 by David Felix, a rational do-gooder. He now believes its time has come, in light of the bleakness of the alternatives, assuming, of course, that social rationality wins out in public decisions as private rationality is alleged to do in private decisions.

FOREIGN DEBT, CAPITAL OUTFLOW, AND FOREIGN ASSET ACCUMULATION, 1971-1985

The formula we use for estimating capital outflow is $CF_t = (\Delta D_t + FDI) - (\Delta R_t - CA_t)$, where CF is net unrecorded capital outflow, ΔD is the change in the foreign debt, CA is the balance of payments on current account and ΔR is the change in official foreign exchange reserves. Positive algebraic differences between the sum of the first two terms and the sum of the second two terms represent net capital outflow, while negative differences represent net capital repatriation. The estimates are annual and thus miss short-circuit capital movements motivated by capital gains from anticipating devaluations and the like. This is not, however, a serious loss for the purpose of this paper, which focuses on longer-term foreign asset accumulation through persistent capital outflow.

A brief comment on the relationship between net capital outflow and capital flight. Ingo Walter (1986) has defined the latter as follows:

> Capital flight is a subset of international asset redeployments of portfolio and adjustments—undertaken in response to significant perceived deterioration in risk-return profiles associated with assets located in a particular country—that occur in the presence of conflict between the objective of asset holders and governments. It may not violate the law. It is always considered to violate an implied social contract.

This definition would exclude some of the net capital outflow from the six Latin American debtor countries. Since the debt crisis broke, their governments may have become desperate to repatriate the foreign assets and, in that sense, refusal of the asset holders to repatriate and continued outflow violates an implied social contract, if not actual laws. But before the crisis broke, most of the six countries had, in at last some years, liberalized their capital markets, implying no conflict then existed between the objectives of asset holders and governments. Moreover, prior to the crisis, some of the capital outflow was associated with a rise of foreign asset yields and no parallel deterioration in yields on home assets. Our formula therefore captures a broader set of capital flows than would be obtained by estimating formulas that focus only on illegal or crisis-motivated outflows. The formula has been used at the World Bank and IMF in (unpublished) estimates of capital flight and, with one modification, by Morgan Guaranty Trust in its published capital flight estimates. That modification is to subtract the increments and add the decrements to the short-term foreign assets of commercial banks from CF. Because Morgan Guaranty is reputedly one of the largest holders of IPB deposits, its modification seems little more than a gratuitous slighting of the capability of Latin American banks for comparable chicanery.

The formula assumes the reliability of the trade and service transaction values that make up most of the current account. Because underinvoicing of exports and overinvoicing of imports are reputedly important channels for capital flight, we tried unsuccessfully to correct for this by pairing exporting and importing data of partner countries of each of the six Latin American countries, using IMF Direction of Trade tapes. Our poor results replicated those of Cumby and Levitch (1986), who found that during 1976-1984

Table 1. Foreign Debt Accumulation and Capital Outflows of Six Major Latin American Debtor Countries, 1971-1985 (In Million U.S. $)

	Increment to Foreign Debt	*Net Capital Flows (+ = outflow)*	*Capital Flows ÷ Debt Increment*
Argentina			
1971-1977	4,340	2,801	0.65
1978-1981	24,228	17,708	0.73
1982-1985	12,678	5,620	0.44
Brazil			
1971-1977	35,325	5,918	0.17
1978-1981	38,642	6,230	0.16
1982-1985	23,931	3,713	0.16
Chile			
1971-1977	2,828	185	0.07
1978-1981	9,835	-1,370	-0.14
1982-1985	13,898	-1,516	-0.39
Mexico			
1971-1977	23,892	11,901	0.50
1978-1981	47,138	20,525	1.08
1982-1985	17,561	24,109	1.37
Peru			
1971-1977	5,864	1,881	0.32
1978-1981	1,166	-1,264	1.08
1982-1985	3,354	-140	-0.04
Venezuela*			
1971-1977	8,989	6,218	0.69
1978-1981	21,199	19,972	0.94
1982-1985	152	14,520	95.53

Note: *Excludes the foreign holdings of the official Venezuelan Investment Fund.
Sources: World Bank (January 1987).
International Monetary Fund (various years).

cumulative import underinvoicing slightly exceeded export underinvoicing in Argentina, Brazil, and Venezuela, and by a considerable amount in Mexico. Underinvoicing of imports motivated by high valorem tariffs could conceivably offset the capital flight motive for overinvoicing imports, but Mexico is the least likely of the four countries for this to happen. Until 1986, Mexico used official reference prices rather than invoice prices to compute import duties, and relied more on import licensing than on tariffs to regulate imports. This suggests that substantial noise is contained in the IMF data: reference prices, leads and lags in reporting, transfer pricing of MNCs, and poor estimates of transport costs. For the pairing method to produce usable results, much data cleansing would be required.

Table 1 aggregates the annual flow data of 1971-1985 into three sub-periods: 1971-1977 when international commercial bank lending was still relatively moderate though accelerating; 1978-1981 the peak years of the bank lending bubble, and 1982-1985, crisis years that followed the collapse of the bubble, when the debt increments mainly represent emergency lending by creditor governments and official international banks, and "involuntary" loans by private creditor banks under IMF-supervised emergency loan packages.

Table 1 shows that in three of the six countries, net capital outflows equalled half or more of their debt increments in at least one of the three subperiods.[4] For Argentina and Mexico this was so in two of the periods, and for Venezuela in all three periods. Although the objective of this part of the paper is merely measurement, with causality examined in the next part, two causal inferences fly out easily from the Table 1 data. Venezuela's massive capital outflow during the OPEC oil boom years indicates that motives for international portfolio diversification other than deteriorating yields on domestic assets have been important. The net capital outflows from all but Chile and Peru during the 1982-1985 period indicates, on the other hand, that the IMF-type retrenchment and restructuring policies, which most of the six countries tried to pursue during 1982-85, failed in most cases to stanch the outflow of capital. Indeed, Mexico's net capital outflow in 1982-85 exceeded the sizeable emergency loans it received in that period. It should also be noted that in Table 1 Peru's capital inflow data after 1977 are misleading; it reflects domestic dollarization during 1977-84, when Peruvian banks were permitted to take dollar-time deposits paying LIBOR minus 3%. The dollar deposits, which had reached 60% of the country's local currency money supply by 1984, were compulsorily converted into *intis* in 1985, and permission to take further dollar deposits was revoked. The size of these dollar deposits relative to other private foreign assets can be computed from the data in Table 2.

Table 2 gives stock estimates for the end of each of the sub-periods. Foreign debt stocks are the debt increments of Table 1 plus the debts outstanding in 1970. The value of foreign assets was estimated using the annual interest rate series on 10-year U.S. Treasury bonds to proxy for the average yield on the foreign assets. The estimating formula is:

$$PFA_{T}, = \sum_{t\,=\,1971}^{T} (CF - Yi)_{T-t}\, \Pi(1 + r_t)^{T-t},$$

where *PFA* are private foreign assets, *Yi* are gross annual return flows of interest and dividends, *CF* is net capital outflow, *T* indexes, alternately, 1977,

Table 2. Cumulated Foreign Debts and Foreign Assets of Six Major Latin American Debtor Countries at end of 1977, 1981, and 1985 (Million of U.S. $)

	Foreign Debts	*Accumulated Net Private Capital Outflow Since 1970*	*Estimated Value of Private Foreign Assets*	*Private Capital Outflow ÷ Foreign Debts*	*Private Foreign Assets ÷ Foreign Debts*
Argentina					
1977	11,429	2,801	3,161	0.25	0.28
1981	35,657	20,509	23,126	0.58	0.65
1985	12,678	5,620	0.44		
Brazil					
1977	41,337	5,918	4,378	0.15	0.16
1981	79,979	12,148	12,750	0.15	0.16
1985	103,910	15,861	20,584	0.15	0.20
Chile					
1977	5,869	185	259	0.03	0.06
1981	15,704	1,185	000	0.088	-0.0
1985	19,595	-2,701	000	-0.14	-0.0
Mexico					
1977	31,170	11,901	12,033	0.38	0.39
1981	78,309	32,426	39,488	0.41	0.50
1985	95,869	56,539	0.59	0.90	
Peru*					
1977	9,117	1,881	2,363 (2,286)	0.21	0.26 (0.25)
1981	10,284	617	6,579 (1,910)	0.06	0.64 (0.19)
1985	13,638	477	2,712 (2,712)	0.03	0.20 (0.20)
Venezuela					
1977	10,727	6,218	4,486	0.58	0.42
1981	31,927	26,190	,25,681	0.82	0.80
1985	32,079	40,710	52,275	1.27	1.63

Note: *See Note 5. Numbers in parentheses are exclusive of domestic dollar deposits.
Sources: Same as Table 1, plus U.S. Federal Reserve Bulletin and Banco Central de Reserva de Peru. International Monetary Fund (various years).

1981, 1985, t indexes the year of the capital outflow, and $\Pi(1 + r_t)^{T-t}$ is the compounded yield over the interval $T - t$ of a 10-year U.S. Treasury bond acquired i year t.

The results are even more startling than the capital flight estimates. At the end of 1985, Venezuela was a net international creditor and Argentina and

Mexico were nearly so. The U.S. 10-year Treasury bond interest rate in 1985 was 10.6%, about equal to the weighted average interest rate on Latin America's foreign debt that year. Had the 1985 *earnings* on the foreign assets been repatriated, each of the three countries could have financed about a doubling of their imports while still servicing their foreign debt and augmenting their foreign exchange reserves. Less spectacularly, Brazil and Peru could have financed a 20% increase of imports. That is to say, three of the six countries could have eliminated the chief impediment and two others could have eased that constraint. Repatriation of earnings in the years preceding the debt crisis might also have prevented its outbreak by reducing the pressure on the countries to run up debt. In sum, it is misleading to model Latin American capital exporters as though they were merely diversifying their portfolios Edwardian-rentier style. Not only has the capital been flowing from poorer to much richer countries, but the Latino foreign investor, unlike the Edwardian, keeps his earnings abroad.

The CF and PFA estimates have three downward biases. They start at zero in 1970; capital outflow via overinvoicing of imports and underinvoicing of exports is not captured by the CF formula, and the World bank's debt statistics are probably underestimates.[5] The PFA estimates have one upward bias: They assume that none of the CF funds were used for unrecorded consumption expenditures abroad. The PFA estimates also assume that CF was placed in assets whose average yield equalled the annual interest rate on 10-year U.S. Treasury bonds during the relevant years, which may be a conservative asssumption.[6] Thus the CF estimates are probably conservative, while the net bias of the PFA estimates is undetermined.

DETERMINANTS OF CAPITAL OUTFLOWS: SOME REGRESSION FINDINGS

This section summarizes the results of preliminary explorations of the relative importance of exchange and interest rate influences on capital flows as against the influence of changes in domestic activity and the foreign debt. Changes of the first two rates will, according to conventional portfolio theory, affect private decisions to hold foreign assets. However, these portfolio variables also have macroeconomic effects; they can alter the levels of economic activity and domestic liquidity, which can also influence portfolio choices between domestic and foreign assets and private and public decisions to acquire foreign debt. The reactions to the macroeconomic variables may, in turn, feedback on the interest and exchange rates, so that ideally, one should test well-articulated general equilibrium or disequilibrium models that specify the expected interactions, their timing, and relative importance. Lacking as yet such model(s), our approach has been the use of the Leamer Specification Search method to identify which of the four plausible explanatory variables are the more statistically robust and thus more likely to show up as causally powerful in more detailed modelling.

The explanatory variables used were percent change of the "real" exchange rate; difference between domestic and U.S. growth rates of real GNP; difference between domestic and Eurodollar real interest rates on time deposits, and percent change of the dollar value of disbursed foreign debt. The dependent variable is the ratio of capital outflow to the export of goods and nonfinancial services. The essence of the Leamer method, described in more detail in the Appendix, is to regress the dependent variable on all possible combinations of the explanatory variables in order to identify those that are statistically robust, that is, whose cofficient values stay within a moderate range and remain statistically significant over the various regressions.

The data, all annual, are described in the Appendix. Here it suffices to mention that, except for the interest rate variable, the data cover 1971-1985 for all six countries. We could find reasonably homogeneous domestic interest rate series covering that entire time span for only three of the countries. This still left us with ample observations, 78, for applying the Leamer method to pooled data, but restricted its applicability as regards individual country regressions.

Table 3 reports the best of the pooled regressions—highest F-value and R^2—from each of four groups of regression runs. Of the four regressions in Group IV, run separately on each of the four explanatory variables, the best, as indicated, is the debt increment regression. Group III contains six regressions on pairs of the four variables. As indicated, the regression on the macro variable pair, that is, the debt increment and the change of the GNP growth ratio, dominated the five remaining regressions, each of which contains one or both of the portfolio variables. Of the four regressions on triplets of the explanatory variables in Group II, the debt, GNP, and interest rate triplet was, as reported in Table 3, the best. Finally, Group I consists of two regressions, each run on all four explanatory variables, but with different definitions of the debt variable. In the best regression, reported in Table 3, only the debt variable is statistically significant (along with two of the country dummies). Debt in this case is the sum of public and private, short and long-term disbursed debt. In the alternative regression, debt is merely public and publicly guaranteed long-term disbursed debt. This narrower definition of debt also produced inferior results in the other three groups of regressions.

A strong, positive relationship between increases of debt and increases of capital flight thus dominated in all of the pooled regressions. The positive relationship between the U.S./debtor country GNP growth ratio and capital flight was a weak second best, the weakness indicated by the large spread between its minimum and maximum coefficient values shown in Appendix Table A-2. Bringing up the rear are the interest rate and exchange rate variables,

Table 3. Best Regressions of Capital Outflow/Exports[a] on Pooled Data, 1971-1985

				Explanatory Variables							
Debt Increment	*Change Exchange Rate (%)*	*Change US/Debtor GNP Growth Rates (%)*	*Change Euro/Debtor Real Interest Rates (%)*	*Intercept Dummies: Argentina*	*Brazil*	*Chile*	*Mexico*	*Peru*	*Venezuela*	*F-Values*	*Adjusted* R^2
I. 0.438***	0.056	0.595	0.044	12.416	-6.528	-18.357**	9.159	-7.352*	8.955*	5.463***	0.343
(3.865)	(1.275)	(1.450)	(1.497)	(1.550)	(-0.970)	(-2,594)	(1.433)	(-1.850)	(1.820)		
II. 0.432***		0.689*	0.045	13.339*	-5.836	-17.587**	9.634	-7.330	9.216*	5.889***	0.337
(3.797)		(1.697)	(1.553)	(1.665)	(-0.866)	(-2.484)	(1.503)	(-1.112)	(1.857)		
III. 0.446***		0.791**		13.805*	-4.759	-13.692**	10.270	-5.696	8.968*	6.259***	0.3235
(3.894)		(1.957)		(1.707)	(0.703)	(-2.047)	(1.590)	(-0.867)	(1.790)		
IV. 0.396***				16.984**	-8.085	-13.588**	8.174	-6.253	10.211**	6.408***	0.2965
(3.479)				(2.102)	(-1.210)	(-1.992)	(1.258)	(-0.934)	(2.016)		

Notes: Observations = 78.

[a]Exports include nonfinancial services.

* = 10% significance.

** = 5% significance.

*** = 1% significance.

in that order. Finally, the coefficient ranges for many of the country dummies in Table A-2 are quite wide, but all the dummy signs conform to expectation. The three heavy capital flight countries have positive coefficients, while the low to moderate capital flight countries have negative ones.

A strong debt-capital outflow relationship has also been uncovered by other recent studies (e.g., see Cuddington 1985, p. 51). The finding supports the current complaints of creditor banks, reluctant to throw in more "involuntary" loans under the IMF adjustment programs, that most of the new loans flow out again as capital flight. The why of the relationship is, however, an unsettled question. Does increased foreign borrowing motivate more capital outflow or vice versa? Vice versa would imply that the governments reacted to the worsening of foreign exchange shortages due to the acceleration of capital flight by increasing their foreign borrowing. The distinctly poorer results we obtained from using government and government debt in place of total disbursed debt would seem to reject this hypothesis, not conclusively, however, since we had to use distorted government debt data. We could not get reliable data on government short-term debt, although the informal evidence is that short-term debt rose considerably at the peak of the foreign borrowing binge. In addition, much of the increase of long-term government debt since 1982 represents merely an accounting transfer, as most debtor governments were forced by the creditor banks and governments to take ex post responsibility for uncollectable private debts as a condition for getting "involuntary" banks loans under the IMF adjustment programs.

The regressions also provide only moderate support for the hypothesis that the retarding effects on capital flight of devaluation and higher real interest rates were more than offset by the depressing macroeconomic consequences of devaluation and higher real interest rates. We interpret this to indicate need to test the hypothesis further on more fully articulated structural models.

A recent article by two IMF economists, offers a model that gives a simple explanation of the positive debt-capital outflow relationship (Khan and Haque 1985). The model is of a one sector, one person, two-period private economy (representative consumer and investor combined) harassed by a sinister government, that is continuously intent on expropriating the private investor. Therefore, he wisely puts some of his wealth abroad and also borrows abroad for domestic investment in order to make his portfolio less accessible and attractive for expropriation. Khan and Haque define expropriation as "any differences between the foreign and home countries in formal taxation, possibilities of confiscation, destruction of private property, changes in politcal and economic regime and so on" (p. 618), which seems much too vague to be analytically useful. This does not deter them from drawing the tautological policy conclusion from their model that if the debtor governments cease doing all those things that cause the private investor to borrow and invest abroad concurrently, he will bring back his foreign assets and curb his foreign borrowing. The model does not fit most of the Latin American cases, where the chief borrower has been the sinister government. It might help explain why Chile is the outlier in our capital flight statistics: the benign Pinochet regime. But the authors spoil that possibility by excluding debt payment crises by assumption from their model (only willful repudiation is allowed). Protection again "expropriation" broadly defined has not prevented private foreign borrowing, largely to feed the Chilean investor's consumption and speculative habits, from plunging Chile into a massive debt crisis requiring the government to socialize the debt.

Clearly, sharper modelling, econometric testing, and tighter findings are needed and will no doubt eventually come forth—most of it after the debt crisis is resolved by actions based on more ad hoc analyses. Meanwhile the offsetting of new debt by new capital outflow remains a major feature of the debt crisis, and the swapping of foreign debt for foreign assets remains a potential solution to that crisis. This bring us to the concluding setion of this paper which analyzes the policy choices ad hocishly.

ALTERNATIVES TO THE CURRENT DEBT CRISIS CONTAINMENT STRATEGY

Latin American debtor countries are trapped in interconnected gridlocks. Sustained revival of economic growth requires a rising flow of imports, but the requisite inflow—higher if the debtors pursue the import-liberalizing, export-oriented strategies urged on them by their creditors—is blocked by the burden of debt services, the near drying-up of foreign loans, the slow economic growth of the creditors, and, for most of the debtors, ongoing capital flight. Repatriating foreign assets, or merely their yields, would lower and, in many cases, eliminate the import financing barrier; directly by augmenting earned foreign exchange and indirectly by reviving the international creditworthiness of the debtors. But inducing repatriation by a sustained improvement of the yield-risk profiles of home assets, or by tightening home credit to generate cash flow shortages sufficient to force some liquidation of foreign holdings, faces Catch 22 dilemmas. Improving yield-risk profiles requires prior improvement of growth prospects, which depends in part on prior reduction of the foreign exchange barrier to revived growth. Forcing repatriation through a liquidity crunch would further depress the real economy and totter the fragile financial structures of the debtors, thereby worsening yield-risk profiles and strengthening the safe-haven motive for capital flight.

The crisis containment strategy of the creditors, orchestrated by the United States in 1982, with the IMF as guest conductor, was intended to restore economic growth and the debt-servicing capability of the debtors within a 3- to 4-year time frame. Now, six years into the crisis with no end in sight, that strategy has become enmeshed in its own gridlock. Political rumblings *a crescendo* are forcing debtor governments to intensify demands for concessionary refinancing or else—the implied threat being unilateral defaulting. This strengthens the reluctance of less exposed lending banks to "throw more good money after bad" as required by the involuntary loan packages. Forced by syndicate defections to assume a rising share of the new involuntary loans, the heavily exposed creditor banks are digging in against further concessions (Truell 1987). Squeezed between rising debtor demands and bank intransigence, the crucial involuntary bank loan component of the crisis containment strategy is in danger of collapse (Pine 1987).

Short of open unilateral default, which the containment strategy was designed to prevent, what alternatives remain? The literature has focused on two: (1) debt-equity exchanges and (2) writing off a substantial part of the debt with the loss shared between the banks and taxpayers of the creditor countries. It is beyond the scope of this paper to explore the many variants of each alternative. But as part of the *mise en scene* for introducing our less-publicized but preferred alternative, it is useful to show the general limitations of the more publicized ones. These are that applied moderately, they would provide inadequate debt relief; applied on a large scale, the immediate debt relief might be substantial but the political cost would be too high.

Consider debt-equity swaps. They require reducing the dollar purchase prices of domestic debtor assets to make swapping attractive. The swaps, to date, have been achieved because asset purchases can be made with discounted bank loan paper obtained in resale markets for such paper. Brazilian paper in Fall 1986 sold at a 25% discount; Chilean, Argentinian, Mexican, and Peruvian paper at discounts, respectively, of 33, 35, 43, and 78%.[7] These large discounts can be interpreted as a financial market judgment that the underlying premise of the current debt strategy is false; the debtors are more than illiquid, they are insolvent. The discounted paper has drawn buyers because it can be resold at near face value for local currency at favorable exchange rates using special central bank facilities of the debtor countries. For multinational firms, the swaps are a cheaper way of financing investments in the debtor countries, so that some of the debt-equity swapping merely reduces FDI in our capital flow formula. The rest, however, may represent added capital inflow, for example, by foreigners and nationals with foreign funds who find purchasing local assets or paying local debts at the cheapened dollar costs attractive. The total dollar amount swapped thus far has, however, been much less than the Latin American debt increments.

This is because the secondary market for Latin American debt has been thin, mainly supplied by banks with low enough Latin American exposure to be able to defect from their loan syndicates and absorb the moderate losses from unloading their Latin American paper,[8] the debt-equity swaps could no doubt rise, but not necessarily the net inflow of foreign exchange to the debtors, because Δ D in our capital flow formula would also shrink. Banks liquidating their Latin American loans could hardly be expected to agree to new involuntary loans, neither is it likely that levelling or reducing their foreign debt by swapping heavily-discounted debt for equity would restore access by the debtor countries to voluntary bank loans. The 1930s Latin American bond defaults were settled with major writedowns that left the debtor countries in 1950 virtually free of foreign debt, but also virtually unable ever since to float new securities in foreign bond markets. In sum, market-based swaps are likely to bring no more than modest debt relief.

More expansive debt-equity swaps involving the sale of major government assets—oil companies, public utilities, steel mills, and so forth—have been proposed. The barely hidden agenda here is to use debt relief to force privatization on the debtor economies, although paradoxically such schemes would necessarily transform debt-equity swapping from a predominantly private to a predominantly intergovernmental transaction. The dollar amounts would rise substantially, but so would the political and financial terms demanded of the debtor governments by the creditors to ensure the long-run profitability and safety of the sizeable assets to be acquired by their foreign investors. Accordingly, debtor governments, however demoralized by the prolonged debt crisis, have thus far shown little enthusiasm for large-scale swap proposals.

They have, however, been enthused by proposals that call for creditors to writedown principal and/or interest, the losses to be shared between banks and taxpayers of the creditor countries. In the creditor countries, the political appeal of such proposals hovers around -60° Celsius, but debtor circles apparently hope the temperature can be raised above freezing by repetitive two-part chorusing: plaintive pleas to creditor humanitarianism and geopolitical concerns over a rumbling continuo of default threats.[9] Were unfreezing to occur, however, the writedowns would undoubtedly come with major restrictions on current and future economic policies of the debtors. Imposed to protect the creditors against moral hazard misbehavior by present and future debtor governments, the policy restrictions would also be shaped by the ideological fantasies and geopolitical perspectives fashionable in Washington, not in the debtor capitals, at the time the proposals were activated. Latin American enthusiasts for major debt writeoffs are usually critics of the IMF adjustment policies and of the close IMF policy monitoring imposed by the short-term emergency loan packages of the current debt containment strategy. Yet they assume, in a strange flight from reality, that they can extract long-term debt writedowns that reduce rather than intensify creditor meddling in their domestic decision making.

This takes us to our preferred alternative: Swaps by debtors of their foreign debt for their foreign assets. Table 2 indicates that even swapping of half their debts would put Argentina, Mexico and Venezuela well along the road to economic recovery and moderately ease the economic travail of Peru and Brazil. In 1985, the senior author (Felix 1985) presented a swap proposal in a paper originally given the Swiftian title, "A Modest Proposal to . . . ." This was to show that the intent was mainly to shock readers into greater awareness of a major scandal—in this case, capital flight, which, until 1985, received even more shadowy treatment in the debt literature than today. However, in the light of the unpleasant alternatives surveyed in the present paper, the proposal may now merit a promotion from "modest" to "desperate but serious."

The proposal is to combine a unilateral cap, Peruvian-style, on the percentage of export receipts devoted by the debtor country to servicing its debt with a compulsory exchange of foreign private assets for negotiable domestic currency bonds. The mobilized foreign assets would be escrowed abroad to meet the unpaid annual debt service and to collateralize the foreign debt. Such socializing of private foreign assets to cover foreign debts is merely the counterpart of the socialization of private foreign debts which the creditor banks with the acquiescence of the IMF have imposed on the debtors in the current crisis. It also has historic precedent in the French compulsory asset mobilization during World War I and the British mobilizations during World Wars I and II.

The precedents, however, only strengthen the legitimacy of mobilizing private foreign assets in dire emergencies, not its practicality. Because the French and British obtained reasonably good compliance from their nationals is no assurance that Latin American nationals steeped in the tradition of "obedecer pero no cumplir" will rush to comply. The proposal calls, therefore, for the collaboration of creditor banks and governments in identifying the foreign assets. The cap on payments from exports is the stick and the escrowing of the mobilized foreign assets is the carrot for inducing collaboration. The cap means partial default; escrowing means collateralizing an otherwise uncollectable debt.

There are many details to be worked out: minimum exemptions on foreign asset conversion to reduce enforcement costs, conversion premia to facilitate compliance, maturity schedules on the domestic bonds to minimize monetary disorder, and so forth. They do not, in any event, gainsay the fact that the proposal offers a positive sum solution to the debt crisis. There are major potential gains in it for both debtor and creditor countries.

For the debtor, the gains include the following. At a minimum, the cap on debt service from exports raises the capacity to import, while the mobilization and escrowing effort, even were it largely ineffective, would still serve as a moral and quasi-legal shield against reprisal by the creditors, should they refuse to collaborate. With collaboration, the effectiveness and the benefits mount. Servicing the debt without writedowns revives the international creditworthiness of the debtors. The negotiable domestic currency bonds create a local market for subsequent issues of long-term government securities. In conjunction with the heightened transactions costs of future capital flight, this substantially broadens the policy space for autonomous monetary-fiscal policies. Successful asset mobilization brings political gains from the more equitable sharing of the debt burden between rich and poor than has been characteristic of IMF adjustment policy packages, while liberation from creditor tutelage of domestic economic policy boosts national morale.

For the creditors, collateralizing Latin American loans strengthens the balance sheets of their banks, an especially timely boon to the overexposed and shaky U.S. banking system. The augmented capacity to import of the debtors and the consequent revival of their economic growth elevates creditor exports and reduces immiserating export competition from debtors desperate for foreign exchange.[10] Collaboration of the creditors in the foreign asset mobilization efforts weakens their role as safe havens for flight capital, allowing the exchange rate, less buffeted by skittish capital movements, to improve its effectiveness as a regulator of trade flows.

The last "benefit" merits brief elaboration, as it is both controversial and important. Observe that the enormous expansion of international financial flows associated with the liberalization and globalization of financial markets since the 1960s has been paralleled by a prolonged slackening of rates of growth of the volume of world output and trade. The parallelism suggests that rather than being a major advance in international allocative efficiency, rapid financial globalization may be a disruptive force. This view is quite compatable with serious economic theory, which accepts that bubbles and breakdowns are logical possibilities inherent in the unavoidable incompleteness of unregulated financial markets. It is also consistent with the view that a necessary if not sufficient requirement for bounding the instability of financial markets is the existence of an outside "lender of last resort," capable of countervailing interventions in emergency and of regulating financial agents against moral hazard excesses during more quiescent periods. The erosion of Britain's power to be the prime international lender of last resort after World War I and the futile efforts of the G-3 of the 1920s to coordinate their financial policies contributed to the international financial collapse of the 1930s. The analogy with the present is obvious. But it may still be possible to salvage the better half of post-World War II international economic liberalism, the multilateral and relatively free commodity trading rules, from disintegration by restraining financial globalism. Redirecting finance toward productive activities, by reviving economic growth, could defuse demands for trade protection. The compulsory asset-debt exchange requires considerable political courage of debtor governments, but considering the bleak alternatives, the courage of desperation could yet carry the day. The potential benefits to the debtor economies are high. And it is not often given to weak peripheral economies to pull themselves out of a desperate crisis by policies that also crucially benefit the capitalist-center countries.

APPENDIX

A Leamer specification search and reporting style consists, broadly speaking, of running all possible regressions with a set of regressors and reporting the bounds obtained for each regressor's coefficient across all model specifications. This methodology is suggested in cases in which economic theory considers some variables as relevant—the so-called focus variables—but, is not certain about which other variables to include in the model. In the case of (international) capital movements we count on portfolio theory which suggests that both interest and exchange rates should be considered in any model trying to explain international capital movements. We include those focus variables in all possible regressions. However, portfolio theory does not tell us which other variables should enter into the explanation of those capital movements. Hence, a specification search including the focus and the explanatory variables about which we do not know much as yet is the best procedure to complete the explanation.

The reporting style suggested by Leamer allows the reader to know whether the different results obtained in all possible regressions are due to model or specification uncertainty or whether they are due to irregularities in the data. A model that is robust and has full explanatory value would show small differences between the minimum and maximum coefficients obtained across all possible model specifications for the regressor's coefficients. Likewise, a robust model would be one in which for different data sets the value of the coefficients of the regressors do not change much.

Table A1. Description of the Variables

I. *Dependent Variable*

For the pooled regressions, the annual capital outflow divided by annual exports plus non-financial services.

II. *Independent Variables*

A. The annual change in the price-deflated dollar value of the total foreign debt, short- and long-term, private and public, for each country in the pool plus the annual change in its IMF position. Price deflation is by the U.S. CPI.

B. The change in the nominal dollar exchange rate of each country multiplied by the ratio of the percentage change of the U.S. CPI to the percentage change of the country's CPI, December to December of each year.

C. The percentage change of the real Eurodollar 90-day deposit interest rate, December to December minus the percentage change of the country's real 90-day deposit rate.

(*continued*)

Table A1. *(continued)*

D. The annual percentage change of U.S. real GDP minus the percentage change of the country's real GDP.

E. Years used in pooled regressions:

Argentina	1978-1984
Brazil	1971-1983
Chile	1971-1983
Mexico	1971-1985
Peru	1971-1985
Venezuela	1971-1985

Table A2. Highest and Lowest Values of Coefficients from Regressions on Pooled Data, 1971-1985, Using Leamer Specification Search

	Coefficient Range	
Explanatory Variable	*Minimum*	*Maximum*
1. Change Real Total Debt (%)	0.387 ***	0.452 ***
	(3.453)	(3.965)
2. Change, Debtor Real Exchange Rate (%)	0.049	0.073
	(1.013)	(1.662)
3. Change US-Debtor Real GNP Growth Rate (%)	0.246	0.791 **
	(0.561)	(1.957)
4. Change US-Debtor Real Interest Rate	0.044	0.058 *
	(1.497)	(1.845)
5. Argentina Dummy	11.624	16.984 **
	(1.324)	(2.102)
6. Brazil Dummy	-10.650	-4.759
	(-1.510)	(-0.703)
7. Chile Dummy	-24.235 ***	-13.588 ***
	(-3.213)	(-1.992)
8. Mexico Dummy	4.171	10.270
	(0.615)	(1.590)
9. Peru Dummy	-14.727 **	-5.696
	(-2.150)	(-0.867)
10. Venezuela Dummy	8.744 *	18.000 ***
	(1.7555)	(3.687)

Notes: * = 10% significance.
** = 5% significance.
*** = 1% significance.

NOTES

1. The Bank for International Settlements reports that in the 3rd quarter of 1986, "there was still hardly any sign of spontaneous new lending to problem debtor countries." Nevertheless, entities from those countries augmented their deposits in financial center banks by $4 billion (Norman 1987).

2. According to a recently cited guesstimate, the four largest U.S. banks hold between $100 and $120 billion IPB deposits, about 70% of which are Latin American (Foweraker 1987).

3. Recent examples are the Mexican government's letter of July 22, 1986 to the Managing Director of the IMF requesting a new loan package and the subsequent IMF document of November 9, 1986 summarizing the approved package. The term, capital flight does not appear in either confidential document.

4. Prior to 1976, the published debt data cover only official and officially guaranteed long-term debt plus borrowings from the IMF. Our debt figures for 1971-1975 are the published long-term figures multiplied by one plus the average ratio per country of short- to long-run debt during the years, 1976-1985.

5. The World Bank estimates of foreign debt, used to compute the capital flight and foreign private asset estimates of Tables 1 and 2, are generally lower than those made jointly by the Organization for European Cooperation and Development and the Bank for International Settlements. The 1985 debt estimate of the OECD/BIS for Argentina is 11% higher than that of the World Bank; their Chilean debt estimate is 24.6% higher, and their Peruvian debt estimate is 11.2% higher than the corresponding 1985 World Bank numbers (cf. OECD [1987] with The World Bank [1987]). The World Bank makes its estimates on data supplied by the debtor governments, whereas the OECD/BIS relies on creditor country reporting. There are three reasons why the latter estimates should be taken as more accurate: (1) Creditor country financial data gathering is more accurate; (2) Heavily-indebted countries may be motivated to give a downward spin to their debt statistics; and (3) The negative 1985 CF estimate for Chile in Tables 1 and 2 makes nonsense of the Chilean government's current effort to induce Chileans to repatriate capital by offering them a favorable swap facility. Putting the OECD/BIS debt figure in our CF formula produces a moderately positive CF that restores sense to the Chilean repatriation effort.

Unfortunately, the OECD/BIS debt series only begins in 1983, whereas the World Bank series goes back to 1970. In the regressions reported in Table 3, we had to use the latter debt series.

6. In 1985, the U.S. Treasury reported that only $12.2 billion of private Mexican bank deposits in the United States were demand deposits. A small sampling of wealthy Mexican expatriates in California uncovered sizeable investments in real estate and businesses as well as in securities (de Murgia 1986).

7. See Weinert (1986-87, p. 85). Weinert's article is a very informative update on the structure and the chief players in the debt-equity swaps.

8. The secondary market prices are also shaped by swaps between heavily-exposed banks. These swaps help the banks to level their country exposures but do not make paper available to third parties. See Weinert (1986-87, pp. 86-87).

9. The papers and pronouncements at the annual ECLAC meetings held in Mexico, January 1987, are a recent example of such two-part chorusing.

10. On March 19, 1986 in testimony to the U.S. Congress, Ms. Paula Stern, Chairwoman of the International Trade Commission attributed a loss of one million U.S. manufacturing jobs to the Latin American debt crisis. Cited in "The Impact of the Latin American Debt Crisis on the U.S. Economy" (1986). The study also blames part of the depth and duration of the U.S. farm depression on the Latin American debt crisis.

REFERENCES

Cuddington, John T. (1985). "Capital Flight: Issues, Estimates and Explanations." CPD, Discussion Paper. Washington, DC: The World Bank.

Cumby, Robert and Richard Levitch. (1986). "On the Definition and Magnitude of Recent Capital Flight." Mimeo, New York University.

Felix, David. (1985). "A Modest Proposal for Alleviating the Latin American Foreign Debt Crisis." Washington University Working Paper No. 81. St. Louis, MO: Washington University.

Foweraker, Joe. (1987). "What's Good for Citicorp ..." *Challenge* 29,6 (January/February), pp. 47-50.

"The Impact of the Latin American Debt Crisis on the U.S. Economy." (1986). A Staff Study of the Joint Economic Committee of the Congress of the United States, May 10.

Khan, Moshin and Nadeem Haque. (1985). Foreign Borrowing and Capital Flight: A Formal Analysis." *IMF Staff Papers* 32,4 (December): 606-628.

de Murgia, Valdemar. (1986). *Capital Flight and Economic Crisis: Mexican Post-Devaluation Exiles in a California Community.* Research Report Series 44, Center for U.S.-Mexican Studies, University of California, San Diego.

Norman, Peter. (1987). "Cross-Border Loans by Bank Surged in 3rd Period of '86." *The Wall Street Journal* (January 26).

OECD. (1987). *External Debt Statistics.* Paris: OECD.

Pine, Art. (1987). "U.S. Policy Makers Fear Citicorp Stance on Debtor Nations Imperials Global Plan." *The Wall Street Journal* (February 13).

Truell, Peter. (1987). "Citicorp's Reed Takes Firm Stance on Third-World Debt: Chairman Aims to Stem Commercial Banks Trend Toward Concessions." *The Wall Street Journal* (February 4).

Walter, Ingo. (1986). "The Mechanisms of Capital Flight." Paper presented at the Conference on Capital Flight and Third World Debt, Institute for International Economics, Washington, D.C.

Weinert, Richard S. (1986-87). "Swapping Third World Debt." *Foreign Policy* 65 (Winter).

The World Bank. (1987, January). The World Bank Data Tape. Washington, DC: The World Bank.

PART III

EVOLVING PATTERNS OF TRADE

THE CHANGING ROLE OF MULTINATIONAL CORPORATIONS IN U.S. INTERNATIONAL TRADE

F. Steb Hipple

INTRODUCTION

Over the past three decades, multinational corporations (MNCs) have become increasingly important in U.S. international trade and investment. The rise of these firms has coincided with the evolution of the United States to a more "open" economy where international trade is a major and growing element in production and consumption.

This paper examines the trading activities of multinational corporations from the perspective of overall U.S. merchandise trade. Trade data for U.S. and foreign multinational corporations are developed for the years 1977 and 1982, based on information in U.S. Government benchmark surveys of direct foreign investment. The analysis utilizes the trade matrix and the flow of funds approach to structure the trading activities of multinational corporations.

The analytical approach used in this paper was originally developed by the author for a 1982 U.S. Government report (Hipple, 1982). That study was limited to a static analysis of 1977 trade data. With the release of additional

Research in International Business and Finance, vol. 7, pages 65-80.

ISBN: 0-89232-906-8

benchmark surveys, trade data can now be developed for 1982, permitting a "dynamic" analysis of changes over the 1977 to 1982 period.

MULTINATIONAL CORPORATIONS AND TRADE FLOWS

The trade flows that link the United States and other countries are composed of many individual transactions. These transactions involve buyers and sellers, domestic corporations and foreign corporations, and the domestic and foreign units of multinational corporations. A trade matrix can effectively show the interlinkages among these different types of trade transactors (Hipple, 1982, pp. 2-3).

To illustrate, divide the world into the United States (U.S.) and the rest of the world (R.O.W.). There are three types of trade transactors: parent corporations (p), affiliated corporations (a), and other corporations (o). The parent corporations in the United States are multinational corporations who control the affiliates in the rest of the world. The R.O.W. parent corporations are multinational corporations who control the affiliates in the United States. "Control" means a 10% or more direct ownership interest. The other corporations are unrelated domestic firms who engage in international trade on an "arms length" basis only.

Exports (X) and imports (M) will be defined from the perspective of the United States. That is, X is imports for the R.O.W., and M is exports for the R.O.W. Total U.S. exports may be shown as:

$$X = Xp + Xa + Xo \tag{1}$$

The terms Xp, Xa, and Xo represent exports by U.S. parent corporations, the U.S. affiliates of foreign (R.O.W.) multinational corporations, and other U.S. corporations, respectively.

The destination of U.S. exports can be shown as:

$$Xp = Xpp + Xpa + Xpo \tag{2a}$$
$$Xa = Xap + Xaa + Xao \tag{2b}$$
$$Xo = Xop + Xoa + Xoo \tag{2c}$$

The first lower case letter represents the domestic U.S. seller, and the second lower case letter represents the R.O.W. buyer. For example, the term Xao is the value of U.S. exports originated by the U.S. affiliates of foreign (R.O.W.) multinational corporations and sold to the "other" group of unrelated foreign corporations.

Similarly, U.S. imports can be shown as follows:

$$M = Mp + Ma + Mo \tag{3}$$

$$Mp = Mpp + Mpa + Mpo \tag{4a}$$
$$Ma = Map + Maa + Mao \tag{4b}$$
$$Mo = Mop + Moa + Moo \tag{4c}$$

The matrix equation system in (2) and (4) can be best analyzed in a flow of funds format.

FLOW OF FUNDS TABLES

Tables 1, 2, 5, and 6 are flow of funds tables based on the matrix equation systems, and show U.S. merchandise trade data for 1977 and 1982. Tables 1 and 2 cover total U.S. trade, while Tables 5 and 6 cover U.S. trade omitting exports and imports of fuels (SITC group 3). The data are displayed in "cells" containing U.S. exports, imports, and the resulting trade balance. The tables are based on the benchmark surveys of foreign direct investment conducted periodically by the U.S. Government. The derivation of the trade data from the benchmark surveys is described in the Appendix.

The direct investment benchmark surveys collect, among other information, data on the exports and imports of U.S. and foreign multinational corporations. The trading activities of MNCs are defined from the perspective of the affiliated corporations. The act of investing in another country "creates" the multinational corporation, and the trade activities of the affiliate distinguish the multinational corporation from other businesses engaged in international trade.

In terms of flow of funds tables, the trading activities of multinational corporations are shown by cells *b, e, f, g, h, j,* and *n*. These cells form a "cross" in the flow of funds matrix. The horizontal row of cells *e, f, g,* and *h* shows the role of foreign (R.O.W.) multinational corporations in U.S. trade through the activities of their affiliates in the United States. Similarly, the vertical row of cells *b, f, j,* and *n* shows the role of U.S. multinational corporations in our merchandise trade through the activities of their affiliates in foreign (R.O.W.) countries. Data cell *f* shows the overlap in the trade activities of the two groups of corporations. This overlap must be taken into account to avoid double counting and exaggerating the importance of multinational corporations in U.S. international trade (Hipple, 1982, pp. 4-5).

Regarding the trade of nonmultinational ("other") corporations, this would be shown by the empty corner cells of the trade flow matrix (cells *a, c, i,* and *k*). There is no way to reasonably estimate the trade flows for these cells. It is possible to determine the total flows in cells *d* and *l,* but there is no rule to allocate these totals into the empty matrix cells. For this reason, cells *d* and *l* have also been left blank.

The trade flow data shown in Tables 1, 2, 5, and 6 are taken from four different U.S. Government benchmark surveys of foreign direct investment. Surveys of U.S. direct investment abroad were conducted in 1977 and 1982. Surveys of foreign direct investment in the United States were conducted in 1974 and 1980. These are sometimes referred to as "outward investment" and "reverse investment" respectively. In the tables, the 1974 and 1980 data from the reverse investment surveys have been rescaled to 1977 and 1982 trade levels. In this manner, the trading activities of both U.S. and foreign MNCs can be compared and measured together.

Three possible problems need to be examined before the trade flows shown in the tables can be accepted as a basis for analyzing the role of MNCs in U.S. international trade. First, we have time-shifted the reverse investment trade data to correspond with the trade data reported in the outward investment benchmarks. Second, two of the benchmark years—1974 and 1982—were recession years, and the data may be affected by cyclical factors. And third, two of the benchmark years—1974 and 1980—followed the two oil price shocks and may be affected by these events.

The trade data from the 1974 reverse investment benchmark has been time-shifted three years to 1977 by a scalar multiplier on exports and imports. The 1980 trade data has been time-shifted two years to 1982 levels by scalar multipliers. The assumption is that the MNC presence in trade flows is unchanged over the period and that the composition of trade is stable. The assumption of a stable MNC presence over short time periods is reasonable. The assumption of a stable trade composition needs to be examined. The following table presents the division of U.S. merchandise trade between manufactures and nonmanufactures over the period 1973 to 1983 (U.S. Department of Commerce, September 1979, pp. 867-870; December 1986, pp. 796-799). The benchmark years are marked by an asterisk.

Composition of U.S. Merchandise Trade 1973-1984
(Percentage Shares)

	Merchandise Exports		*Merchandise Imports*	
Year	*Manufactures*	*Other Exports*	*Manufactures*	*Other Imports*
1973	63.6	36.4	64.4	35.6
1974*	65.3	34.7	55.0	45.0
1975	66.6	33.4	52.9	47.1
1976	67.9	32.1	53.5	46.5
1977*	67.4	32.6	51.8	48.2
1978	67.0	33.0	58.3	41.7
1979	65.3	34.7	54.4	45.6
1980*	66.4	33.6	51.1	48.9
1981	67.4	32.6	54.6	45.4
1982*	67.4	32.6	59.0	41.0
1983	67.6	32.4	63.3	36.7
1984	67.5	32.5	68.0	32.0

On the export side, the data shows an amazing stability in trade composition. Between 1974 and 1977, the shift was only 2.1 share points; between 1980 and 1982, the shift was only 1.0 share points. Both share shifts were in favor of manufactures trade and away from nonmanufactures. In both the 1974 benchmark and the 1980 benchmark, the foreign MNC export trade presence is primarily in the nonmanufactures area, thus the time-shifting to 1977 and 1982 will slightly overstate the trade magnitudes associated with foreign MNCs. In terms of trade shares presented in Tables 4 and 8 these effects are fractions of a share percent.

The import composition shares are not as stable as the export shares. Between 1974 and 1977, there was a 3.2 share point shift away from manufactures, while between 1980 and 1982, there was a 7.9 share point jump in favor of manufactures. In both the 1974 and 1980 benchmarks, the foreign MNC import presence was slightly higher in manufactures. Thus the 1974 to 1977 shift will slightly overstate the foreign MNC trade presence in 1977; the 1980 to 1982 time shift will understate the import trade levels of foreign MNCs in 1982. Again, in terms of trade shares shown in Tables 4 and 8 these effects are fractions of a share percent.

A second concern deals with the effects of the severe recessions in 1974-1975 and 1981-1982 on the data collected in the 1974 and 1982 benchmarks. On the export side, the 1974 shares are in line with a trend shift between 1973 and 1976; the 1982 shares are nearly identical to adjacent years. On the import side, once the 1973 oil price hikes had been absorbed, the 1974 trade composition shares are reasonably typical for the period. The 1982 trade composition shares are in line with the trend shift between 1980 and 1984. In short, the trade composition shares do not show any significant movements that can be attributed to the business cycle. In contrast, the dollar value and real volume of trade display definite cyclical linkages.

The final concern addresses the affects of the oil price shocks in 1973 and 1979 on the benchmark surveys of the following years. Driven by higher energy prices, between 1973 and 1975, the nonmanufactures share of U.S. imports increased from 35.6% to 47.1%. Between 1978 and 1980, the share increase was from 41.7% to 48.9%. The approach here was to recalculate MNC trade flows omitting exports and imports of fuels (SITC group 3). These results are shown in Tables 5, 6, 7, and 8, which exactly parallel the format of Tables 1, 2, 3, and 4. This alternate view of the data does not reveal any significant differences, and the principal conclusions of the study remain unaffected.

MULTINATIONAL CORPORATIONS AND U.S. INTERNATIONAL TRADE

The major findings of the study are presented in Tables 1, 2, 3, and 4. Tables 1 and 2 present MNC-related trade flows for 1977 and 1982. Table 3 summarizes the dollar value of U.S. exports and imports originated by multinational corporations. Table 4 converts the dollar values into percentage shares of total U.S. trade.

In Table 3 trade data are shown for U.S. multinational corporations, rest of world MNCs, and combined domestic and foreign MNCs. Total shipments and intrafirm shipments are presented for 1977 and 1982. Total shipments are all corporate sales which entered into U.S. merchandise trade. The bulk of total shipments represents sales to related corporations, and is shown as intrafirm shipments. These intrafirm shipments may be from parent to affiliate, or from affiliate to parent.

The trade data in Table 3 are based on the flow of funds tables. The values shown for combined MNCs have been adjusted for the overlap in trade (cell *f*) between U.S. and R.O.W. multinational corporations. For analytical purposes, Table 3 also shows trade balances and changes in shipments between 1977 and 1982. Total U.S. merchandise trade figures are provided as a reference at the bottom of the table.

Table 4 converts the dollar values into percentage shares of U.S. merchandise trade. The multinational corporation trade shares are the ratio of the MNC shipments to total U.S. trade. The format of Table 4 is identical to Table 3, except that overall shares are shown in place of balances. The overall shares are a trade-weighted average of the export and import shares.

Four major findings emerge from the data in Table 4. First, multinational corporations accounted for half of the value of U.S. international trade in 1982. Second, some one-third of U.S. trade in 1982 was intrafirm shipments and was valued by transfer prices. Third, the share of trade held by the multinational corporations fell significantly between 1977 and 1982 (roughly seven share points). And fourth, the share decline reflects a reduced role of U.S. multinational corporations in our own trade activities.

Between 1977 and 1982, the combined MNC share of U.S. trade decreased from 57.5% to 50.7%, a drop of nearly seven share points. This decline was caused by important shifts which occurred between the trade shares of U.S. MNCs and foreign MNCs. In 1977, U.S. multinational corporations had a 30.8% overall share of U.S. exports and imports, while the R.O.W. share was 27.8%. By 1982, the U.S. share had dropped to 23.7% while the R.O.W. share was unchanged. As a result, foreign multinational corporations held the larger share in total U.S. trade.

A similar pattern emerged in intrafirm shipments. In 1977, intrafirm shipments accounted for over 40% of merchandise trade. This share fell in 1982 to 33%, again linked to a declining role of U.S. multinational corporations in our own trade.

As previously mentioned, the MNC trade flows in Tables 1 and 2 were recalculated omitting fuels (SITC group 3). These results are presented in Tables 5 and 6. Tables 7 and 8 present the summary information on trade values and trade shares. In general, this alternative view of the data leads to the same four major findings presented above. It does present additional detail on the role of multinational corporations in U.S. international trade. In particular, Table 8 shows that foreign MNCs already had the larger share of U.S. nonfuels trade in 1977, a position which they continued to hold in 1982.

Table 1. U.S. Merchandise Trade Flows in 1977 (Billions of U.S. $)

		REST OF WORLD			
		Parent	Affiliate	Other	Total
	X		32.397		
Parent	M		32.639		
	B		-0.242		
		a	*b*	*c*	*d*
	X	14.384	1.746	13.512	29.642
Affiliate	M	31.426	1.421	11.815	44.662
	B	-17.042	0.325	1.697	-15.020
UNITED STATES		*e*	*f*	*g*	*h*
	X		6.644		
Other	M		7.465		
	B		-0.821		
		i	*j*	*k*	*l*
	X		40.787		120.101
Total	M		41.525		146.817
	B		-0.738		-26.716
		m	*n*	*o*	*p*

Table 2. U.S. Merchandise Trade Flows in 1982 (Billions of U.S. $)

		REST OF WORLD			
		Parent	Affiliate	Other	Total
	X		46.559		
Parent	M		41.598		
	B		4.961		
		a	*b*	*c*	*d*
	X	20.186	2.097	27.932	50.215
Affiliate	M	47.621	1.849	27.318	76.788
	B	-27.435	0.249	0.613	-26.573
UNITED STATES		*e*	*f*	*g*	*h*
	X		8.062		
Other	M		7.959		
	B		0.102		
		i	*j*	*k*	*l*
	X		56.718		212.193
Total	M		51.406		243.952
	B		5.312		-31.759
		m	*n*	*o*	*p*

Table 3. U.S. Trade Originated by Multinational Corporations (Billions of U.S. $)

	Total Shipments			Intrafirm Shipments		
	1977	*1982*	*Chg*	*1977*	*1982*	*Chg*
United States MNCs						
Export Value	40.787	56.718	+15.931	32.397	46.559	+14.162
Import Value	41.525	51.406	+9.881	32.639	41.598	+8.959
Balance	-0.738	+5.312	+6.050	-0.242	+4.961	+5.203
Rest of World MNCs						
Export Value	29.642	50.215	+20.573	14.384	20.186	+5.802
Import Value	44.662	76.788	+32.126	31.426	47.621	+16.195
Balance	-15.020	-26.573	-11.553	-17.042	-27.435	-10.393
Combined MNCs						
Export Value	68.683	104.836	+36.153	45.035	64.648	+19.613
Import Value	84.766	126.345	+41.579	62.644	87.370	+24.726
Balance	-16.083	-21.510	-5.427	-17.609	-22.723	-5.114
Total U.S. Trade						
Export Value	120.101	212.193	+92.092			
Import Value	146.817	243.952	+97.135			
Balance	-26.716	-31.759	-5.043			

Table 4. Multinational Corporation Shares of U.S. International Trade (Percentage Shares)

	Total Shipments			*Intrafirm Shipments*		
	1977	*1982*	*Chg*	*1977*	*1982*	*Chg*
United States MNCs						
Export Share	33.96	26.73	-7.23	26.97	21.94	-5.03
Import Share	28.28	21.07	-7.21	22.23	17.05	-5.18
Overall Share	30.84	23.70	-7.13	24.37	19.33	-5.04
Rest of World MNCs						
Export Share	24.68	23.66	-1.02	11.98	9.51	-2.46
Import Share	30.42	31.48	+1.06	21.40	19.52	-1.88
Overall Share	27.84	27.84	0.00	17.16	14.87	-2.30
Combined MNCs						
Export Share	57.19	49.41	-7.78	37.50	30.47	-7.03
Import Share	57.74	51.79	-5.94	42.67	35.81	-6.85
Overall Share	57.49	50.68	-6.81	40.34	33.33	-7.01

Table 5. U.S. Merchandise Trade Flows Less Fuels in 1977 (Billions of U.S. $)

UNITED STATES		REST OF WORLD: Parent	Affiliate	Other	Total
Parent	X		31.900		
	M		17.781		
	B		14.119		
		a	*b*	*c*	*d*
Affiliate	X	14.158	1.772	13.263	29.193
	M	28.115	1.059	9.933	39.107
	B	-13.957	0.714	3.329	-9.914
		e	*f*	*g*	*h*
Other	X		6.461		
	M		4.395		
	B		2.065		
		i	*j*	*k*	*l*
Total	X		40.133		115.902
	M		23.235		102.530
	B		16.898		13.372
		m	*n*	*o*	*p*

Table 6. U.S. Merchandise Trade Flows less Fuels in 1982 (Billions of U.S. $)

UNITED STATES		REST OF WORLD: Parent	Affiliate	Other	Total
Parent	X		45.508		
	M		27.724		
	B		17.784		
		a	*b*	*c*	*d*
Affiliate	X	16.640	1.913	24.648	43.201
	M	45.451	1.325	20.253	67.029
	B	-28.811	0.589	4.394	-23.828
		e	*f*	*g*	*h*
Other	X		7.976		
	M		5.143		
	B		2.832		
		i	*j*	*k*	*l*
Total	X		55.397		199.416
	M		34.192		178.543
	B		21.205		20.873
		m	*n*	*o*	*p*

Table 7. U.S. Trade Less Fuels Originated by Multinational Corporations
(Billions of U.S. $)

	Total Shipments			*Intrafirm Shipments*		
	1977	*1982*	*Chg*	*1977*	*1982*	*Chg*
United States MNCs						
Export Value	40.133	55.397	+15.264	31.900	45.508	+13.608
Import Value	23.235	34.192	+10.957	17.781	26.724	+9.943
Balance	+16.898	+21.205	+4.307	+14.119	+17.784	+3.665
Rest of World MNCs						
Export Value	29.193	43.201	+14.008	14.158	16.640	+2.482
Import Value	39.107	67.029	+27.922	28.115	45.451	+17.336
Balance	-9.914	-23.828	-13.914	-13.957	-28.811	-14.854
Combined MNCs						
Export Value	67.554	96.685	+29.131	44.286	60.235	+15.949
Import Value	61.283	99.896	+38.613	44.837	71.850	+27.013
Balance	+6.270	-3.212	-9.482	-0.552	-11.616	-11.064
Total U.S. Trade						
Export Value	115.902	199.416	+83.514			
Import Value	102.530	178.543	+76.013			
Balance	+13.372	+20.873	+7.501			

Table 8. Multinational Corporation Shares of U.S. International Trade Less Fuels (Percentage Shares)

	Total Shipments			*Intrafirm Shipments*		
	1977	*1982*	*Chg*	*1977*	*1982*	*Chg*
United States MNCs						
Export Share	34.63	27.78	-6.85	27.52	22.82	-4.70
Import Share	22.66	19.15	-3.51	17.34	15.53	-1.81
Overall share	29.01	23.70	-5.31	22.74	19.38	-3.37
Rest of World MNCs						
Export Share	25.19	21.66	-3.52	12.22	8.34	-3.87
Import Share	38.14	37.54	-0.60	27.42	25.46	-1.96
Overall Share	31.27	29.16	-2.10	19.35	16.43	-2.92
Combined MNCs						
Export Share	58.29	48.48	-9.80	38.21	30.21	-8.00
Import Share	59.77	55.95	-3.82	43.73	40.24	-3.49
Overall Share	58.98	52.01	-6.97	40.80	34.95	-5.85

APPENDIX

The trade data shown in Tables 1, 2, 5, and 6 are developed from the benchmark surveys of direct investment conducted periodically by the U.S. Government. Benchmark surveys of foreign investment in the United States were conducted for the years 1974 and 1980. Benchmark surveys of U.S. direct investment abroad were conducted for the years 1977 and 1982. The surveys collected data on many topics, including trade flows. The trade data from the 1974 and 1980 surveys have been rescaled to 1977 and 1982 levels respectively, so that the trading activities of U.S. multinational corporations and foreign multinational corporations may be directly compared.

The U.S. Government benchmark surveys of direct investment are now on a seven-year cycle. The next benchmark survey of foreign direct investment in the United States will cover 1987, while the next benchmark survey of U.S. direct investment abroad will cover 1989. Given the normal data processing lags, the information from this next set of benchmark surveys will not be available until 1992 at the earliest. Thus, the composite information presented in these tables is the best available data for the next several years.

The derivation of individual data cells in Tables 1, 2, 5, and 6 is discussed below. Tables 5 and 6 are derived from Tables 1 and 2 by subtracting exports and imports of fuels (SITC group 3). Insufficient data exist to estimate the trade flows in empty data cells. Tables 3 and 4 are based on the trade data in Tables 1 and 2, while Tables 7 and 8 are based on the trade data in Tables 5 and 6.

Data Cells in Table 1

b. (U.S. Department of Commerce [DOC], April 1981, pp. 156, 160.)

e. Adjustment factors are used to convert 1974 data to a 1977 basis. For exports, the factor is 1.227 which is the ratio of 1977 merchandise cxports to 1974 exports. For imports, the factor is 1.465 which is the ratio of 1977 merchandise imports to 1974 imports. (DOC, December 1974, pp. 9, 18; April 1976, p. 51; December 1977, p. 9.)

f. The trade flow data for cells *b, e, h, n,* and *p* are known. The residual amounts (*n* - *b*) and (*h* - *e*) must be allocated into cells *f* and *j* and cells *f* and g, respectively. The unallocated level of trade within the matrix is *p* - (b + *e*). R.O.W. affiliates account for (*n* - *b*), thus the ratio (*n* - *b*) / *p* - (b + *e*) is used to allocate (*h* - *e*) into cell *f*. Or, U.S. affiliates account for (*h* - *e*) and the ratio (*h* - *e*) / *p* - (b + *e*) is used to allocate (*n* - *b*) into cell *f*.

g. Residual of *h* - (e + *f*).

h. Adjustment factors are used to convert 1974 data to a 1977 basis. See the discussion under cell *e*. (DOC, April 1976, p. 51.)

j. Residual of *n* - (b + *f*).
n. (DOC, April 1981, pp. 154, 158.)
p. (DOC, December 1977, p. 9.)

Data Cells in Table 2

b. (DOC, December 1985, pp. 129, 133.)
e. Adjustment factors are used to convert 1980 data to a 1982 basis. For exports, the factor is 0.962 which is the ratio of 1982 merchandise exports to 1980 exports. For imports, the factor is 1.013 which is the ratio of 1982 merchandise imports to 1980 imports. (DOC, December 1980, p. 11; December 1982, p. 9; October 1983, p. 141.)
f. The trade flow data for cells *b, e, h, n,* and *p* are known. The residual amounts (*n* - *b*) and (*h* - *e*) must be allocated into cells *f* and *j* and cells *f* and *g*, respectively. The unallocated level of trade within the matrix is *p* - (b + *e*). R.O.W. affiliates account for (*n* - *b*), thus the ratio (*n* - *b*) / *p* - (b + *e*) is used to allocate (*h* - *e*) into cell *f*. Or, U.S. affiliates account for (*h* - *e*) and the ratio (*h* - *e*) / *p* - (b + *e*) is used to allocate (*n* - *b*) into cell *f*.
g. Residual of *h* - (e + *f*).
h. Adjustment factors are used to convert 1980 data to a 1982 basis. See the discussion under cell *e*. (DOC, October 1983, p. 141.)
j. Residual of *n* - (b + *f*).
n. (DOC, December 1985, pp. 127, 131.)
p. (DOC, December 1982, p. 9.)

Data Cells in Table 5

Note: The following discussion details the derivation of exports and imports of fuels (SITC group 3). These amounts are subtracted from the trade flows shown in Table 1.

b. Adjustment factors are used to convert majority owned affiliate data to affiliate data. For exports, the factor is 1.139 which is the ratio of affiliate exports to majority owned affiliate exports. For imports, the factor is 1.093 which is the ratio of affiliate imports to majority owned affiliate imports. (DOC, April 1981, pp. 154, 158, 336, 340, 353, 356.)
e. Adjustment factors are used to convert 1974 data to a 1977 basis. For exports, the factor is 1.219 which is the ratio of 1977 fuels exports to 1974 exports. For imports, the factor is 1.747 which is the ratio of 1977 fuels imports to 1974 imports. (DOC, December 1974, pp. 10, 17; April 1976, p. 51; December 1977, pp. 10, 17.)

f. The trade flow data for cells *b, e, h, n,* and *p* are known. The residual amounts (*n* - *b*) and (*h* - *e*) must be allocated into cells *f* and *j* and cells *f* and *g* respectively. The unallocated level of trade within the matrix is *p* - (b + *e*). R.O.W. affiliates account for (*n* - *b*), thus the ratio (*n* - *b*) / *p* - (b + *e*) is used to allocate (*h* - *e*) into cell *f*. Or, U.S. affiliates account for (*h* - *e*) and the ratio (*h* - *e*) / *p* - (b + *e*) is used to allocate (*n* - *b*) into cell *f*.

g. Residual of *h* - (e + *f*).

h. Adjustment factors are used to convert 1974 data to a 1977 basis. See the discussion under cell *e*. (DOC, April 1976, p. 51.)

j. Residual of *n* - (b + *f*).

n. Adjustment factors are used to convert majority-owned affiliate data to affiliate data. See discussion under cell *b*. (DOC, April 1981, pp. 336, 352.)

p. (DOC, December 1977, pp. 10, 17.)

Data Cells in Table 6

Note: The following discussion details the derivation of exports and imports of fuels (SITC group 3). These amounts are subtracted from the trade flows shown in Table 2.

b. Adjustment factors are used to convert majority-owned affiliate data to affiliate data. For exports, the factor is 1.075 which is the ratio of affiliate exports to majority-owned affiliate exports. For imports, the factor is 1.115 which is the ratio of affiliate imports to majority-owned affiliate imports. (DOC, December 1985, pp. 127, 131, 264, 268, 281, 285.)

e. Adjustment factors are used to convert 1980 data to a 1982 basis. For exports, the factor is 1.567 which is the ratio of 1982 fuels exports to 1980 exports. For imports, the factor is 0.827 which is the ratio of 1982 fuels imports to 1980 imports. (DOC, December 1980, p. 17; December 1982, p. 15; October 1983, pp. 154, 166; March 1985, p. 38.)

f. The trade flow data for cells *b, e, h, n,* and *p* are known. The residual amounts (*n* - *b*) and (*h* - *e*) must be allocated into cells *f* and *j* and cells *f* and g, respectively. The unallocated level of trade within the matrix is *p* - (b + *e*). R.O.W. affiliates account for (*n* - *b*), thus the ratio (*n* - *b*) / *p* - (b + *e*)) is used to allocate (*h* - *e*) into cell *f*. Or, U.S. affiliates account for (*h* - *e*) and the ratio (*h* - *e*) / *p* - (b + *e*)) is used to allocate (*n* - *b*) into cell *f*.

g. Residual of *h* - (*e* + *f*).

h. Adjustment factors are used to convert 1980 data to a 1982 basis. See the discussion under cell *e*. (DOC, October 1983, pp. 152, 164.)

j. Residual of *n* - (b + *f*).

n. Adjustment factors are used to convert majority-owned affiliate data to affiliate data. See discussion under cell *b*. (DOC, December 1985, pp. 264, 281.)

p. (DOC, December 1982, p. 15; March 1985, p. 38.)

ACKNOWLEDGMENTS

The author is indebted to numerous colleagues at the U.S. Department of Commerce for their assistance and comments; in particular, the special help given by Victor Bailey on data and Jeff Lins on methodology. The author also acknowledges the useful suggestions made by the editor of this volume. Final responsibility for the methodology and analysis rests, of course, with the author.

REFERENCES

Hipple, F.S. (July 1982). *The Role of Multinational Firms in U.S. International Trade.* Washington, DC: Department of Commerce, International Trade Administration.

U.S. Department of Commerce, Bureau of the Census. (December 1974). *FT990.* Washington, DC: U.S. Government Printing Office.

________. (December 1977). *FT990.* Washington, DC: U.S. Government Printing Office.

________. (September 1979). *Statistical Abstract of the United States 1979.* Washington, DC: U.S. Government Printing Office.

________. (December 1980). *FT990.* Washington, DC: U.S. Government Printing Office.

________. (December 1982). *FT990.* Washington, DC: U.S. Government Printing Office.

________. (December 1986). *Statistical Abstract of the United States 1987.* Washington, DC: U.S. Government Printing Office.

U.S. Department of Commerce, Bureau of Economic Analysis. (April 1981). *U.S. Direct Investment Abroad, 1977.* Washington, DC: U.S. Government Printing Office.

________. (October 1983). *Foreign Direct Investment in the United States, 1980.* Washington, DC: U.S. Government Printing Office.

________. (December 1985). *U.S. Direct Investment Abroad: 1982 Benchmark Survey Data.* Washington, DC: U.S. Government Printing Office.

U.S. Department of Commerce, International Trade Administration. (March 1985). *1984 U.S. Foreign Trade Highlights.* Washington, DC: U.S. Government Printing Office.

U.S. Department of Commerce, Office of the Secretary. (April 1976). *Foreign Direct Investment in the United States: Benchmark Survey, 1974.* Washington, DC: U.S. Government Printing Office.

INTRA-INDUSTRY TRADE PATTERNS:
A TEST OF THE VARIETY HYPOTHESIS

Kay A. Smith

INTRODUCTION

International trade theory explains why nations trade. The most basic reason for trade is that all nations gain in welfare because of the exchange of goods. Explaining the pattern of this exchange of goods is the main goal of trade theories. The factor proportions theory (also known as the Heckscher-Ohlin-Samuelson theory) emphasizes comparative advantage and focuses attention on different supply capabilities rather than demand patterns among nations. Other trade theories, such as the availability theory or neo-technology theories, also emphasize supply characteristics and focus upon differences in the attributes of firms or industries to explain international trade flows.

This paper examines trade patterns of countries with similar factor endowments, thereby focusing on demand variables as being crucial in understanding the pattern of international trade. The trade theory presented, the variety hypothesis, is not applicable to a broad number of nations and goods. The main premise is that the variety hypothesis is useful when examining trade in manufactured goods among industrialized trading partners, and that, when combined with the factor proportions theory and other trade theories

Research in International Business and Finance, vol. 7, pages 81-127.

ISBN: 0-89232-906-8

emphasizing supply factors, it presents a more complete understanding of the pattern of international trade. The remaining section of this introduction will quickly explore the reasoning behind the idea that the variety hypothesis is just a part to be fit into the total picture of international trade theories.

The factor proportions theory of international trade emphasizes differences in factor endowments as the reason for trade. Its two principal propositions can be stated fairly simply:

1. Countries export commodities whose production requires relatively intensive use of productive factors found locally in relative abundance.
2. Commodity trade tends, generally, to reduce international discrepancies in wages, rents, and other factor returns of similar types of factors.

Except for the possibility that biases in tastes will outweigh the effect of differences in resource endowments, the relationship between demand factors and the pattern of trade has never been described explicitly. Demand is a function of tastes and income, and tastes are exogenous. One assumes that the impact of any change in total income upon the autarkic pattern of demand is negligible.[1]

The factor proportions theory argues that international trade takes place because of different supply characteristics. In autarky, different nations have different factor endowments which cause different relative costs in production. International trade takes place when the money prices of goods differ in autarky. A country will export those goods whose autarkic money costs are smaller. Given tastes, factor prices in autarky will reflect factor endowments. Goods with low autarkic money costs are those which use relatively intensively the cheap (and therefore, plentiful) factors of production. The opening of international trade will cause similar factors of production to earn similar returns. The primary reason for trade is different factor endowments. This reason for trade stresses the fact that nations will differ more in supply characteristics (i.e., factor endowments) than demand characteristics.

Trade flows of manufactured goods between developed countries are not really explained by the factor proportions theory. The factor proportions theory suggests that the larger trade flows would take place among nations with markedly different factor endowments. However, similarity of income reflects similarity in endowments. Why does a large percentage of world trade take place among nations with relatively small differences in income? Some economists have suggested that the factor proportion theory can explain trade between developed and developing nations but that the explanation for trade among developed nations must rely on other theories that emphasize demand factors (Gray 1976).

The explanation of trade in manufactured goods has been developed into two separate but overlapping theories: The neo-technology and the differentiated goods theories (Gray 1980). These theories are complementary rather than competitive explanations. The neotechnology theories focus on differences in the attributes of firms and industries in the trading nations to explain international trade flows. Variation in individual firms and their expertise can make international trade possible even though factor prices may be similar. The differentiated goods or variety theories are based essentially on very close similarities of supply characteristics so that goods are distinct only by design and quality. These theories emphasize demand variables to explain the trade flows of manufactured goods.

Linder first attempted to explain trade in manufactured goods among developed countries by focusing on the role of income rather than factor endowments (Linder 1961). A domestic market is needed in order for domestic producers to be able to achieve the necessary economies of scale for international trade. Producers of manufactured goods are likely to succeed in catering to domestic majority tastes. The type of goods that the home markets desire will depend on the level of income per capita. Nations with similar incomes will have similar tastes insofar as the type of goods and sophistication of those goods are concerned. Similarity of tastes will increase the number of products manufactured domestically that are potential exports and the number of foreign commodities that are potential imports. Countries with similar levels of per capita income and similar tastes may trade in large volumes of manufactured goods that differ only in design—these types of goods are differentiated goods. The volume of trade that actually takes place depends upon the volume of potential trade and the degree to which there are trade-breaking forces such as tariffs, transportation costs, and nontariff barriers. There have been several attempts to verify Linder's hypothesis (Sailors 1973; Hoftyzer 1975).

Recently Barker has proposed another explanation for the importance of income in explaining trade in manufactured goods (Barker 1978). Barker notes two tendencies: (1) that during the period of 1950-1970 there has been a strong bias of world trade among developed countries, and toward manufactured goods relative to other commodities; and (2) that there has been a substantial growth of world trade relative to the growth in income. Although there may be other explanations of these two tendencies, Barker develops a new theory to explain the strong income-biased growth of world trade. The variety hypothesis directly answers the question of why trade increased proportionally greater than income or production. The variety hypothesis emphasizes the demand-side explanations of trade in manufactured goods.

Another set of theories that explain trade in manufactured goods focuses upon the supply-side explanations. In 1956, Kravis introduced the availability theory which disagreed with the assumption that all factors of production are generally available. This theory emphasized the notion that trade occurs because some goods are unable to be produced domestically. Several reasons for a good to be unavailable are:

1. A product-specific input is not available in all countries.
2. Technological innovation is not yet available in all countries
3. Product differentiation causes one country to have a monopoly in producing the good in question.

Technological innovations repeatedly have transformed trade patterns, threatening the markets for traditional goods (for example, natural rubber and jute) or adding new products to the export lists. The group of theories that explain trade in terms of these *technological* innovations are known as neotechnological theories of international trade. A new product or production process is developed and tested in the home market. If the innovation proves profitable, wider markets are sought and exports grow. The innovation, unless fully protected by patents, is likely to attract imitation. This causes the innovator's original gain to disappear as successful imitation takes place abroad. However, some countries may prove regularly to be frequent sources of innovation. Therefore, their (the innovators') trade is explained in terms of *technological gap* exports and not solely in terms of factor endowments or productivity advantages (Hufbauer 1970).

Another closely-related theory explaining trade in manufactured goods is Vernon's product life cycle (Vernon 1966). The model of the product life cycle suggests that changes occur in the input requirements of a new product as it becomes established in markets and standardized in production. These changes may shift the cost advantage from one country to another. At the first stage of production, a new product is manufactured on a small scale and its market success is uncertain. Production techniques will probably require large inputs of skilled labor. The good must be produced near its market, because the producer needs a quick feedback of information in order to improve its performance, reliability, and general appeal. When the product is established at home, the product will begin to be exported. Standardization of product will allow mass production. As the product becomes standardized and its market is more competitive, the pull of cost advantages on the location of production grows stronger. Unless the innovating country has an ultimate comparative advantage, production will shift to other countries as the product matures. This model helps explain changes in production and trade in terms of new product lines. Furthermore, for goods whose manufacturing is spread abroad, we observe a shift from processes heavily dependent on skilled labor to automatic assembly processes using relatively more capital and unskilled labor.

While there are degrees of overlap, it is useful to identify the two stands of theory that are used to explain trade in manufactured goods. The neotechnological theories identify stages of development of a product from the first nonstandardized to the ultimate standard version under the lable of *product differentiation.* Generally, the neotechnological theories emphasize the role of supply-side (cost-affecting) variables in explaining international trade flows of manufactured goods.

The differentiated goods or variety hypothesis is based essentially on the assumption that countries have very close similarities of supply characteristics so that goods are distinct only by design and quality. These explanations emphasize demand variables to explain trade flows of manufactured goods. The variety hypothesis is one theory that tries to explain trade flows by means of focusing on demand variables.

This study attempts to verify the demand side explanation of manufactured goods trade flows by trying to determine if the variety hypothesis can be empirically-verified. Four types of goods will be used for the empirical work: automobiles, television and radio receivers, and domestic electrical applicances for four Western European nations during the years of 1955-1978. The most important good (and therefore most of the analysis concerns this product) is automobiles.[2]

THE VARIETY HYPOTHESIS

The variety hypothesis was first described by Barker (1978). In his article he notes two tendencies: (1) that during the period of 1950-1970, there has been a strong bias of world trade toward developed countries and a bias toward trade in manufactured goods; and (2) that there has been a substantial growth of world trade relative to the growth in real income. Barker develops the variety hypothesis to explain the strong income-biased growth of world trade. The variety hypothesis directly answers the question of why increases in trade tend to be proportionally greater than increases in income or production.

Barker implies a causality from income to increased trade because with increases in income, consumers are better able to satisfy desires for variety from sources abroad. However, there may be other reasons for this observed relationship between real income and trade.

The first explanation—the demand-side approach—is essentially the approach used by Barker and his predecessors. Real income increases and this increase leads to increases in trade because of demand reasons. Countries have the same supply capabilities and therefore the emphasis is on the demand side to explain the positive relationship between increases in real income and increases in trade.

A second explanation of this observed relationship, the "spurious" interpretation, states that this relationship is merely coincidential. There is no causality between these variables. This relationship is observed because there is an omitted regressor that explains the observed relationship between income and trade. The validity of this explanation can be determined in part by the econometric work presented in this study.

A third explanation, the supply-side approach, states that the reasons why there is an observed relationship between increased trade and income is attributed to different supply capabilities. In the introduction, this approach was referred to as the neotechnological theories.

A fourth explanation, the customs-union approach, states that because of increased importance of common markets in the last 20 years (especially in Western Europe), tariffs have decreased particularly on manufactured goods among common market members. The common market may have caused greater specialization and trade. One does observe a positive relation between income and trade but the explanation is attributed to a third variable: importance of customs unions. These countries obey Ohlin's precepts of a single nation and, therefore, common markets have transformed international trade to intranational trade (Ohlin 1967).

The variety hypothesis is a special case of the first approach with overtones of the last approach. This section will fully delineate the assumptions and model of the variety hypothesis. The variety hypothesis emphasizes the effects of real income and its growth on trade. The argument is as follows: As real income increases, purchasers are now able to buy more varieties of a product. Because a greater number of these varieties is available from abroad, the share of imports will increase. In general, the quantity of imports will rise more than proportionally with an increase in income per capita.

To explain this conclusion, Barker uses a version of Lancaster's model of consumer demand (Lancaster 1966). Each good has a set of desired characteristics and a commodity group consists of a set of similar goods. These characteristics are features of a good that the consumer deems important—price is only one of many characteristics. As their real incomes increase, purchasers are able to buy more varieties of a product and since a greater number of these varieties is available from abroad rather than domestic sources (because of economies of specialization), the share of imports in demand as the number of characteristics available in a commodity group increases. The main explanatory variable for the rapid increase in trade of these differentiated goods becomes income. These differentiated goods used in verifying the variety hypothesis must be a collection of commodities, having similar types of characteristics. Each commodity group would have a fixed combination of characteristics.

The assumptions and analysis have to be explored in greater detail. The assumptions of the variety hypothesis are:

1. Purchasers desire goods because of the combination of characteristics that the goods contain.
2. Diversity of preference for different combinations of characteristics exists.

3. Fixed number of purchasers and goods are available: Tastes, characteristics (including prices), and the total number of goods themselves are each unaffected by the growth in real income.
4. Domestic producers in a commodity group will not offer all the combinations of characteristics desired. The cost of adding new variants of products is high to the domestic producer. International trade is due to the purchaser's desire for variety and the domestic producers having to limit the goods they produce due to *economies of specialization.* Economies of specialization mean that there are increasing costs of producing new desired varieties of the commodity and that foreign sources will add to the number of varieties of goods within a commodity group available in a country.
5. The purchaser can buy only one unit of the good and not a combination of goods. Barker argues that this is the case in most durable goods markets.
6. Domestic consumers do not have strictly national tastes.

There are four sets of goods. The first is the available set which comprises all available goods. The second set, the efficient set, consists of those goods that are not dominated by any other goods in *all* desired characteristics. The strongly efficient set is those goods that are not dominated by any other goods in the nonprice characteristics. Finally, the feasible set is those goods that are within the budget constraint. With an increase in real income, the purchaser is able to exercise his/her preference for more elaborate combinations of characteristics contained within each set of goods. In any market of tradeable goods, international trade will exist, because the foreign goods will offer combinations of characteristics preferred by diverse purchasers. The greater the number of goods that have different combinations of characteristics, the greater the probability of a foreign supplier. This is due to the economies of specialization coupled with the purchaser's desire for variety. Given diversity of preferences, the strongly efficient set (where nonprice characteristics are more important) will grow faster than the efficient set. Imports comprise the majority of the strongly efficient set. The reason is that imports are subject to costs that domestic goods are not (e.g., increased transportation costs). Any general differential that raises the price of foreign goods relative to domestic goods has two effects: (1) it removes some of the imported goods from the feasible set and (2) it removes the imported goods from the efficient set. However, it can never remove any goods from the strongly efficient set since this set is defined by nonprice characteristics. Thus, as real incomes increase, the feasible set increases and proportionately more of the strongly efficient goods are brought and since imports will comprise the majority of the strongly efficient goods, the share of imports in demand will increase.

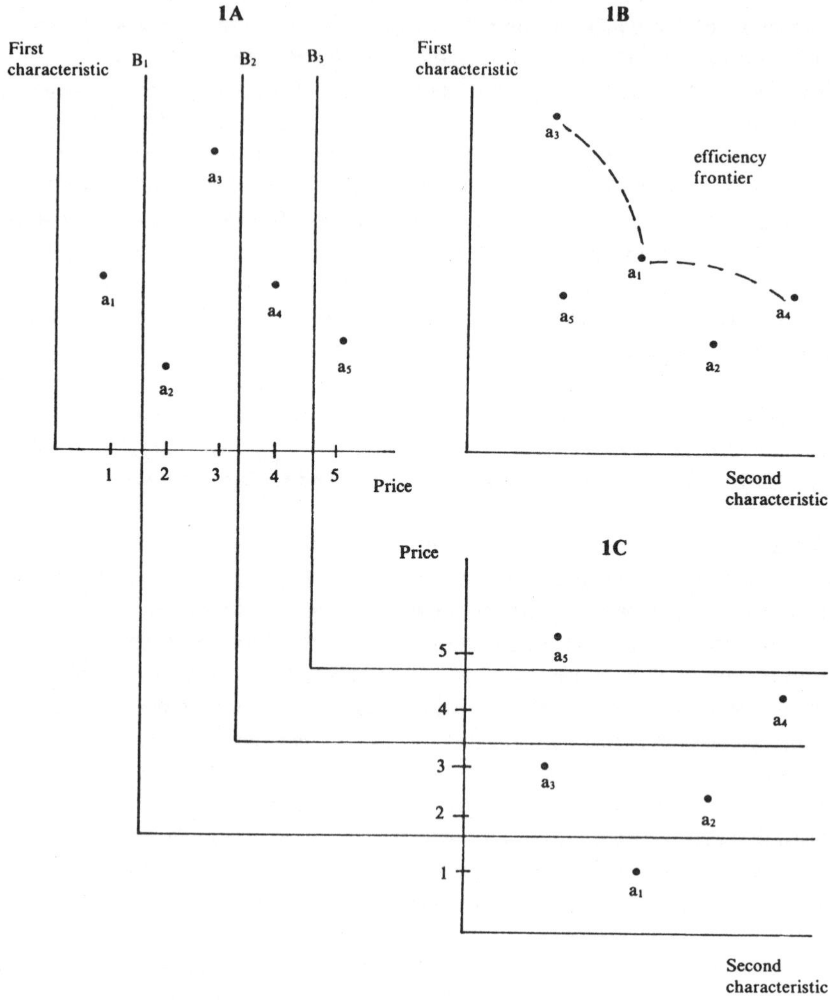

Figure 1. Derivation of Efficiency Frontier

The choice for the purchasers can be represented in Figure 1. Each purchaser has two constraints: The budget constraint and the availability constraint which is determined by the physical characteristics of the good, the desires of other purchasers, and the realized economies of scale in production. In Figure 1, there are three characteristics (with price being one of the characteristics). There are five goods labeled a_1, a_2, a_3, a_4, a_5. Each good consists of a different combination of characteristics. Figure 1a shows the first characteristic plotted against the price for each of the five goods. Figure 1b shows the different combinations of the two physical characteristics available. Figure 1c plots the second characteristic against the price of the good. Since only one of the goods is to be purchased, the budget allocated by the purchaser is represented by the maximum price he/she is prepared to pay. The lines B_1, B_2, and B_3, represent different budget lines. There are as many lines as there are different budgets. Now using Figure 1, it is easier to understand the differences among the various sets of goods described above. The available set consists of goods a_1, a_2, a_3, a_4, and a_5. The efficient set consists of those goods that are not dominated by any other good in all three characteristics. The only good that is excluded is a_5 which as a higher price than any other good and has a lower amount of both of the other two characteristics. Figure 1b (the efficiency frontier in Barker's terms) shows the efficient set. The strongly efficient set consists of a_1, a_3, and a_4. A_2 is excluded because a_2 has less of both the first and second characteristics compared to a_4. The feasible set comprises those goods that are within the budget constraint. If the budget constraint is B_1, then the feasible set is a_1. If the budget constraint is B_3, then the feasible set would be a_1, a_2, a_3, and a_4.

The effects of increasing real per capita income are as follows. The budget lines shift out (from B_1 to B_3) as real income increases. Each purchaser is able to buy his/her preferred combinations of characteristics. Given diversity of preferences, the strongly efficient set (a_1, a_2, a_4—read off the efficiency frontier in Figure 1b), which is the set of goods that is not dominated by any other good in *nonprice* characteristics, grows faster than the efficient set.

There are some theoretical similarities and differences between the variety hypothesis and the Heckscher-Ohlin-Samuelson (H-O-S) theory of international trade. The H-O-S theory assumes identical production functions and similar homogeneous factors as does the variety hypothesis. The H-O-S theory assumes tastes are identical for countries and purchasers. The variety hypothesis states that tastes are diverse for purchasers but may be identical over countries. The H-O-S theory assumes homogeneous goods; the variety hypothesis is described in terms of differentiated consumer durables whose characteristics are important in the purchaser's choices. The variety hypothesis rests on the assumption that when demand increases (due to increases in income), there are more different goods available from abroad rather than from domestic sources.

Barker attempted to empirically estimate the variety hypothesis using the following model.[3]

$$M_i = c_1 + c_2 Y + \text{capacity, price, and trend terms} + \text{error term}$$

where M_i is imports of commodity i (constant prices), Q_i is domestic production of commodity *i* (constant prices), and Y is real per capita income. The prediction of the variety hypothesis is that c_2 is greater than 0. He estimated this equation for U.K. imports from 1955-1972 and found that most of the manufactured goods provided confirmation of the variety hypothesis.

The variety hypothesis also suggests one explanation for intra-industry trade. A large proportion of trade in manufactures among developed countries takes place with goods that are simultaneously exported and imported. One type of simultaneous exporting and importing of the same good occurs because two different goods with two different production functions and end uses are included in the same SITC level. Such trade would be present when aggregated at the one or two digit SITC level. This type of trade is known as categorical aggregation and is explained by the factor proportions theory (Gray 1979). Another type of simultaneous exporting and importing is called two-way trade. This is described as trade in closely-related but not identical goods. These goods have different end uses and somewhat different production functions. The last type of simultaneous exporting and importing of the same good is called pure intra-industry trade. This trade involves the exchange of a good that has the same end use and the same production function (Gray 1980).

Because of economies of specialization (in Barker's terms), intra-industry trade should increase as income increases. Another reason for an increased importance of intra-industry trade is the assumption of the variety hypothesis that preferences are diverse over purchasers but may be identical over countries. If this is true, the variety hypothesis predicts that intra-industry trade should increase as income increases.

The previous section explained why the various hypothesis emphasized income as the major explanatory variable for increased international trade in manufactured goods. With increases in income, the strongly efficient set of goods increases at the expense of the efficient set. Because of economies of specialization, the source of the strongly efficient set of goods will be imports. Income, not price, is the major explanatory variable for increases in trade in manufactured consumer goods.

In the economic literature, studies using disaggregated manufactured goods have emphasized the role of income and domestic demand in explaining import share.[4] Most of these studies have used import unit value as a price variable and real per capita GNP as a domestic-demand variable. Some studies have used the characteristics approach to estimate the hedonic price equation but relatively few studies have estimated a hedonic price equation and then estimated import demand using the hedonic price and income variables as part of the import demand equation. Toder et al. (1978) was one of the few studies that estimated an import share demand equation in this manner. The empirical results reported in the study are: (1) high price elasticity in the short-run with ranges between -.945 to -1.754; (2) long-run price elasticity is very unstable; and (3) very high income elasticities in some equations. The fact that the long-run price elasticity is unstable might suggest that price changes have not been the major determinant of changes in the share of imported cars sold in the

United States. All of the estimated import share equations had elastic income elasticities of demand. The problem of applying their methodology to a study involving Western Europe is that the detailed data is not available.

THE MODEL FOR TESTING

The goods used to verify the variety hypothesis must be differentiated with approximately the same cost and technology conditions in the different sample countries. The goods used in this study are passenger motor vehicles; television and radio receivers; washing machines and vacuum cleaners. The countries in the sample are United Kingdom, France, Federal Republic of Germany, and Italy during the period of 1955-1978.

Motor vehicles have been one of the most dynamic commodity groups in the world economy. During the period of 1953-1964, motor vehicle production grew more rapidly than industrial production as a whole, and world trade in motor vehicles expanded more rapidly than world vehicle production, total world commoduty exports, or world exports of manufactured goods. The results of the equations using motor vehicles will form the major test of verifying the variety hypothesis.

The other four goods chosen, television and radio receivers, washing machines and vacuum cleaners, are also differentiated goods having the same cost and technology conditions within the four European countries. The time span for these goods is 1966-1978.

There will be two tests of the variety hypothesis. The first test pertains to the import share in demand and specifically predicts that the elasticity of import share with respect to real income is greater than zero. The second test expands the variety hypothesis as an explanation for intra-industry trade and predicts that the income coefficient will be positive when using an intra-industry trade index as the dependent variable. The first section will describe the first test; the second section will describe the intra-industry test.

The Model Using Import Share

The first test of the variety hypothesis is estimated using an equation of the following form:

$$\frac{Q_{m_i}}{Q_{p_i} - Q_{x_i}} = a_0 + a_1 \frac{P_f}{P_d} + a_2 Y + a_3 \frac{\text{ADV}}{\text{SALES}} + a_4 \frac{U_t}{U_{min}} + E_i \text{ (error term)}$$

where Q_{m_i} is the quantity of imports of commodity *i*; Q_{p_i} is the quantity of commodity *i* produced domestically; Q_{x_i} is the quantity of commodity *i* exported; P_f/P_d is a relative price variable; Y is real per capita income (base

1970) of the importing country; U_t is unemployment rate at times t; U_{min} is minimum unemployment rate over the time span of 1955-1978, and Adv/Sales is advertising expenditure per unit of sales in industry i. There will be four import share equations estimated, corresponding to the four goods used in the sample. For motor vehicles only, four import equations will be estimated, one for each of the four Western European countries. For the other goods, the number of years available make it impossible to estimate an import share equation for each country as there would be only 13 observations per country. The analysis that follows is a more detailed description of the methodology and variables used.

The Import-Share Variable

The central tenet of the variety hypothesis is that as income increases, consumers will be able to obtain the desired combination of characteristics. The source of these increased goods most likely will be foreign because of economies of specialization. Therefore, the correct dependent variable to use in verifying the variety hypothesis is import share of domestic consumption of commodity i in country j. Because this study is concerned with four Western European countries, the imports will be the quantity of commodity i, that is, imported from the three remaining countries. If the variety hypothesis is to have any validity across countries, it should hold for those four countries.

The Relative Price Variable

The variety hypothesis attempts to apply Lancaster's model of consumer demand to an international setting. It emphasizes all characteristics that a particular good contains as important decision elements for a consumer. The previous literature that applied differentiated goods to an international setting tended to view these goods in terms of standardized units rather than in Chamberlinian terms of product differentiation with design and feature differences (Gray and Martin 1980). What follows is a brief exposition of the hedonic price technique and reasons why this technique is inapplicable to this study.

Hedonic regression technique is based on a model of product differentiation that states that goods are valued for their utility-bearing characteristics. Hedonic prices are defined as the implicit prices of attributes and are revelaed from observed prices of differentiated products and the specific amounts of characteristics associated with each observed price. Econometrically, implicit prices are estimated by obtaining hedonic price regressions (which are observed prices regressed on characteristics).

Consider a class of commodities that are described by n attributes or characteristics, $z = (z_2, z_2, \ldots z_n)$. The terms *product* or *model* or *brand* are used interchangeably to describe commodities of a given quality or specification, or to designate commodities of a given design or quality. It is assumed that there exists a large number of *models* such that the choice among various combinations of z is continuous.

Each product has a quoted market price and is also associated with a fixed value of the vector z, so that the product market implicitly reveals a function $p(z) = p(z_1,z_2, \ldots z_n)$. This function is the observed price function relating observed prices and characteristics and is the hedonic price regression. It gives the minimum price of any package of characteristics as a positively desired characteristic. Then firms can change their products (by increasing the amount of z) only by the use of additional resources, and $p(z_1,z_2, \ldots z_n)$ must be increasing in all its arguments. Graphically the $p(z_1,z_2, \ldots z_n)$ function becomes:

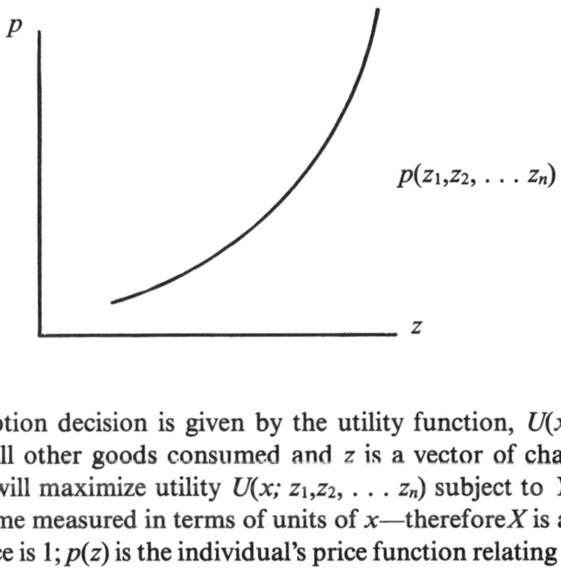

The consumption decision is given by the utility function, $U(x; z_1,z_2, \ldots z_n)$ where x is all other goods consumed and z is a vector of characteristics. The consumer will maximize utility $U(x; z_1,z_2, \ldots z_n)$ subject to $Y = x + p(z)$ where Y is income measured in terms of units of x—therefore X is a composite good whose price is 1; $p(z)$ is the individual's price function relating the product price and different characteristics. Maximization of utility required choosing x and $(z_1,z_2, \ldots z_n)$ to satisfy budget and the first order conditions. A value or bid function is defined as $T(z_1,z_2, \ldots z_n; Y^0; U^0)$ according to $U(Y\text{-T}; (z_1,z_2, \ldots z_n) = U^0$. $T(z_1,z_2, \ldots z_n; U^0; Y^0)$ is the expenditure a consumer is willing to pay for alternative values of $(z_1,z_2, \ldots z_n)$ at a given utility index U^0 and at a given income Y^0. T_i (for the ith consumer) defines a family of indifference curves relating the zth characteristic and money (i.e., X forgone). Utility is maximized when $\text{p}(z_1,z_2, \ldots z_n) = T_i(z_1,z_2, \ldots z_n)$; U^0; Y^0); $p(z)$ is the minimum price the consumer pays in the market. $T_i(z_n; U^0; Y^0)$ is the amount the consumer is willing to pay at a fixed utility index and income. Graphically, the utility maximization decision becomes:

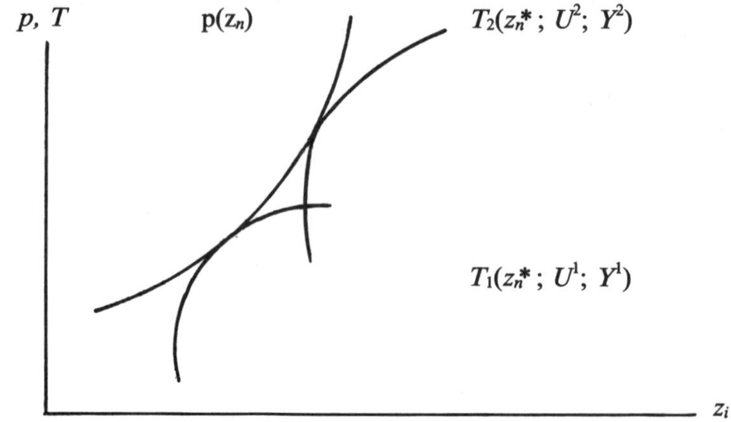

So for each value function (T), there is a different income level. Each observed price, $p(z_i)$, has an implied different income level. Because each equilibrium price that is observed has a given income level, to use income as an additional independent variable would be a clear case of misspecification. The misspecification would occur if income was regressed on observed price as an additional independent variable along with the other characteristics (the z_i's) in the hedonic price regression. When two independent variables are highly correlated, the problem of multicollinearity exists. Multicollinearity does not really raise problems in predicting the dependent variable, provided that there is no attempt to estimate what the individual effects of the two highly-correlated independent variables are on the dependent variable. Because the major explanatory variable of import share is income, one cannot use the hedonic price equation (observed price is a function of characteristics and income) to estimate what income's effect of the import share would be. This is especially important when the hypothesis used is the variety hypothesis which states that income is the major explanatory variable in describing an increasing import share in demand.

As a result, three different measures of competitiveness will be used in this study to capture the relative price effect. Competitiveness may be defined as the advantage in price, speed of delivery, or design which enables a country to secure sales at the expense of its competitors.

The price of imports is set by world market considerations. To obtain a relative price of imports, one has to examine the market structure under which domestic firms produce the import substitute. If the producers of import substitutes are producing goods that are effectively identical to the imports and, therefore, adjust their prices fully to the world price, then relative prices (i.e., the price of imports relative to a price index of domestically-produced goods) tell nothing. The variety hypothesis asserts that goods are differentiated and, therefore, imports and import substitutes possess different characteristics and that international as well as domestic markets are imperfectly competitive.

The use of import unit values is the most common method of measuring the foreign price index. The use of published import unit values as foreign prices has many limitations. Because this is a disaggregated study, there exists no published unit value indices for separate goods. For this study, a unit value measure will be used as one foreign price variable. Specifically this measure is:

$$P_f = \frac{\dfrac{TV_{ij}}{U_{ij}}}{\dfrac{TV_{1970}}{U_{1970}}}$$

where TV is the total value of imports of country i of commodity j; U_{ij} is units of commodity j imported by country i; TV_{1970} and U_{1970} is the number of units of commodity j imported by country i during 1970. This unit value measure has 1970 as a base because all domestic price variables and income variables use 1970 as a base. The domestic price used is the wholesale price index for the four countries.

As an alternative approach, instead of focusing on import unit values, is to focus on the share that each country has in the total world exports, which is, to some extent, a consequence of price movements. The share of a given country in total exports might rise or fall for a variety of reasons. One group of factors consists of shifts in demand. A country's export share might grow because importers' tastes shifted toward its products, or because its exports benefitted from high income elasticities of demand in the importing countries (explained by the variety hypothesis), or because its traditional markets were enjoying a period of particularly rapid economic growth. The focus on the share that each country has in the total world exports as a measure of competitiveness was first introduced by Balassa in 1967.

The concept of *revealed* comparative advantage introduced by Balassa pertains to the relative trade performance of individual countries in particular commodities. On the assumption that the commodity pattern of trade reflects intercountry differences in relative costs, the measure is assumed to reveal the comparative international advantage of the trading countries. The Balassa-type approach to international competitiveness measures arose from the difficulties of (1) accounting for all the factors that influence an industry's comparative advantage and (2) actually measuring and comparing these factors between countries and industries. Balassa argued that the apparent or revealed performance of a country's trade pattern would serve as an adequate indicator of that country's revealed comparative advantage in international trade.

The revealed comparative advantage method would reflect costs of production as well as nonprice factors in an industry's operations. Two indices that will be used are:

$$A_{ij} = \frac{\dfrac{|X_{ij} - M_{ij}|}{X_{mj} - M_{mj}}}{\dfrac{|X_i - M_i|}{X_m - M_m}} \quad \text{of the three remaining countries}$$

and

$$B_{ij} = \frac{\dfrac{X_{ij}}{X_i} \text{ of commodity } i \text{ in country} \neq j}{\dfrac{X_{mj}}{X_m} \text{ of manufactured commodities in country} \neq j}$$

where X_{ij} is exports of commodity *i* of country *j*; M_{ij} is imports of commodity *i* of country *j*; X_{mj} is manufactured imports of country *j*. These two indices are (1) a measure of the relative export performance of an industry involving the relative share of a country's total share in world exports (in this case, the world is the three remaining countries) of individual commodities suitable normalized by that country's share in total world exports in manufactured goods and (2) a measure of the industry's trade balance. The measure A_{ij} can be used to check B_{ij}. That is to say, if country *j*'s relative share in world exports of commodity *i* is greater than its overall share in total world exports of manufactured goods then country *j* has a revealed comparative advantage in exporting commodity *i*. There also should be a positive balance of trade in commodity *i*.

Capacity Utilization

U_t/U_{min} is a proxy for capacity utilization in the industry. The problems with capacity utilization figures published by national sources are (1) different countries use different definitions of capacity and (2) not all countries have series over time that directly measure capacity. Arena stated that imports and a capacity utilization variable were very sensitive to each other.[7] His study linked imports to capacity-use variables for all merchandise imports and for 15 specific industries in the United States. His equation was

$$\frac{I_t}{O_t} = B_1 \frac{1}{C^* - C_t} + B_2 \frac{P_t}{F_t} + B_3 T + B_4 K$$

where I_t is imports of the commodity, O_t is domestic production. C^* *is desired operating rate as a percent of capacity,* C is actual operating rate, P_t in U.S. wholesale price index for each industry, F_t is unit value index of finished manufactures for the United States, T is a trend variable, and K is constant 1. The problem with using his capacity-use variable is that the industry data are not available for the European countries. However, his study did imply that the U.S. import share in production was extremely sensitive to his measure of capacity utilization. One would expect the proxy used in this study, U_t/U_{min}, to decrease as full employment is reached and thus as full capacity is approached.

Marketing Variable

Adv/Sales ratio is a proxy trying to capture the importance of marketing effort and as a measure of entry barriers. Hitiris states three reasons why Adv/Sales ratio can be used as a measure of entry barriers (Hitiris 1978). First, advertising can deter entry by influencing firms' cost conditions. Cost conditions are affected by causing either scale economies or by creating absolute cost differences between established firms and new entrants, especially if the latter must advertise by relatively larger amounts. Second, this variable measures the degree of product differentiation or, more specifically, the degree to which the product and market characteristics permit heavy advertising expenditures to differentiate the products effectively. Finally, advertising leads to brand loyalty that acts as a barrier to entry. The data for this variable are available for the motor vehicle industry only for the years of 1955-1975 in the United States.[7]

Methodology

The major test of the variety hypothesis concentrates upon the income coefficient; if the coefficient is positive and significant, the hypothesis is supported. That is to say, if the import share of demand increases as income increases for all countries, then the variety hypothesis may be one explanation of international trade flows among these four European countries in differentiated goods.

In Barker's original article, this hypothesis was only tested for Great Britain. Barker used all of Great Britain's imports as his sample and found that the income variable was positive and significant for most manufactured goods. However, he failed to define his capacity, price, or trend terms (the other independent variables). He also used imports as a percentage of total production for the dependent variable.

The ways in which this study differs from Barker's original attempt to verify this hypothesis are: (1) the number of countries involved; (2) the dependent variable will be the import share of consumption rather than import share of production; and (3) the type of goods involved. This study uses only differentiated goods, the type of goods implied by Lancaster's characteristics theory of demand.

The Model Using Intra-Industry Trade

A number of studies (Balassa 1966; Grubel 1967; Grubel and Lloyd 1971, 1975; Gray 1973; Pagoulatos and Sorenson 1974; Aquino 1978) have found that the pattern of international trade of manufactures in Western Europe is best characterized by intra-industry trade. Grubel first presented a formal theoretical analysis of intra-industry trade. He defined intra-industry trade as occurring when "free international trade will result in a situation where each country simultaneously produces, exports, and imports products which are very close substitutes in consumption, production, or both" (Grubel 1967, p. 375). Inter-industry specialization results when countries produce and export but do not import the output of some industries. Grubel presented theoretical reasons for intra-industry trade, and Grubel and Lloyd (1971, 1975) suggested empirical measures to determine the importance of intra-industry trade for various countries.

Once the assumptions of zero transportation costs and concentrated production are relaxed, then intra-industry trade can be explained. Possible reasons for intra-industry trade are: joint production (between countries), combination of natural resource deposit (between countries), combination of natural resource deposit and transportation costs, border trade, seasonal fluctuations in demand, and differentiated products. He stated "the more interesting and probably more quantitatively important intra-industry trade takes place in commodities where there are no joint products and transportation and other distribution costs are small relative to the total price of the product" (Grubel 1967, p. 381). That is, the case of differentiated goods explanation is probably the most significant explanation.

Grubel and Lloyd (1971, 1975) developed the empirical measures of intra-industry trade in more detail and estimated the importance of intra-industry trade for Australia. Later studies used a wider sample to demonstrate that intra-industry trade was an important phenomenon, especially in explaining trade flows of manufactured goods.

Subsequent articles have used either a weighted version of Balassa's index or an index based on Grubel and Lloyd's measures of intra-industry trade (Gray 1973; Giersch 1979). The index used in this study is a version of Grubel and Lloyd's measures. Aquino (1978) used the measure for several reasons. First, it corrects the downward bias of Grubel and Lloyd's measure when aggregate trade is imbalanced. Second, it is a measure that moves in the same direction as the proportion of intra-industry trade.

The variety hypothesis suggests that intra-industry trade will increase as income increases. Consumers' desire for variety will be satisfied by foreign differentiated products.

Aquino's study investigated the relationship between export and import patterns of manufactures. His study used three and four digit SITC level categories and calculated the value of an intra-industry index which was corrected for imbalances in trade of each of the SITC categories. If comparative advantage was an important explanation of trade in all types of goods, then a country should either export or import a commodity, depending on if the country has a comparative advantage in producing that good. He tested this proposition by investigating the relationship between export and import patterns of manufactures. His empirical test of this relationship was to estimate, for each industry and country, the elasticities of the share of each industry in the country's total exports of manufactures (normalized by the share of the industry in world exports of manufactures) with respect to the industry's share in the country's total imports of manufactures (normalized by the industry's share in the world imports of manufactures). The values of the elasticities turned out to be positive much more often than negative (Aquino 1978, pp. 286-287). This means that relatively high values of exports are more often associated with relatively *high* values of imports. In his industry elasticities, both passenger motor cars and domestic electrical appliances had positive and significant elasticities. However, television receivers had a negative, but statistically insignificant, elasticity. He found that when a country exports a relatively large quantity of a manufactured good, most likely it will also import a large quantity of the same commodity. The fact that export shares and import shares turn out to be positively correlated clearly indicates that the pattern of home demand has an impact on the trade flows of manufactures as suggested by the variety hypothesis.

The measure used in the intra-industry model is Aquino's measure. The test of the variety hypothesis using intra-industry trade is:

$$Q_j = f(\text{Adv}/\text{Sales};\ Y;\ U_t/\ U_{min})$$

The measure, Q_j, is Aquino's measure and is:

$$Q_j = \frac{\sum_j (X_{ij} + M_{ij} - \sum_j |X_{ij}^e - M_{ij}^e|)}{\sum (X_{ij} + M_{ij})}$$

where i = commodity, j = country, and X_{ij}^e and M_{ij}^e are estimates of what the values of exports and imports of each commodity would have been adjusting for the importance of the commodity in the trade of the sample countries:

$$X_{ij}^e = X_{ij} * \frac{X_{ij}}{\sum_j (X_{ij} + M_{ij})}$$

$$M_{ij}^e = M_{ij} * \frac{M_{ij}}{\sum_j (X_{ij} + M_{ij})}$$

The income coefficient should be positive and significant.

Sumary of Empirical Tests of the Variety Hypothesis

Import Share Equations

The model is of the following form:

$$\frac{Q_m}{Q_p - Q_x} = a_0 + a_1 \frac{P_f}{P_d} + a_2\, Y + a_3 \frac{U_t}{U_{min}} + a_4 \frac{\text{ADV}}{\text{SALES}} + E_i$$

The variety hypothesis predicts that the income coefficient (a_2 above) will be positive and significant. One would expect a_1, the price coefficient, to be negative. A_3, a coefficient measuring the effect of a change in capacity, should be negative. As full capacity is reached ($U_t/\ U_{min}$ decreases), the share of imports in demand should increase. A_4, the coefficient that measures the effect of a change in the advertising/sales ratio, should be negative. Assuming that the advertising/sales ratio for the U.S. motor vehicle industry is a good proxy for the advertising/sales ratio for Western European industry and that an increase in the U.S. advertising per unit of sales does not mean that the increase in advertising is directed solely to foreign markets, then one would expect a_4 to be negative. The results of a_4 could be ambiguous as it was not possible to separate domestic and foreign expenditures on advertising for the U.S. motor vehicle industry.

The empirical test using the three other goods (vacuum cleaners, washing machines, and television receivers) uses the same set of variables excluding the advertising/sales variable. The advertising data for those particular industries were not available. The predictions concerning the signs of the remaining coefficients remains the same.

Intra-Industry Trade Equations

In this section, the model is:

$$Q_{ij} = \frac{1}{1 + e} - (b_0 + b_1 Y + b_2 \frac{U_t}{U_{min}} + b_3 \frac{\text{ADV}}{\text{SALES}} + U_i)$$

The variety hypothesis suggests that intra-industry trade will increase as income increases. Because the dependent variable lies between 0 and 1, the equation used in estimation is a logistic transformation. To show that as income increases so will intra-industry trade, one has to show that the estimated coefficient for income (b_1) in the logistic transformation is positive and significant. The capacity coefficient (b_2) should be negative. As full capacity is approached, intra-industry should increase. The marketing coefficient (b_3) should be positive. As the marketing effort increases then intra-industry trade should also increase.

The empirical test using the other three goods is identical with the exception of not using advertising/sales. The predictions concerning the signs of each coefficient remains the same.

THE EMPIRICAL RESULTS

Import-Share Equations

In order to calculate an import-share equation for each good, one had to determine if pooling the data across countries was feasible. By pooling data of several subsets (in this case, the subsets were countries) and trying to estimate one regression, the subsets must come from the same underlying structure. If the countries had significantly different slope and intercept terms (especially slope terms), then the countries could not be combined to obtain an efficient estimate of common slope and intercept terms. The Chow test is designed to test whether the regression coefficients estimated by assigning subsets of a given set of observations to two or more different structures do, in fact, belong to the same structure. In this case, the Chow test would determine if the observations from the four countries can be combined over time into the same

Table 1. Results of Chow Tests: Import Share Equations for Cars Corrected for Serial Correlation

Various Price Specifications	*F Ratio*	*df*[a]	*Critical F Ratio*[b]
Unit value (using P_f as foreign price)	17.836[c]	15,64	2.19
A_{ij}	24.016[c]	15,64	2.19
B_{ij}	26.83[c]	15,64	2.19

Notes: Null hypothesis: equality of coefficients in four countries.
[a] *df* is degrees of freedom in numerator and denominator, respecitively.
[b] Value of F that has to be exceeded with significance level of 1% in order to reject null hypothesis.
[c] Reject null hypothesis.

Table 2. Results of Chow Tests: Import Share Equations for Television Receivers Corrected for Serial Correlation

Various Price Specifications	*F Ratio*	*df*[a]	*Critical F Ratio*[b]
Unit value (using P_f as foreign price)	1.74	8,18	3.71
A_{ij}	2.18	8,18	3.71
B_{ij}	6.03[c]	8,18	3.71

Notes: Null hypothesis: equality of coefficients in four countries.
[a] *df* is degrees of freedom in numerator and denominator, respecitively.
[b] Value of F that has to be exceeded with significance level of 1% in order to reject null hypothesis.
[c] Reject null hypothesis.

Table 3. Results of Chow Tests: Import Share Equations for Vacuum Cleaners Corrected for Serial Correlation

Various Price Specifications	*F Ratio*	*df*[a]	*Critical F Ratio*[b]
Unit value (using P_f as foreign price)	20.67[c]	8,18	3.71
A_{ij}	8.52[c]	8,18	3.71
B_{ij}	3.05	8,18	3.71

Notes: Null hypothesis: equality of coefficients in four countries.
[a] *df* is degrees of freedom in numerator and denominator, respecitively.
[b] Value of F that has to be exceeded with significance level of 1% in order to reject null hypothesis.
[c] Reject null hypothesis.

Table 4. Results of Chow Tests: Import Share Equations for Washing Machines Corrected for Serial Correlation

Various Price Specifications	F Ratio	df[a]	Critical F Ratio[b]
Unit value (using P_f as foreign price)	94.08[c]	8,18	3.71
A_{ij}	29.36[c]	8,18	3.71
B_{ij}	8.25[c]	8,18	3.71

Notes: Null hypothesis: equality of coefficients in four countries.
[a] *df* is degrees of freedom in numerator and denominator, respecitively.
[b] Value of *F* that has to be exceeded with significance level of 1% in order to reject null hypothesis.
[c] Reject null hypothesis.

regression equation. The application of the Chow test involves estimating a serial correlation factor for each country, combining the different factors into one regression, and then applying the Chow test to that corrected set of equations. The correction is necessary since adjacent errors among subsets are correlated in the presence of serial correlation and the Chow test requires independence.[8] Tables 1-4 report the results. The majority of the goods using the import-share equations could not be pooled. In this case, the results of country equations will be reported with sufficient caveats when the lack of degrees of freedom becomes a problem. The functional form chosen in the import-share equation was a double log equation and thus the coefficients can be interpreted as elasticities.

Using the results of the Chow test, none of the equations using motor vehicles could be pooled. Each country had significantly different slope and intercept terms for all equations. In the instance of cars, there is a sufficient number of observations available for each country to have confidence in the results of the separate country equations.

Tables 5-10 report the import-share equations for cars using different price specifications. Each equation was tested for the presence of serial correlation of error terms. The presence of serial correlation will not affect the unbiasedness or consistency of the OLS regression estimators, but it does affect their efficiency. In the case of positive serial correlation, this loss of efficiency will be masked by the fact that the estimates of the standard errors obtained by OLS will be smaller than the true standard errors. The regression estimators will be unbiased, but the standard error of the regression will be biased downward. This will lead to the conclusion that the parameter estimates are more precise than they actually are. In the case of cars, all four country equations were in the uncertain range of accepting the hypothesis that the serial correlation factor was zero.[9]

Table 5. Regression Results of Import Share Equations—Cars—Country Equations—Unit Value as Price Uncorrected for Serial Correlation

Variable	*France*	*United Kingdom*	*Italy*	*Federal Republic of Germany*
Intercept				
estimate	-15.182*	-26.953*	-13.819*	-14.133*
t	-2.783	-5.03	-7.614	-7.61
P_f/P_d				
estimate	-1.134*	.110	-.091	-.716
t	-3.886	.4371	-.35	-1.80
Y				
estimate	2.788*	4.798*	2.692*	3.44*
t	2.476	3.75	7.685	13.688
$U_t/_{min}$				
estimate	-.203	.755	-1.26*	.171
t	-.499	2.04	-4.02	1.72
Adv/Sales				
estimate	-.228	-.424	-.102	.671*
t	-.512	-1.2	-.419	2.57
Durbin-Watson	2.19	1.59	1.809	1.56
R^2	.8988	.8803	.9642	.9425
df	16	16	16	16
Regression sum of squared errors	3.051	1.977	.964	.719

Note: * Significant at the 95% confidence interval.

The range of the Durbin-Watson statistic was between .73 and 1.84. The serial correlation factor was estimated and a generalized differencing procedure was used to calculate new estimates of the regression parameters. These results are in Table 6. In both cases for all countries, the income coefficient is positive and significant at the 95% confidence interval. In Table 6, the price coefficients were negative for all countries as expected, but were significant at the 95% confidence interval for France only. The price specification used in this import-share equation was the unit value index divided by the domestic wholesale price index. The result that the price variable was not significant across all countries may suggest that price may not be as important as income in explaining the import share in consumption.

The results of the capacity variable are mixed. Theory expects the sign of this coefficient to be negative. As full employment is approached (U_t/U_{min} decreases), the import share of consumption would increase. This variable is

Table 6. Regression Results of Import Share Equations—Cars—Country Equations—Unit Value as Price Corrected for Serial Correlation

Variable	*France*	*United Kingdom*	*Italy*	*Federal Republic of Germany*
Intercept				
estimate	.999*	.97*	1.02*	.994*
t	2.75	4.86	7.51	7.16
P_f / P_d				
estimate	-1.22*	-.036	-.049	-.722
t	-4.28	-.1478	-.1875	-1.93
Y				
estimate	2.88*	4.813*	2.65*	3.44*
t	2.33	3.66	7.33	10.34
U_t / U_{min}				
estimate	-.275	.756	-1.26*	.188
t	-.629	2.04	-3.98	1.76
Adv/Sales				
estimate	-.158	-.251	-.208	.694*
t	-.357	-.5749	-.765	2.28
Regression Sum of Squares	2.902	1.762	.904	.684
R^2	.9836	.9846	.9914	.9871
df	15	15	15	15
Durbin-Watson	2.202	1.6431	1.8507	1.8351

Note: * Significant at the 95% confidence level.

significant and of the expected sign for only one country; for the rest of the countrics, it is insignificant and of mixed signs.

The advertising/sales variable was insignificant (though of the expected signs) in three of the four equations. For West Germany, however, it was significant at the 95% confidence interval and positive. This may be explained by the importance of the U..S market for the West Germany motor vehicle industry. During the time span of the study, one author suggests that the main German car export production level (the Volkswagen) was highly dependent on the U.S. market (Rhys 1972, pp. 145-149). In addition, in terms of shares of the German market, the American firms have done much better compared to the rest of the European countries' market share, mainly improving their position at the expense of Volkswagen. An increase in the advertising/sales ratio of the U.S. motor vehicle industry might cause an increase in the ratio for West German exports—causing exports to increase at a higher rate than

Table 7. Regression Results of Import Share Equations—Cars—Country Equations—A_{ij} as Price Uncorrected for Serial Correlation

Variable	*France*	*United Kingdom*	*Italy*	*Federal Republic of Germany*
Intercept				
parameter estimate	-30.837*	-24.321*	-13.116*	-11.871*
t	-5.43	-5.96	-6.69	-8.43
A_{ij}				
parameter estimate	-.154	-.133	-.078	.068
t	-.978	-1.37	-.919	.747
Y				
parameter estimate	6.584*	4.472*	2.47*	3.32*
t	6.20	4.74	5.74	12.49
U_t / U_{min}				
parameter estimate	-1.055	.433	-1.36*	.074
t	-2.34*	1.00	-6.28	.872
Adv/Sales				
parameter estimate	-.052	-.18	-.132	.974*
t	-.085	-.469	-.56	4.22
R^2	.8144	.8916	.9657	.9331
df	16	16	16	16
Durbin-Watson	.8212	1.729	1.95	1.7124
RSS	5.596	1.791	.9223	.8355

Notes: * Significant at the 95% confidence interval.

imports—thus causing the quantity of cars produced for domestic consumption to decrease. This might explain the positive coefficient of the advertising/sales ratio for West Germany (especially when the ratio is in terms of the U.S. industry).

The results of the car import-share equations lead to the definite conclusion that real per capita income is a major and significant explanatory variable.[10] For all countries, the income coefficient was positive, elastic, and significant. The variety hypothesis is confirmed using cars and should be included as an explanation of trade for this differentiated good. So far the results described above have utilized an average unit value as the foreign price of cars.

Tables 7 through 10 provide evidence to indicate that the positive and significant income coefficients hold up for various relative price specifications.

Table 8. Regression Results of Import Share Equations—Cars—Country Equations Using A_{ij} as Price Corrected for Serial Correlation

Variable	*France*	*United Kingdom*	*Italy*	*Federal Republic of Germany*
Intercept				
parameter estimate	.697*	1.032*	1.00*	.999*
t	3.02	5.79	7.07	7.39
A_{ij}				
parameter estimate	-.075	-.103	-.102	.072
t	-.61	-1.06	-1.2	.76
Y				
parameter estimate	3.90*	4.76*	2.28*	3.33*
t	2.32	4.66	5.35	9.785
U_t/U_{min}				
parameter estimate	-.139	.51	-1.35*	.0855
t	-.299	1.14	-6.64	.889
Adv/Sales				
parameter estimate	-.432	-.07	-.295	.987*
t	-.655	-.16	-1.17	3.37
R^2	.8827	.9876	.9935	.9872
df	15	15	15	15
Durbin-Watson	.797	1.86	2.06	1.8
RSS	2.838	1.687	.8315	.8177

Note: * Significant at the 95% confidence interval.

The results, using different specifications of a Balassa-type, revealed comparative advantage index as prices are identical. The income variable is always positive and significant. The price variables are negative but insignificant using both A_{ij} and B_{ij} as price. The capacity variable is significant for one country (Italy) and is of the expected sign. The advertising variable is negative and insignificant for all countries except West Germany. This result tends to confirm the special relationship that the West German car industry has with the U.S. market. All of the variables have the same sign and same degree of significance whether using A_{ij} or B_{ij} as price. This tends to confirm the hypothesis that A_{ij} and B_{ij} can be used as checks for one another.

Table 9. Regression Results of Import Share Equations—Cars—Country Equations Using B_{ij} as Price Uncorrected for Serial Correlation

Variable	*France*	*United Kingdom*	*Italy*	*Federal Republic of Germany*
Intercept				
parameter estimate	-29.56*	-17.25*	-15.27*	-11.797*
t	5.40	3.26	5.42	8.01
B_{ij}				
parameter estimate	-.549	-1.34*	-.414	-.039
t	1.02	2.19	.6096	.161
Y				
parameter estimate	6.28*	2.37*	2.88*	3.24*
t	6.44	5.27	7.466	13.16
U_t?U_{min}				
parameter estimate	-.965	.336	-1.18*	.053
t	2.03	.888	3.57	.602
Adv/Sales				
parameter estimate	.056	-.357	-.112	.942*
t	.087	1.16	.4716	4.04
R^2	.8153	.9070	.9647	.9309
df	16	16	16	16
Durbin-Watson	.8287	1.743	1.7898	1.77
RSS	5.57	1.537	.949	.8633

Note: * Significant at the 95% confidence interval.

Using cars, the results of the import-share equations have confirmed the main prediction of the variety hypothesis. The prediction remains valid using any of the proposed different price specifications. The next part of this section will report the results obtained with the three other differentiated goods.

According to the results of the Chow tests, it was possible to pool time and cross-sectional observations for television receivers (using all price specifications except B_{ij}), and vacuum cleaners using B_{ij} as price. Before describing the results, a short description of the problems of pooling and the estimation method used follows.

The case of pooling cross-sectional and time-series observations has interesting estimation problems. Here, the behavior of the disturbances over

Table 10. Regression Results of Import Share Equations—Cars—Country Equations Using B_{ij} as Price Corrected for Serial Correlation

Variable	*France*	*United Kingdom*	*Italy*	*Federal Republic of Germany*
Intercept				
parameter estimate	.694*	1.08*	1.02*	.996*
t	3.11	3.36	5.53	7.12
B_{ij}				
parameter estimate	-.243	-1.18	-.398	-.00137
t	-.579	-1.92	-.602	-.0054
Y				
parameter estimate	3.81*	2.85*	2.81*	3.231*
t	2.4	2.10	7.06	10.47
U_t/U_{min}				
parameter estimate	-.094	.393	-1.15*	.0693
t	-.205	1.02	-3.46	.701
Adv/Sales				
parameter estimate	-.262	-.232	-.231	.939*
t	-.354	-.624	-.85	3.26
R^2	.8851	.9862	.9915	.9877
df	15	15	15	15
Durbin-Watson	.85	1.901	1.835	1.832
RSS	2.879	1.453	.8846	.8497

Note: * Significant at the 95% confidence interval.

the cross-sectional units (in this case, countries) is likely to be different from the behavior of the disturbances of a given cross-sectional unit over time. In particular, the relationship between the disturbances of two countries at some specific time may differ from the relationship between the disturbances of a given country at two different periods of time. Clearly, various kinds of prior specifications with respect to the disturbances will lead to different methods of estimating the pooled equation.

The approach used in this study is an extension of the seemingly unrelated regression technique. The seemingly unrelated equations model consists of a series of equations linked because the error terms across equations are correlated. Zellner suggests that efficiency in estimation can be gained if one

Table 11. Parks Method Estimates—Television Receivers—Import Share Equations using A_{ij} as Price[a]

Variable Specification	*Estimated Coefficients*	*t Values*
Intercept	-20.823[b]	-5.934
A_{ij}	-.0878	-1.91
Y	4.039[b]	5.19
U_t/U_{min}	-.431[b]	-2.80

Notes: [a] 29 *df.*
[b] Significant at 95% confidence interval.

views the system of seemingly unrelated equations as a single large equation to be estimated, *especially* if there is knowledge that the disturbance in one regression might be correlated with the disturbance term in another regreession. Estimation of this single equation is accomplished through the use of generalized least-squares estimation which takes into account the fact that cross-equation error correlations may not be zero. The application of generalized least squares necessitates obtaining estimates of the error covariances among equations. Zellner obtains these estimates by first estimating an OLS equation on each cross-sectional unit and obtaining variances and covariances of the estimated residuals. The variances and covariances of the estimated residuals provide consistent estimators of the error variances and covariances. The problem with using Zellner's approach is that it accounts for autocorrelation of error term at the same point in time, but it does not allow serial correlation over time. Parks presents an extension of Zellner's method that allows autocorrelation of error terms over time as well as at the same point in time.[11] This study uses the Parks method.

Not all the goods chosen were eligible to be pooled. Using the import-share equations, the following goods were pooled: (1) television receivers using P_f/P_d and A_{ij} as price, and (2) vacuum cleaners using B_{ij} as price. Tables 11 through 13 report the results of the Parks method of combining time-series and cross-sectional data. The results of using television receivers, in Tables 11 and 13, substantiate the predictions of the variety hypothesis. All of the income coefficients are positive and significant. The capacity coefficient was negative and significant in all of the equations using different price specifications for television receivers. The price coefficients for the television receivers are not significantly different form zero using all of the various price specifications. Table 13 presents the results of combining cross-sectional and time-series data for only one price specification (B_{ij}) using vacuum cleaners. These results also confirm the predictions of the variety hypothesis. The income coefficient is

Table 12. Parks Method Estimate—Television Receivers—Import Share Equations using Unit Value as Price[a]

Variable Specification	*Estimated Coefficients*	*t Values*
Intercept	-20.44 [b]	-5.52
A_{ij}	-.099	-.593
Y	3.96 [b]	4.7777
U_t / U_{min}	-.359[b]	-2.49

Notes: [a] 29 *df.*
[b] Significant at 95% confidence interval.

Table 13. Parks Method Estimates—Vacuum Cleaners—using Import Share Equations and B_{ij} as Price[a]

Variable Specification	*Estimated Coefficients*	*t Values*
Intercept	-16.355[b]	-3.61
B_{ij}	-.396[b]	-2.87
Y	3.241[b]	3.25
U_t / U_{min}	-.2[b]	-1.29

Notes: [a] 29 *df.*
[b] Significant at 95% confidence interval.

positive and significant. The capacity variable is negative as expected but is not significant at the 95% confidence interval. The price coefficient is negative and significant. All of the variables are of the expected signs and all, except the capacity variable, are significant.

The next set of reported results deal with equations that were impossible to pool. As a result, the lack of degrees of freedom is a major problem. Not a great deal of confidence can be put on the significance of these coefficients. Tables 14 to 19 report the results of those goods on which the data could not be pooled as determined by the Chow tests. All of the income coefficients are positive; but not all of the income coefficients are significant at the 95% confidence interval. Out of 18 country regressions, the income coefficient is positive and significant in 10 regressions. No other variable (except the intercept) is significant in as many regressions as the income coefficient. However, because of the lack of observations in each regression, the most that one could say is that the major premise of the variety hypothesis is supported tentatively by the data using television receivers, vacuum cleaners, and washing machines.

Table 14. Import Share Equations using B_{ij} as Price—Television Receivers

Variable Specification	*France*	*Italy*	*Federal Republic of Germany*
Intercept			
parameter estimate	.875	.754*	.607*
t	.748	2.89	2.93
B_{ij}			
parameter estimate	-.307	-3.07	-.62
t	-1.85	-1.82	-2.33
Y			
parameter estimate	.645*	7.79*	1.87*
t	2.85	2.81	3.23
U_t/U_{min}			
parameter estimate	-.23	-3.07	-.26
t	-.212	-1.82	-1.60
R^2	.999	.9417	.9934
df	8	8	8
Durbin-Watson	1.8905	1.8142	1.7834
RSS	.2026	.5575	.3735

Note: * Significant at the 95% confidence interval.

The price coefficients are negative and significant in 6 out of 18 regressions. The capacity coefficients are uniformly insignificant and of mixed signs. The major hypothesis regarding the income coefficient is supported, however, the confidence attached to these results must necessarily be less than the confidence attached to the reported results of the country equations using cars and the pooled equations using television receivers and vacuum cleaners.

Intra-Industry Trade Equations

Methodologically, the intra-industry trade equations have an interesting problem. The dependent variable, Q_{ij}, is constrained to lie between the values of 0 and 1, by definition of the intra-industry trade index. The OLS assumption of the dependent variable having a normal distribution is no longer valid. One

Table 15. Import Share Equations using Unit Value as Price—Vacuum Cleaners

Variable Specification	*France*	*Italy*	*Federal Republic of Germany*
Intercept			
parameter			
estimate	-4.47	-21.93*	-12.24*
t	-.77	-7.03	-3.30
P_f / P_d			
parameter			
estimate	-1.149*	-1.197[a]	-.39
t	-2.81	-13.77	-5.72
Y			
parameter			
estimate	.402	4.75*	2.28*
t	2.11	7.00	2.786
U_t / U_{min}			
parameter			
estimate	.70	1.18*	.055
t	.299	3.67	.3908
Durbin-Watson	1.394	1.6823	1.7295
R^2	.834	.9755	.639
df	8	8	8
RSS	.4328	.4526	.5193

Note: * Significant at the 95% confidence interval.

way of dealing with this problem is to use logistic transformation. This is a method that deals with an intrinsically nonlinear model represented as:

$$U_i = \frac{\delta}{1 + e^{(a + B_i X_i + E_i)}} \qquad \delta > 0 \ ; \ B_i < 0$$

In this case, the population regression line is given by a logistic growth curve as shown below:

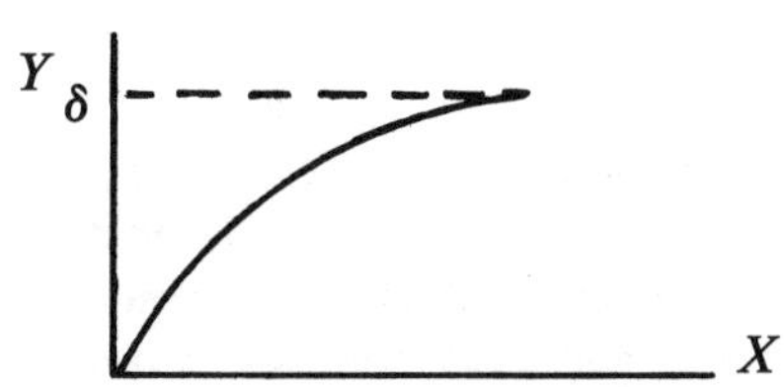

Table 16. Import Share Equations using Unit Value as Price—Washing Machines

Variable Specification	*France*	*Italy*	*Federal Republic of Germany*
Intercept			
parameter			
estimate	6.8	-3.38 *	-7.52*
t	.8966	-.8441	-2.91
P_f / P_d			
parameter			
estimate	-1.45*	-.918	-1.97*
t	-2.52	-2.38	-2.95
Y			
parameter			
estimate	1.76	.023	1.48*
t	1.01	1.03	2.62
U_t / U_{min}			
parameter			
estimate	-.063	-.31	.042
t	-.1528	-.0272	.46
R^2	.5469	.5962	.7566
df	8	8	8
Durbin-Watson	1.4032	2.1659	2.5096
RSS	.7347	.398871	.2354

Note: * Significant at the 95% confidence interval.

The slope of this cumulative logistic distribution is greatest at $Y_i = 1/2$. In terms of the regression model, this implies that changes in the independent variables will have their greatest impact on the probability of choosing *Y* at the midpoint of the distribution. The rather low slopes near the endpoints of the distribution imply that large changes in *X* are necessary to bring about a small change in the probability of *Y*. The interpretation of the individual estimated parameters must be done with care. The numerical effect of a 1% change in the independent variable on the intra-industry trade index depends upon the value of the index itself. When the index is close to one, then the effect of an increase in the independent variable is less than if the index is in the midpoint of the distribution. What is of importance to the variety hypothesis is the sign of the estimated coefficient. If the coefficient is positive, then as the independent variable increases, the dependent variable increases also. What is not so self-evident is the numerical amount that a given change in the independent variable will affect on the dependent variable.

Table 17. Regression Results of Import Share Equations using A_{ij} as Price—Vacuum Cleaners

Variable Specification	*France*	*Italy*	*Federal Republic of Germany*
Intercept			
parameter estimate	-8.26	-23.97*	-12.462*
t	-1.07	-2.28	-3.79
A_{ij}			
parameter estimate	.057	-.485*	-.127
t	1.04	-3.05	-1.58
Y			
parameter estimate	1.28	5.09*	2.25*
t	1.76	2.3	3.11
U_t/U_{min}			
parameter estimate	.4	2.17	.163
t	.954	2.02	1.12
Durbin-Watson	1.74	2.716	1.978
R^2	.709	.7214	.7137
df	8	8	8
RSS	.7585	5.154	.412

Note: * Significant at the 95% confidence interval.

Empirical Results of the Intra-Industry Trade Equations

The model estimated is:

$$\log\left(\frac{Q_{ij}}{1-Q_{ij}}\right) = b_0 + b_1 Y_t + b_2 \frac{\text{ADV}}{\text{SALES}} + b_3 \frac{U_t}{U_{min}} + E_i$$

where i refers to country i and j refers to good j. For goods other than cars, the advertising/sales variable was omitted. The variety hypothesis is concerned with the effect of income on the index of intra-industry trade. The variety hypothesis implies that as income increases, so will the index Q_{ij}. If the income coefficient is positive and significant, the variety hypothesis can be used as an explanation for increasing intra-industry trade in these goods.

Table 18. Import Share Equations using A_{ij} as Price—Washing Machines

Variable Specification	*France*	*Italy*	*Federal Republic of Germany*
Intercept			
parameter estimate	-.217	-10.05*	-10.14*
t	-.024	-2.59	-2.9
A_{ij}			
parameter estimate	-.089	-.011	-.079
t	-.1135	-.1528	-.8089
Y_t			
parameter estimate	.239	1.43*	1.96*
t	1.5	2.3	2.58
U_t/U_{min}			
parameter estimate	-.055	-.426	.00998
t	-.1129	-1.09	.0718
Durbin-Watson	1.477	1.939	1.727
R^2	.3675	.3116	.5309
df	8	8	8
RSS	1.0257	.6799	.4537

Note: * Significant at the 95% confidence interval.

Table 20 applies the Chow test to the intra-industry trade equations that were converted to the logistic transformation. Table 21 summarizes the results of country equations for cars which is the product whose data could not be pooled. Tables 22-24 report the results of the goods that could be pooled using Parks' method of estimation.

Table 21 describes the results using cars. In all country equations, the income coefficient is positive and significant at the 95% confidence interval. The capacity is negative for two countries, Italy and the United Kingdom, but is significant only for the United Kingdom. So only for that country can one state that as full capaciety approaches and U_t/U_{min} decreases, does Q_{ij} increase. The advertising/sales coefficients are positive but significant for all countries. There is no evidence of serial correlation in any of the equations.

The results using the remaining three goods do not support the main prediction of the variety hypothesis as strongly as the results using cars. The

Table 19. Import Share Equations using B_{ij} as Price—Washing Machines

Variable Specification	*France*	*Italy*	*Federal Republic of Germany*
Intercept			
parameter estimate	7.088	-6.55	-9.93*
t	.7095	-1.35	-2.54
B_{ij}			
parameter estimate	-.347	-1.05*	-.154
t	-.7346	-2.46	-1.33
Y			
parameter estimate	1.67	.846	1.9
t	1.595	.851	2.19
U_t / U_{min}			
parameter estimate	-.179	.473	.065
t	-.3007	.342	.45
Durbin-Watson	1.9627	2.3355	1.4135
R^2	.4722	.6453	.601
df	8	8	8
RSS	.8415	.3342	.3518

Note: * Significant at the 95% confidence interval.

Table 20. Chow Test—Intra-Industry Trade Equation—Logistic Transformation

Goods	*F Ratio*	*Critical F Ratio*
Cars	5.595*	1.83 *df* = 12,68
Television receivers	.2113	2.46 *df* = 6,27
Vacuum cleaners	.1525	2.46 *df* = 6,27
Washing machines	.2455	2.46 *df* = 6,27

Notes: Null hypothesis: equality of coefficients in four countries.
* Reject null hypothesis.

Table 21. Regression Results of Intra-Industry Trade Equation—Cars—Logistic Transformation

Variables Specified	*France*	*United Kingdom*	*Italy*	*Federal Republic of Germany*
Intercept				
parameter estimate	.071	-.588*	.228	-.169
t	.4853	-2.77	.947	-.893
U_t				
parameter estimate	.013*	.016*	.014*	.016*
t	6.88	6.19	8.19	12.28
U_t/U_{min}				
parameter estimate	.017	-.16*	-.028	.011
t	.78	-3.86	-.589	.914
Adv/Sales				
parameter estimate	17.45	9.94	.897	11.658
t	1.30	.9323	.067	.888
Durbin-Watson	1.497	1.8833	1.9842	1.8594
R^2	.9075	.9329	.8981	.9109
df	16	16	16	16
RSS	.174	.1263	.1918	.1676

Note: * Significant at the 95% confidence interval.

Table 22. Television Receivers—Regression Results of Intra-Industry Trade Equations—Parks Estimates—Pooled Equations, Logistic Transformation

Variable Specification	*Estimated Coefficients*	*t Values*
Intercept	.745	.852
Y^*	.087	.646
U_t/U_{min}	-.00007	-.022

Notes: 33 *df.*
* Significant at 95% confidence interval.

Table 23. Vacuum Cleaners—Regression Results of Intra-Industry Trade Equations—Parks Estimates—Pooled Equations, Logistic Transformation

Variable Specification	*Estimated Coefficients*	*t Values*
Intercept	4.42	3.03*
Y	.5	1.57
U_t / U_{min}	-.007	-1.37

Notes: 33 *df.*
* Significant at 95% confidence interval.

Table 24. Washing Machines—Regression Results of Intra-Industry Trade Equations—Parks Estimates—Pooled Equations, Logistic Transformation

Variable Specification	*Estimated Coefficients*	*t Values*
Intercept	1.22	2.39*
Y	.076	1.63
U_t / U_{min}	-.0035	-.0687

Notes: 33 *df.*
* Significant at 95% confidence interval.

income coefficient is of the expected sign for all three goods but the coefficient is not significant at the 95% confidence interval. In two of the goods, vacuum cleaners and washing machines, the income coefficient comes close to approaching significance. The capacity variable also was not significant in any of the equations. The best that could be said regarding the predictions of the variety hypothesis is that there is an indication that income's effect on intra-industry trade is positive, but one cannot declare that statement with a high degree of certainty using vacuum cleaners, television receivers, and washing machines as a sample of differentiated goods.

Analysis Including Tariffs

This section will answer the question of whether the results reported on cars can be explained by the lowering of tariffs in the Common Market. This issue is addressed by deleting the years that the Common Market did not exist. A set of regressions was run for the time span of 1962-1978 for all countries using

Table 25. Cars—Regression Results Using Import Share Equations, Time Span: 1962-1975, Country Equations using P_f/P_d as Price

Variable Specification	*France*	*United Kingdom*	*Italy*	*Federal Republic of Germany*
Intercept				
estimate	.38	-35.72*	-12.33*	-11.16*
t	.112	-9.66	-4.94	-2.72
P_f/P_d				
estimate	-.397	.323	.588	.132
t	-.4312	.426	.731	.177
Y				
estimate	.34	7.375*	2.36*	2.82*
t	1.438	9.61	4.43	4.31
U_t/U_{min}				
estimate	.379	.868*	-.102	.051
t	1.679	4.3	-.2528	.415
Adv/Sales				
estimate	.193	.235	-1.71	.669*
t	.997	.6911	-2.05	2.25
Durbin-Watson	1.6847	2.2719	1.5577	1.5293
R^2	.7302	.9751	.756	.9176
df	9	9	9	9
RSS	.2156	.2459	.6537	.1866

Note: * Significant at the 95% confidence interval.

all price specifications. If the income coefficient is positive and significant during that time span, then the variety hypothesis is confirmed using imports that were not subject to tariffs. The model is:

$$\frac{Qm_{EEC}}{Q_p - Q_x} = c_0 + c_1 Y + c_2 \frac{P_f}{P_d} + c_3 \frac{\text{ADV}}{\text{SALES}} + c_4 \frac{U_t}{U_{min}} + E_i$$

where Qm_{EEC} is the quantity of imports of cars in units from the three remaining countries; Q_p is quantity of cars produced in units in country i; Q_x is quantity of cars exported in units from country i; P_f is total value of cars imported from the three remaining countries divided by quantity of cars imported from the three remaining countries (1970 = 100); P_d is the domestic wholesale price index (1970 = 100); Y is real per capita income (1970 = 100); ADV is advertising of the U.S. motor vehicle industry; U_t is unemployment rate at time t; and U_{min} is minimum unemployment rate over the time span used.

Table 26. Cars—Regression Results Using Import Share Equations, Time Span: 1962-1975, Country Equations A_{ij} as Price

Variable Specification	*France*	*United Kingdom*	*Italy*	*Federal Republic of Germany*
Intercept				
estimate	.35	-36.73*	-12.142*	-11.545*
t	.091	-10.14	-5.05	-6.46
A_{ij}				
estimate	.034	.011	-.104	-.024
t	.7	.192	-1.06	-.356
Y_t				
estimate	.397	7.47*	2.052*	2.815*
t	.431	9.28	3.44	6.28
U_t / U_{min}				
estimate	.4	.88*	-1.47	.072
t	1.6	3.55	-2.15	.872
Adv/Sales				
estimate	.131	.106	-.32	.6*
t	.61	.47	-.87	3.05
Durbin-Watson	1.867	2.346	1.9132	1.6088
R^2	.6854	.9747	.7701	.9184
df	9	9	9	9
RSS	.2515	.2499	.6158	.1846

Note: * Significant at the 95% confidence interval.

This equation was estimated using the two other price specifications, A_{ij} and B_{ij}, for the same time span of 1962-1978. Using Balassa's comparative advantage indices as price, one would expect the income coefficients to be positive and significant if the variety hypothesis is confirmed. Table 25 summarizes the regression results using the average unit value as foreign price. For all countries, the income coefficient is positive. However, the income coefficient is significant at the 95% confidence interval for all countries except France. No other variable (except the intercept) was consistently significant for more than one country. No variable was significant in France's equation. The lack of degrees of freedom is a problem in all of these equations. The regression results using the different price specifications (summarized in Tables 26 and 27) are similar to the results described above. All income coefficients are positive for all countries. Only France's estimates are consistently insignificant. The income coefficient and the intercept were the only variables that were significant and positive for the three countries.

Table 27. Cars—Import Share Equations, Time Span: 1962-1975, B_{ij} as Price

Variable Specification	*France*	*United Kingdom*	*Italy*	*Federal Republic of Germany*
Intercept				
estimate	-1.13	-33.25*	-14.84*	-11.29*
t	-.303	-6.878	-3.55	-7.45
B_{ij}				
estimate	-.083	-.336	-.517	-.22
t	-.497	-.875	-.564	-1.38
Y_t				
estimate	.011	6.617*	2.63*	2.72*
t	.013	5.614	3.67	7.74
U_t / U_{min}				
estimate	.378	.764*	-1.33	.074
t	1.53	3.409	-1.86	.99
Adv/Sales				
estimate	.197	.11	-.238	.587*
t	.902	.542	-.638	3.49
Durbin-Watson	1.9415	2.324	1.694	1.9827
R^2	.6771	.9766	.7503	.9318
df	9	9	9	9
RSS	.2581	.2313	.6689	.1544

Note: * Significant at the 95% confidence interval.

The variety hypothesis is tentatively confirmed by three countries. However, the lack of degrees of freedom is a problem. In addition, since none of the variables in any of France's equations are significant, the confirmation of the variety hypothesis is tentative. During the period of 1962-1978, France may have had a more *nationalistic* taste for cars than the other countries.

SUMMARY AND CONCLUSIONS

The empirical results presented in this study support the main prediction of the variety hypothesis. This study is a disaggregated one, concentrating on 4-digit SITC and 6-digit NIMEXE categories. The goods are consumer durable goods whose supply characteristics are similar across the countries chosen for the sample. If the variety hypothesis can be used to explain trade flows of differentiated manufactured goods, the main prediction (that the income coefficient is positive and significant) must be supported by this study.

The model that directly tests the predictions of the variety hypoethsis is the import-share model. The import share will increase as income increases, because, with higher incomes, purchasers are able to buy goods which contain a more preferred combination of characteristics. The source of these increased number of goods will be imports. Therefore, as income incrcases, the import share in demand will also increase.

There were three different price specifications used in this study. Using cars and television receivers, the major prediction of the variety hypothesis—that the income coefficient was positive and significant—was supported by all four countries and all three price specifications. Using vacuum cleaners, the income coefficient was positive and significant for Italy and the Federal Republic of Germany. Using washing machines, the income coefficient was positive and significant for Italy employing the two measures of revealed comparative advantage as price. When unit value was used as price, then the income coefficient was positive and significant for the Federal Republic of Germany alone. The variety hypothesis is confirmed using cars, television receivers, and vacuum cleaners. The results of washing machines do not have significant statistical support of the variety hypothesis across countries.

The variety hypothesis can be used to explain trade in manufactured goods which have similar supply characteristics among countries. This hypothesis augments the factor-proportions theory by explaining trade flows of manufactured goods among nations of relatively similar factor endowments. The variety hypothesis cannot explain all trade in manufactured goods. It must be used in conjunction with theories that emphasize supply characteristics in order to explain the more general trade in manufactured goods.

Because the variety hypothesis explains trade in differentiated goods, it also constitutes an explanation for intra-industry trade. The hypothesis predicts that as incomes increase, the index of intra-industry trade will increase if the country will not experience long-term problems in the balance of trade. If the country is not to experience these long-run problems, then increases in a country's exports (as will its imports) will be proportionately greater than the increases in its real income per capita. Another way of testing this proposition is to use an index of intra-industry trade. As incomes increase, then the index of intra-industry trade should also increase. Using cars, this prediction of the variety hypotehsis is confirmed for all countries. Using the other three goods this prediction does not have significant statistical support. The income coefficient is positive but not significant at the 95% confidence interval. However, these three goods are a relatively unimportant element in the total trade of manufactured goods when compared to the importance of passenger cars. Therefore, the result that the variety hypothesis is confirmed using cars is not surprising.

While the model must be viewed as preliminary and the results as tentative, they are, nonetheless, encouraging. The variety hypothesis does have a place in international trade theory. It must be used as an additional explanation for trade in manufactured goods rather than the sole explanation. The variety hypothesis is more useful in explaining trade in differentiated goods which belong to the same commodity group, having similar supply characteristics. This study should be viewed as an empirical verification of an explanation of trade flows of differentiated products focusing on demand variables, and thus, should be considered as part of the total solution of the international trade puzzle.

NOTES

1. See Caves (1960, Chapter 6) for a review of the studies that analyze demand factors. In Meade's *Geometry of International Trade* (1952), to obtain the trade indifference curves, he assumes all tastes are identical—which ignores the demand aspects when there is a change in the pattern of international trade.

2. The main source of the dependent variable for the car equation was the *World Motor Vehicle Data* (1979 ed.) publishd by the Motor Vehicle Manufacturing Association. This source gave exports, imports, and production of cars in units for the years of 1955-1978. To obtain imports of cars from the three remaining countries, the following assumption was made: The imports of cars from the four Western European countries were of the same weight. This assumption was needed in order to compute the number of units imported from the three remaining countries. Figures breaking down total imports (measured in weight) according to source are available but only measured in metric tons. Therefore, using the assumption, if 18% of the total imports of United Kingdom (measured in metric tons) came from the Federal Republic of Germany, France, and Italy, then 18% of the United Kingdom's total imports (measured in units) came from the Federal Republic of Germany, France, and Italy. The source for the data in metric tons was the United Nations *Commodity Trade Statistics.* The source of the income variable for all countries was various issues of the United Nations *Statistical Yearbook,* converted to a 1970 base. The source of the unemployment figures was from various issues of the International Labor Organization *Yearbook of Labor Statistics.* The advertising/sales ratio for the U.S. motor vehicle industry was various issues of the U.S. Government *Statistics of Income.* The source of the domestic wholesale price indices was various issues of the *Statistical Yearbook* and all indices were converted to a 1970 base. For the remaining three goods, the only different statistical source was used in the collection of the imports, exports, and production both in value and unit terms. The Common Market publishes unit and value figures for production exports and imports of these three goods in *Analytical Tables of Foreign Trade.* The time span for these variables is from 1966 through 1978.

3. In the *Cambridge Journal of Economics,* Barker (1978) does not define his capacity, price, or trend terms, saying that a previous reference discusses the functional form and data sources. That source is published in France and I have not been able to obtain a copy of the source in the United States.

4. Houthakker and Magee (1969). See Leamer and Stern (1975) for a good summary in Chapter 2.

5. See note 2.

6. Arena set C^* to 93 because McGraw-Hill Department of Economics estimated it to be 93 in April 1966.

7. An attempt to obtain data from any (preferably all) European car manufacturers was unsuccessful.

8. The Chow test breaks down in the presence of heteroskedasticity. See Toyoda (1974).
9. The range of the Durbin-Watson stastistic is:

.73	d	1.84:	uncertain
1.84	d	2.16:	accept hypothesis that there exists no serial correlation
2.16	d	3.27:	uncertain

Outside of these ranges, reject the hypothesis that there is no serial correlation.

10. During the time span of 1955-1975, incoem and time were highly collinear. A set of regressions of import-share equations for cars was estimated using time instead of income as an independent variable. The time coefficient was significant and positive for all four countries. These results suggest that for the time period and sample chosen, it is difficult to separate the income and time effects. However, time as an explanatory variable is not appealing since it includes such factors as number of characteristics that each good contains, total number of goods offered as well as other factors that are important in explaining consumer durable goods.

11. See da Silva (1975) for a discussion of all of the methods for pooling data; sespecially see pp. 33-45 for a discussion of the Parks method.

REFERENCES

Aquino, A. (1978). "Intra-Industry Trade and Inter-Industry Specialization as Concurrent Sources of International Trade in Manufactures." *Weltwirtshaftleches Archiv* 114(2): 275-296.

Arena, J. (1967). "U.S. Imports and the Manufacturing Utilization Rate." *New England Business Review* (August):1-7.

Balassa, B. (1966). "Tariff Reductions and Trade in Manufactures Among the Industrial Countries." *American Economic Review* 56: 466-473.

________. (1967a). "Trade Liberalization and 'Revealed' Comparative Advantage." *The Manchester School of Economic and Social Studies* 33(2): 99-123.

________. (1967b). "Trade Creation and Trade Diversion in the European Market." *Economic Journal* 77.

Barker, T. (1978). "International Trade and Economic Growth: An Alternative to the Neoclassical Approach." *Cambridge Journal of Economics* 1: 153-171.

Caves, R. (1960). *Trade and Economic Structure.* Cambridge, MA: Cambridge University Press.

Caves, R. and R. Jones. (1977). *World Trade and Payments.* Boston, MA: Little, Brown.

Davies, R. (1978). "Trade Overlap and Intra-Industry Trade: A Comment." *Economic Inquiry* 16(July): 470-474.

European Economic Community. *Analytical Tables of Foreign Trade.* Various issues.

Finger, J.M. (1975). "Trade Overlap and Intra-Industry Trade." *Economic Inquiry* (December): 581-589.

Giersch, H. (1979). *On the Economics of Intra-Industry Trade.* Tubingen, W. Germany: J.C.B. Mohr.

Gray, H.P. (1973). "Two-Way International Trade in Manufactures: A Theoretical Underpinning." *Weltwirtschaftleches Archiv* 109: 19-38.

________. (1976). *A Generalized Theory of International Trade.* London: Macmillan.

________. (1977). "Two-way International Trade: Reply." *Weltwirtschaftleches Archiv* 113: 182-184.

________. (1979). "Intra-Industry Trade: The Effects of Different Levels of Data Aggregation." In H. Giersch (ed.) *On the Economics of Intra-Industry Trade.* Tubingen, W. Germany: J.C.B. Mohr.

________. (1980). "The Theory of International Trade Among Industrial Nations." *Weltwirtschaftleches Archiv* 116.

Gray, H.P. and J. Martin. (1980). "The Meaning and Measurement of Product Differentiation in International Trade." *Weltwirtschaftleches Archiv* 116: 322-329.

Gray, H.P. and K. Smith. (1978). "The Income Sensitivity of International Trade." Mimeo.

Grubel, H. (1967). "Intra-Industry Specialization and the Pattern of Trade." *Canadian Journal of Economics and Political Science* 33: 374-388.

Grubel, H. and P. Lloyd. (1971). "The Empirical Measurement of Intra-Industry Trade." *Economic Record* 47: 494-517.

________. (1975). *Intra-Industry Trade.* London: Halsted.

Hitiris, T. (19787). "Effective Protection and Economic Performance in the U.K. Manufacturing Industry, 1963 and 1968." *Economic Journal* 88: 107-120.

Hoftyzer, J. (1975). "Empirical Verification of Linder's Trade Thesis: Comment." *Southern Economic Journal:* 694-698.

Houthakker, H.S. and S.P. Magee. (1969). "Income and Price Elasticities in World Trade." *Review of Economics and Statistics* (May): 111-125.

Hufbauer, G.C. (1970). "The Impact of National Characteristics and Technology on Commodity Composition of Trade in Manufactured Goods." In R. Vernon (ed.), *Technology Factor in International Trade.* New York: National Bureau of Economics.

International Labor Organization. *Yearbook of Labor Statistics.* Various issues.

Kmenta, J. (1971). *Elements of Econometrics.* New York: Macmillan.

Kravis, I.B. (1956). "Availability and Other Influences on the Commodity Composition of Trade." *Journal of Political Economy* 64.

Kravis, I.B. and R. Lipsey. (1971). *Price Competitiveness in World Trade.* New York: National Bureau of Economic Research.

Krenin, M.E. (1960). "U.S. Imports and Income in the Postwar Period." *Review of Economics and Statistics:* 223-225.

________. (1967). "Price Elasticities in International Trade." *Review of Economics and Statistics:* 510-516.

________. (1973). "Disaggregated Import Demand Functions: Further Results." *Southern Economic Journal* 40: 19-25.

Lancaster, K. (1966). "A New Approach to Consumer Theory." *Journal of Political Economy* 74: 132-156.

Leamer, E. and R. Stern. (1975). *Quantitative International Economics.* Cambridge, MA: Harvard University Press.

Linder, S.B. (1961). *An Essay on Trade and Transformation.* New York: Wiley.

Loertscher, R. and F. Wolter. (1980). "Determinants of Intra-Industry Trade Among Countries and Across Industries." *Weltwirtschaftleches Archiv* 116(2): 280-293.

Magee, S. (1975). "Prices, Incomes and Foreign Trade." In P. Kenen (ed.), *International Trade and Finance for Research.* Cambridge, MA: Cambridge University Press.

Meade, J. (1952). *Geometry of International Trade.* London: Allen & Unwin.

Motor Vehicle Manufacturer Association. (1980). *World Motor Vehicle Data.* Detroit: Author.

Ohlin, B. (1967). *Interregional and International Trade.* Cambridge, MA: Cambridge University Press.

Pagoulatos, E. and R. Sorenson. (1974). "Two-Way Trade: An Econometric Analysis." *Weltwirtschaftleches Archiv* 110.

Pindyck, R. and D. Rubenfeld. (1976). *Econometric Models and Economic Forecasts.* New York: McGraw-Hill.

Rhys, D.G. (1972). *The Motor Vehicle Industry: An Economic Survey.* London: Butterworth.

Sailors, J. et al. (1973). "Empirical Verification of Linder's Trade Thesis." *Southern Economic Journal* (October): 262-268.

da Silva, J. (May 1975). "The Analysis of Cross-Sectional Time Series Data." Institute of Statistics Mimeograph Series No. 1011. Raleigh, NC: Institute of Statistics.

Toder, E., E. Burton, and N.S. Cardell. (1978). *Trade Policy and the U.S. Automobile Industry: A Charles River Associates Research Report.* New York: Praeger.

Toyoda, T. (1974). "Use of the Chow Test Under Heteroskedasticity." *Econometrica* (May): 601-608.

United Nations. (1955-1979). *Commodity Trade Statistics, Series D.* New York: Author.

________. (1955-1979). *Statistical Yearbook.* New York: Author.

United States Government. (1955-1975). *Statistics of Income.* Washington, D.C: Treasury Department (I.R.S.).

Vernon, R. (1966). "International Investment and International Trade in the Product Cycle." *Quarterly Journal of Economics:* 160-207.

Zellner, A. (1962). "An Efficient Method of Estimating Seemingly Unrelated Regressions and Tests For Aggregation Bias." *Journal of the American Statistical Association* (June): 348-368.

MARKET SHARE EFFECTS OF THE LOMÉ CONVENTION AND THE GSP

Demetri P. Tsanacas

INTRODUCTION

The current pattern of international trade is, to a great extent, the result of political-economic consideration. In particular, the existence of preferential treatment in the structure of commercial policy has led to the regionalization of both patterns of international trade and industrial production beyond the degree that would be expected as a result of lower transportation costs. The actual structure of tariffs and other impediments have led to reduced access to the markets of developed countries by all or some developing countries.

The theory of regional or bloc-discrimination of tariffs and other barriers to trade has been developed by Viner (1950) and Meade (1955) in their analysis of the problems of customs unions. In general, preferential treatment increases the accessibility of goods from the region enjoying the preference and displaces goods from other regions even in static equilibrium. The institution of preferences has the same effect, but analysis, through time, must recognize that many other factors affect any changes in the pattern of trade; elasticities of supply of different goods, as well as, changes in tastes in different goods. Further, for goods which require some kind of marketing effort, preferential

Research in International Business and Finance, vol. 7, pages 129-207.

ISBN: 0-89232-906-8

treatment in one area may cause a conscious effort on the part of the producing country to expand its sales to another, third area. These efforts are usually referred to, summarily, as trade creation and trade diversion. This study develops and tests two hypothesis: (a) that the preferential commercial treatment incorporated in the Lomé Convention has drastically reduced the effects of the Generalized System of Preferences (GSP) in the European Economic Community (EEC) for other non-Lomé developing nations; and (b) that the exports from the Lomé beneficiaries have been diverted away from Japan and the United States making GSP in these countries more beneficial for non-Lomé nations.

This study (1) summarizes the characteristics of two important innovations in preferential arrangements; (2) sets out the methodology of the test; (3) examines the hypothesis in terms of aggregate data; and (4) considers them on the basis of 3-digit commodity data.

PREFERENTIAL TREATMENT INSTITUTED DURING THE 1970s

The problems of the developing world have been discussed extensively at the various UNCTAD Conferences, but it was not until 1971 through the implementation of the GSP that the emphasis on finding meaningful solutions to these problems shifted to access to markets, rather than aid.

The GSP was designed as a means of improving access to the markets of the developed nations for manufactured exports of developing nations through a series of preferential tariffs. According to the scheme, exports from a developing nation would be charged a lower (preferential) tariff than would exports from competing developed nations which would continue to be charged the most-favored nation (MFN) tariff on similar products. The GSP would thus provide developing nations with a margin of preferences equal, at a maximum, the MFN tariff in the industrialized nations, making developing country exports more competitive even if some industrialized nations enjoyed a slight cost advantage for the product in question. Such a price advantage is expected to stimulate new investment in export capacity, thus leading to economic development through industrialization (for a detailed explanation of GSP see Murray [1977]).

Preferential trading arrangements have traditionally been analyzed in terms of trade creation and trade diversion concentrating specifically on whether world welfare increases or decreases (Balassa 1967). In the case of the GSP, world welfare is secondary, because the GSP aims at increasing the welfare of the developing countries, measured in higher volume of export, to developed countries. Under the trade creation effect, imports from a preferred source displace less-efficient domestic production; while, under the trade diversion, effect imports from a preferred source displace more-efficiently produced imports from a nonpreferred source. Both of these effects operate in favor of the developing countries. The total impact of the GSP which both liberalizes and distorts world trade depends upon the relative magnitudes of trade creation and trade diversion. A large trade creation will result if there are similarities in the economic structure of the preferred sources and the importing countries. If there are substantial differences in the economic structure, the scope of the trade creation is significantly reduced. Likewise, the magnitude of the trade diversion effect is enhanced by the similarities in the economic structures of preferred sources and nonpreferred sources.

The scope of the GSP was, however, limited to the manufactured products falling under the 25-99 chapters of the Brussels Tariff Nomenclatura (BTN) classification and it excluded the processed agricultural and fishery products which are of special interest to a large number of developing nations. In addition, its effectiveness was greatly reduced through a whole series of safeguard measures instituted by the preference-granting developed nations. These measures range from outright exclusion on import-sensitive products to restrictive ceiling limitations and maximum amounts. Two of these measures, the ceiling allocation of the EEC[1] and the competitive-need criterion of the United States[2] have been instrumental in reducing the projected GSP benefits. Under the ceiling allocation, the fixed shares of the EEC quota, allocated to member states, do not reflect the actual trade patterns and have sterilized the trade-expanding incentives of the GSP even when the total ceiling is not exhausted. Under the U.S. competitive-U.S. imports of a particular product from a particular beneficiary country exceed (1) $25 million annually[3] or (2) 50% of total U.S. imports of the product. The rationale for such criteria is that for developing countries, which can export products competitively under the MFN tariff, there is no need for preferential treatment. The ambiguity, however, in defining product groups at various levels of aggregation under the U.S. Tariff Schedule (T.S.U.S.), did lead to the automatic denial of preferential entry for a substantial volume of GSP trade.

The reclassification of imports into sensitive, semi-sensitive, and nonsensitive introduced an uncertainty element as to the expected tariff upon presentation for customs clearance, since a different tariff quota and maximum amounts applies to different products depending on the import sensitivity of the domestic producers.

The expected GSP benefits were further curtailed by a set of rules of origin and process requirements which, although designed to prevent a mere deflection of trade from one industrialized nation to another via a beneficiary country, were too strict and rigid and could not be met by the vast majority of developing countries. The major problems surrounding the rules of origin revolve around what constitutes substantial transformation of imported material. The definition of substantial transformation, either under the process criterion of Japan and the EEC or the value added criterion of the United

States, failed to account for the imported components of GSP exports which originated in other developing countries. There were no provisions for cumulative origin during the early years of the GSP. Recently the EEC has granted cumulative rules of origin to three regional groupings of developing countries,[4] while the United States permitted cumulative origin for those developing country associations which are formal free-trade areas or customs unions.

The benefits that did accrue to the developing countries are nonetheless quite substantial especially for certain categories of manufactured products. Interestingly enough, these categories of products are no longer isolated to low-skilled labor intensive production such as apparel, footwear, and textiles, but are widespread to electronics, communications, and light electrical machinery. The concentration ratio of the benefits is extremely high; evidence of the unequal degree and type of industrialization experiences of industrial developing countries and regions. Over half of the preferential EEC imports in 1974 originated in four beneficiary countries (Yugoslavia, Brazil, Hong Kong, and India), over one-third of preferential Japanese imports originated in the Republic of Korea and Taiwan, while over half of the estimated 1974 U.S. preferential imports originated in three beneficiaries (Mexico, Hong Kong, and Taiwan). The concentration ratio would have been even higher if beneficiary exports were not denied preferential entry through the various quantitative limitations instituted by the importing countries.

The Lomé Convention, implemented on January 1, 1975, affords 46 countries in Africa, the Caribbean, and the Pacific (the so-called ACP countries) a comprehensive preferential entry to the European Community markets beyond that of the GSP (July 1971) which was given to all the developing countries. This preferential entry is clearly a departure from the MFN principle of the General Agreement on Tariffs and Trade (GATT) and even though given without reciprocity, it could very well lead to a regionalization of world trade on selective preferences between trading blocs.

The preferences under the Lomé Convention are an extension of the preferences under the Yaounde Convention (January 1971) and the Arusha Agreement (January 1971). They represent a compensation to former colonies for the loss of their preferential status after the implementation of the GSP scheme by the EEC. This compensation extends beyond trade preferences into areas of trade promotion, trade cooperation, and assistance in the agricultural, financial, and industrial sectors of the economy (for more information see Frans 1977). Although the main objective is one of trade creation and trade promotion, the secondary objectives of cooperation and assistance are an integral part in accelerating the rate of growth of the export industries and in strengthening the existing trade patterns and information links between the ACP countries and the European Community.

Generally, most products originating in the ACP countries, with the exception of certain agricultural products, enter the markets of the Community free from customs duties or charges having equivalent effect. Moreover, these imports face relaxed rules of origin and process requirements and are not subject to any quantitative limitations in the form of ceilings or maximum amounts.

The preferential treatment granted to the ACP countries combines free access with a comprehensive program for industrial, technical, and regional cooperation which is intended to promote both the development and the diversification of industry in these countries. This will serve a dual purpose: (a) it will expand the industrial capacity of the ACP countries and will allow a fuller use of their preferential market access; and (b) it will increase the ability of these countries to absorb a larger volume and a higher level of manufactured imports from the EEC Given the limited export capacity of the ACP countries in the area of manufactures and the lack of an adequate infrastructure, the importance of the industrial and technical cooperation as an initial step towards realizing the benefits of their preferential entry is unquestionable.

Several developments could effect the ACP preferential states currently protected by Article 11 of the Lomé Convention: The enlargement of the EEC to include Greece, the establishment of a free trade area for industrial products moving between the enlarged EEC and the remaining European Free Trade Association (EFTA) countries, the formation of a special relationship between the enlarged EEC and the developing countries of the British Commonwealth, the reduction of the trade barriers through multilateral trade negotiations, and future modification of the EEC's GSP scheme. The enlargement of the EEC to include European nations which have already applied for membership to the Community—Spain, Portugal, and possibly Turkey—will lead to the domination of the special tariff advantages enjoyed by the ACP countires, only if, exports from these new EEC members displace ACP exports in the Community markets. Given the respective levels of industrialization of the proposed new members and the ACP countries, the similarities of their economic structures would suggest a substantial displacement of certain ACP exports. The enlarged EEC markets might be good outlets for certain ACP products; products not produced in the new EEC members' countries. The overall effect, however, will probably be against the trade interests of the ACP countries.

The GSP, which was designed as a measure of improving the disadvantaged position of the developed world, can be considered a weak version of the Lomé Convention, since this Convention contains all the elements that a truly Generalized System of zero-tariff Preferences should contain. Although their respective scopes, their beneficiaries, and the time of implementation are quite different, the fact that the product coverage shows an important degree of similarity provides enough ground for a meaningful comparison of the two preferential schemes, and an examination of their interaction, at least for the EEC, because the EEC implemented both schemes albeit at different time periods.

The expected results can be summarized as follows. The ratio of the non-OECD imports to OECD imports will rise after the implementation of the GSP scheme, especially for those groups of manufactured commodities which are produced competitively in the OECD and the non-OECD countries. Within the group of non-OECD nations, the pre-Lomé market share of the Lomé beneficiaries will fall after the GSP implementation, especially in the European Economic Community, because their preferential status is eroded. The post-Lomé market share of the Lomé beneficiaries will increase as the preferential access is restored and strengthened through a series of quantitative restrictions imposed by the EEC on GSP. During the post-Lomé period, exports from Lomé beneficiaries will be diverted to the EEC and away from the United States and Japan, because they enjoy greater preferences there. The expected results can be analyzed either by looking at the Lomé/non-Lomé ratio or through the competitiveness residuals. It is not expected that all non-OECD regions will be affected to the same degree and for the same commodity groups. Certain regions either possess a distinct comparative advantage in the production of certain goods, or have established and diversified export industries and are, therefore, able to switch their exports drive toward those commodity groups which are not highly disadvantaged by the EEC's Lomé Convention. The so-called Newly Industrializing Countries (NICs) (Krueger 1980), will be in a privileged position not only as recipients of the GSP preferential treatment, but also in the ability to divert their exports to other markets. The greatest effect of the Lomé Convention will be felt by those developing countries and regions which show important similarities in their export patterns to those of the Lomé beneficiaries.

STATISTICAL METHODOLOGY

The demand for imports from various sources and the relative competitiveness of these sources in a given world market is affected by a number of factors including differentials in productivity, prices, quality of products, delivery and service schedules, and tariff treatment. In the absence of analyzing these prices and nonprice determinants of changes in competitiveness, the changes in a country's import shares can be analyzed as ex-post reflections of changes in the relative competitiveness of the various sources of supply. Although the substitution between the various sources is not entirely determined by changes in relative competitiveness, an analysis of the relative shares can, nonetheless, be taken as a good proxy of overall change in the competitiveness of one source of supply vis-à-vis other sources.

The demand for imports in a given market from two competing sources of supply may be described in the following relationship:

$$q_1/q_2 = f(p_1/p_2) \tag{1}$$

where q_i and p_i are quantity sold and price of the commodity from the ith supply source. The assumption made is that the total worldwide demand for a commodity is given, in the sense that it does not depend on the price of one source or on the ratio of this source's price to a price of other sources (Flanders 1963)[5]. But the ratio of total imports of that commodity from the specific source does depend on the ratio of the price charged by this source to the prices charged by the other sources. The demand function then states that the ratio of quantities of a given commodity demanded by a country, from two competing sources or groups of sources, is a function of the ratio of their prices. The elasticity of substitution[6] is measured by a percentage change in market share divided by the percentage change in the price ratio.

$$\delta_{1/2} = \frac{d\left(\frac{q_1}{q_2}\right)}{d\left(\frac{p_1}{q_2}\right)} \quad \bullet \quad \frac{\frac{p_1}{p_2}}{\frac{q_1}{p_2}} \tag{2}$$

The p's and q's are defined as prices and quantities of goods of the same nature, but differentiated because of different origin, differentiated sufficiently to make the cross-elasticities of demand high and the case of the price ratios meaningful. The elasticity of substitution can be computed using quantity data for single commodities, but it is not very useful if commodity groups are analyzed. Value figures will be used instead in the computation of the market shares.

Equation (2) indicates that country one's share of the market in question will remain constant except as p_1/p_2 varies. This establishes the validity of the constant share norm and actual import growth may be attributed to price changes. Changes in trade preferences expressed in reduced and/or zero tariff rates for one source of supply versus other sources will be an important factor, but not the only factor, affecting the price ratios and, therefore, the market shares and the trade patterns for various commodity groups. Other factors affecting the ratio are: demand and supply conditions, rates of inflation, productivity increases, various types of government assistance, volumes of infrastructure, and the like. All these factors not only vary across different sources, but they also vary across products within the same source. It is not, therefore, expected that changes in trade preferences will have the same impact on all trade categories.

A useful and traditionally-accepted model for analyzing a country's or a region's relative import performance is the Constant Market Share (CMS) model (Leamer and Stern 1970). The model divides the actual growth of a country's imports into four components: the world trade effect, the commodity effect, the market effect, and the competitiveness effect. The first three components are designed such that they reflect the extent to which a country's imports from particular sources of supply have either maintained the same rate of growth as world trade, or have deviated from a constant share norm; and further, the extent to which this deviation can be explained by the concentration of country's imports in either commodities or markets with above or below average rates of growth. The fourth component in the CMS identity is derived as a residual and represents the difference between the actual increase in a country's imports and the increase that would have occurred had the country maintained a constant share in each market for each commodity.

Formally, the CMS identity can be written as:

$$M^{oo} - M^{o} = rM^{o} + \sum_{i}(r_i - r)\, M_i^{o} + \sum_{i}\sum_{j}\ (r_{ij} - r_i)\, M_{ij}^{o}$$
$$+ \sum_{i}\sum_{j}\ (M_{ij}^{oo} - M_{ij}^{o} - r_{ij}\, M_{ij}^{o})$$

where:

r	=	the growth rate of total world trade in value terms;
r_i	=	the growth rate of international trade in commodity $_i$;
r_{ij}	=	the growth rate of total imports of commodity $_i$ from country $_j$;
M	=	total imports of the focus country;
o	=	initial period;
oo	=	second period;
i	=	commodity group;
j	=	country of origin.

The first term on the right-hand side of this identity, world trade effect, indicates what the imports would have been had they expanded at the same rate as world trade. If the other terms were zero, the imports would be completely undifferentiated as to the commodity and the region of origin and the increase would depend only on the unbiased growth in demand in the importing country.

The second term, the commodity effect, indicates the influence of the change in the commodity mix of the country's imports on growth. The commodity composition effect will be positive if the importing nation's demand for that commodity has increased faster than the average for all commodities. In this case, $(r_i - r)$ is positive and the value taken by the commodity effect will be relatively large if the imports of commodity $_i$ are large. If $(r_i - r)$ is negative, the commodity effect will be negative.

The third term indicates the market distribution effect. If the importing country seeks markets which are experiencing relatively rapid growth, imports from these markets would increase faster than if the importing country concentrates on stagnating foreign markets. The effect would not only indicate the importance of the various regions as producers of international commodities, but also the importing country's preferences towards particular sources of supply for particular commodities. Traditional trade links and trade routes will figure predominantly in this effect.

The last term on the right hand side of the CMS identity is referred to as the competitiveness effect, and it is obtained as a residual of the growth in imports which is not explained by any of the other three effects. A negative competitiveness residual reflects a failure to maintain market shares, while a positive one shows an increase in the market shares. The value taken by the residual may be due to both demand and supply factors such as, changes in productivity, marketing conditions, monetary inflation, domestic levels of absorption, and government policies. The changes in government policy could either affect total imports (reduction or increase in trade interference) or the imports from certain regions. In the latter case, imports from certain regions could be more preferred than imports from other regions either through a series of preferential tariff rates or through import quotas, maximum amounts, and ceiling limitations. The use of quantitative restrictions would increase the level of uncertainty as to the tariff status of the imported commodity at the time of entry and it would discourage potential importers. The interpretation of the competitiveness residual is complicated not only by the general equilibrating system that lies behind it, but also by the necessarily arbitrary selections of the base period and the level of disaggregation of the commodity and market groups.

This analysis is thus quite inflexible, in the sense that its implications may apply only to a specified time period with a particular breakdown of commodities and market groups. Possibly different conclusions will emerge on the relative importance of the various factors isolated, if various sensitivity tests as to the base-year period and the level of aggregation are conducted.

The CMS methodology is a useful tool in analyzing and evaluating the achieved import growth from the various competing sources by making possible the separation of this growth into the world trade effect, the commodity composition effect, the market distribution effect, and the competitiveness effect. However, the methodology is hampered by a number of conceptual limitations as well as problems of empirical application (Richard 1971). On a conceptual basis, the CMS equation is an identity and, therefore, cannot provide any casual explanation of the country's import expansion. Because the analysis is based on value shares and not on quantity shares, price movements would hamper the interpretation of the various components. Finally, the CMS procedure is an ex-post methodology and it evaluates past shifts in import shares.

The CMS methodology will be applied to the growth of manufacturing imports of the EEC-6, the EEC-9, the United States, and Japan for three selected subperiods between 1969 and 1978 from various groups of non-OECD nations. The three selected subperiods are the following: subperiod 1 from 1969-1971, labelled as the pre-GSP period; subperiod 2 from 1971-1974, labelled as the post-GSP or pre-Lomé period; and subperiod 3 from 1974-1978, labelled as the post-Lomé period. During the last subperiod, both the Lomé and the GSP were in operation. Certain problems could arise for the United States, because its GSP scheme was not implemented until 1976.

The sources of import for the three countries are grouped into regions based on the preferential access to the markets of the three regions: The Sino-Soviet region covering all communist countries in Europe and Asia, excluding Yugoslavia (Some of these countries are beneficiaries under the EEC and the Japanese GSP schemes); the Lomé region consisting of all ACP countries, signatories of the Lomé Convention; the South American region; the Central American region, inclusive of Mexico; the Far East region, excluding mainland China; and, finally, the rest of the non-OECD countries region consisting mainly of Middle Eastern states, North African states, Malta, and Yugoslavia. The most preferred region is the Lomé region for the EEC, while the least preferred region, for all importing nations, is the Sino-Soviet bloc.

The data were collected for imports by the EEC-6, the EEC-9, Japan, and the United States from the non-OECD regions for 27 SITC categories of manufactured goods at the three-digit level (see Table 1). A specific category is considered part of the sample if imports by the EEC-9 in 1978, the last year of the test, from all non-OECD regions were at least 10% of total EEC imports during the same year. Sources for the data were various years of the OECD "Trade by Commodities, Series C." The collection of the data necessitated the use of a conversion table relating the BTN classification to the corresponding SITC classification[7] because GSP was written under the BTN classification but the data were recorded under SITC classification.

The CMS methodology was applied to the analysis of the imports by the original EEC, by the enlarged EEC, by the United States, and by Japan from the various non-OECD regions. The effects of the differential tariff treatment were expected to result in substitution among the sources of supply and, therefore, in indentifiable changes in market shares. The impact on traditionally-established trade routes was not expected to be as great as on newly-established ones, while certain commodity groups were expected to weigh more predominantly than others in explaining the changes in the market shares.

A preliminary investigation of the data indicated that the CMS approach, had to be modified prior to its application in the present study[8]. The modification was required mainly because of the rampant inflation in the trading countries and the tremendous increases in the demand for imports, by value, which resulted in a world trade effect which completely dominated the three remaining effects.

Table 1. Sample of SITC Commodity Groups

SITC Classification	*Description*
512	Organic Chemicals
513	Inorganic Chemicals
532	Dyeing and Tanning Extracts
541	Medicinal and Pharmaceutical Products
551	Essential Oils and Perfume
561	Fertilizers, Manufactured
611	Leather
612	Manufactures of Leather
631	Veneers, Plywood Boards, etc.
632	Wood Manufacturers
651	Textile Year and Thread
652	Cotton Fabrics, Woven
653	Textile Fabrics, Woven
656	Made-up Articles of Textile Material
657	Floor Coverings, Tapestries
667	Pearls, Precious and Semi-Precious Stones
696	Cutlery
697	Household Equipment of Base Metal
724	Telecommunications Apparatus
729	Other Electrical Machinery
735	Ships and Boats
821	Furniture
831	Travel Goods and Handbags
841	Clothing (Except Fur Clothing)
851	Footwear
864	Watches and Clocks
894	Permulators, Toys, and Games

The modification in the CMS analysis was carried out in a series of steps with the intention of adjusting the data for the world trade effect and the inflation effect. This adjustment led to a more meaningful explanation of the commodity composition effect and the competitiveness residuals. A demonstration of the various steps is provided below using the EEC-6 and the 1969-1971 subperiod.

- *Step 1:* Calculate the growth rate of total imports for 1969-1971 for the EEC for all commodity groups:

$$r/g = \frac{\sum_{i=1}^{27} M_i^{1971}}{\sum_{i=1}^{27} M_i^{1969}}$$

- *Step 2:* Calculate the 1971 adjusted imports by dividing every commodity group for all regions by $r/g_{69,\ 71}$. The data are now for 1971 adjusted and the total is equal to the actual imports in 1969.
- *Step 3:* Calculate the 1971 expected imports for each region and each commodity group assuming that the shares were the same as in 1969. The difference between the expected value and the actual value in 1969 is the commodity composition effect. The 1971 expected is given by:

$$\sum_{i=1}^{27} r_i M_i^{1969}$$

- *Step 4:* Calculate the competitiveness residual by substracting the 1971 expected imports for every commodity group from the 1971 adjusted value for every commodity group.

To verify the expectation that the differences in the preferential tariff treatment lead to substantial changes in the market shares, the chi-square test was performed for all the commodity groups of the sample and the four importing countries.

The chi-square test involves a comparison of the expected frequencies with the observed frequencies (adjusted from the original data) in order to determine whether the difference between the expected and the observed values is greater than might reasonably be anticipated to occur by chance. The null hypothesis is that there is no significant difference. The commodity groups for which the hypothesis was rejected were especially effected by the differential tariff treatment and they were very important in explaining the damages in the market shares. The commodities for which the hypothesis was accepted were not important in explaining the changes in the market shares, since the competitiveness residuals were insignificant. The chi-square statistic is:

$$X^2 = \sum \frac{(|f_o - f_e|)^2}{f_e}$$

where f_o equals observed (sample) frequencies (in this case, adjusted frequencies) and f_e equals expected (theoretical) frequencies (Blalock 1960).

The calculated value was compared to the value for X^2 taken from the table for five degrees of freedom and an appropriate level of significance. If the calculated value exceeded the table value, the null hypothesis was rejected, indicating significant differences between the observed and the expected frequences. This implied that the competitiveness residuals were important in explaining the changes in the market shares.

RESULTS ON AGGREGATE DATA

Table 2 presents the estimation of the source of growth in the imports of the EEC in each of the three subperiods, adjusted for inflation and growth, while Table 3 presents the same estimates for the United States and Japan. The commodity composition reflects the changes in the demand for imports brought about by changes in the level and structure of income and output while the competitiveness effect reflects the residual growth in imports from the various competing sources of supply.

These results indicate that over the 1969-1971 period for the EEC-9 the only regions which were experiencing substantial increases in their market shares were the Sino-Soviet bloc and the Lomé region; the Sino-Soviet bloc mainly because of a positive commodity composition and the Lomé because of a positive competitiveness residual. All of the other regions experienced a decrease in their share of the EEC market. The results indicate that the enlargement of the EEC to nine members negatively affected the previously gainers, but was beneficial mainly for the Far East region, for the region covering the rest of the developing countries, and, to a lesser degree, for the South American region.[9] The results for the United States and Japan indicate a substantial increase in the market share of the Far East region in both importing markets. In addition, the South American region increased its share of the U.S. market because of a favorable competitiveness residual, and the Lomé region achieved the same result for the Japanese market. All the other regions experienced a decrease in their market shares, either because of a negative commodity composition or competitiveness residual, or a combination of both.

During the 1971-1974 period, positive sources of growth were achieved by the Far East region in the EEC-6, the EEC-9, and Japan, but not in the United States. The Lomé region did experience a decrease in its share of the market in all the importing countries. The South American region registered important gains in all markets. The biggest increase was observed in the U.S. market because of a large positive competitiveness residual. The Sino-Soviet bloc increased its share of all markets with the exception of the Japanese markets. The shares of the two remaining regions decreased in all markets except for the Central American region which increased its share of the U.S. market.

Table 2. Analysis of EEC Imports by Region (1969-1978)
(Thousands U.S. $)

Year / Region	*Sino-Soviet*	*Lomé*	*South America*	*Central America*	*Far East*	*Other Devel.*	*Total*
EEC-6							
A. 1969-1971							
Commodity composition	+28,511	-66	-13,381	-2,053	-11,774	-9,377	-8,145
Competitiveness residual	-347	+21,077	+12,530	-3,638	-12,179	-9,297	+8,145
B. 1971-1974							
Commodity composition	+25,966	-26,721	-12,083	-10,757	+65,393	-41,928	-8,585
Competitiveness residual	-10,125	-30,638	+47,674	-3,844	+74,229	-77,211	+8,585
C. 1974-1978							
Commodity composition	-74,9296	-14,773	-48,256	-34,219	+126,987	+43,956	-1,234
Competitiveness residual	-223,135	+99,542	+23,430	-31,987	+290,804	-157,419	+1,234
EEC-9							
A. 1969-1971							
Commodity composition	+1,878	-110,336	-12,046	+-5,262	+85,954	+29,183	-105
Competitiveness residual	-80,748	+19,342	+21,192	-8,396	+29,594	+19,122	+105
B. 1971-1974							
Commodity composition	+8,393	-23,027	-14,834	-11,620	+77,706	-36,744	-125
Competitiveness residual	+19,009	-38,802	+61,746	-28,765	+28,962	-42,025	+125
C. 1974-1978							
Commodity composition	-47,444	-62,664	-49,367	-44,600	+125,900	+99,941	+21,775
Competitiveness residual	-304,542	+126,824	+30,355	-35,506	+244,847	-83,752	-21,775

Source: Tsanacas (1982), Statistical Appendix B, Tables B-4 and B-6.

Table 3. Analysis of U.S. and Japanese Imports by Region (1969-1978) (Thousands U.S. $)

Year / Region	*Sino-Soviet*	*Lomé*	*South America*	*Central America*	*Far East*	*Other Devel.*	*Total*
			United States				
A. 1969-1971							
Commodity composition	-3,158	-4,026	-2,794	+5,571	+40,794	-36,454	-67
Competitiveness residual	-7,660	-6,735	+18,853	-8,738	+10,674	-6,327	+67
B. 1971-1974							
Commodity composition	+3,694	-20,464	+9,332	+79,430	-62,081	-10,023	-112
Competitiveness residual	+18,202	-21,106	+94,841	-16,782	-33,548	-41,494	+112
C. 1974-1978							
Commodity composition	-12,131	-37,207	-17,108	-122,453	+316,416	+89,336	+216,853
Competitiveness residual	+67,705	-10,078	-133,773	-59,506	+13,796	-94,997	-216,853
			Japan				
A. 1969-1971							
Commodity composition	+7,777	-1,805	-4,157	-3,870	+3,926	-1,695	+176
Competitiveness residual	-12,935	+7,423	-4,557	-4,557	+16,532	-1,164	-1,164
B. 1971-1974							
Commodity composition	+20,596	-23,833	-9,599	-3,465	+27,706	-13,839	-2,434
Competitiveness residual	-27,174	-721	+12,689	-3,959	+32,518	-10,919	+2,434
C. 1974-1978							
Commodity composition	-6,388	+18,167	+1,007	+1,827	-42,089	+26,950	-526
Competitiveness residual	-86,127	-17,327	-51,775	+5,891	+152,771	-2,906	+526

Source: Tsanacas (1982), Statistical Appendix B, Tables B-11 and B-9.

During the 1974-1978 period, a reversal in the trend occurred in the Lomé share of the market for the EEC-6 and the EEC-9. The principal factor expanding the share was a large competitiveness effect. The Sino-Soviet bloc suffered tremendous losses in all markets except the United States where it improved further on its previous gain. The Far East region continued to dominate in all markets reaching very high levels of concentration. The remaining regions did not favor very well in any of the importing countries with minor exceptions reported in the case of the rest of the developing countries region (increase for the EEC-9 and Japan).

The results suggest that, during the 1969-1978 period, the competitiveness residual was the major factor accounting for changes in the market shares of the non-OECD regions, even though the commodity composition effect was extremely important for the Far East and the Central American regions in explaining the U.S. imports. The values of the competitiveness residual in the post-Lomé period, especially for those exporting regions whose preferential status was eroded by both the GSP and the Lomé Convention, provide strong indication that preferential tariff arrangements are an important determinant of competitiveness. The two regions mostly affected were the Sino-Soviet bloc and the region consisting of the rest of the developing countries. On the other hand, the competitiveness of the Lomé region increased mainly because of the new preferential arrangements.

It is to be noted that the value of the residual depends on demand and supply factors in both the exporting and the importing regions. Any changes in the demand and supply conditions in the importing countries would have an impact on the primary as well as on the secondary or residual foreign suppliers. Decreases in demand would have a great impact on the residual suppliers, while increases in demand would benefit these suppliers only if the additional demand could not be satisfied by the primary suppliers. Any changes in the relative prices of the exporting regions would directly affect their attractiveness as suppliers of manufactured products and it would influence their relative market shares. These relative price changes do not necessarily have to be real as long as the decision of the importer is clouded by uncertainty as to the tariff status of various commodities and as to the continued availability of preferences for certain countries within the regions.

The uncertainty is expected to have its greatest impact on the market shares of those regions whose exports face a series of ceilings, tariff quotas, maximum amounts, or a reclassification of their commodities as sensitive or semi-sensitive. In addition, the administration of these quantitative restrictions on a daily or monthly basis could very well divert exports away from certain markets. The size of the export sector and the degree of market familiarity which are associated with established exporters will provide these exporters with a competitive edge over newly-establishing exporters, in the interpretation of the complex rules regarding preferential tariff trade.

The Lomé region did not have to cope with these rules for its exports to the EEC, because preferential entry was unlimited. Exports to the EEC continued long after the various quantitative limitations were exhausted. The fact that the EEC preserved a part of its import market for the Lomé beneficiaries' exports does necessarily imply that the other non-OECD regions had to compete rigorously for the rest of the market. The non-OECD regions, whose countries were at advanced stages in their development process, were most likely to capture the biggest share of the market. These countries possessed not only the necessary infrastructure, the human capital, and the large and diversified export capacity, but were also receptive to foreign technology and innovative techniques. The flexibility of their domestic factors of production facilitated the shifting of their productive efforts towards those goods for which foreign demand was rising or foreign restrictions were easing. Countries fitting this mode are labelled as Newly Industrializing Countries (NICs). The majority of these countries are members of the Far East Region (Hong Kong, Korea, Singapore, Taiwan, India[10]). Their success is testimony to the effectiveness of export-led growth and it is evident in the increased share of the market in all importing countries (Table 4) as well as in the values of the commodity composition and competitiveness residuals (Tables 2 and 3). It should be pointed out that, during the 1971-1974 period, the values of the competitiveness and the commodity composition effects for the Far East region in the U.S. import market were both negative. The explanation for the sign as well as for the decrease in the market share during that period is partially due to the fact that the U.S. GSP scheme was not in operation.

The uncertainty as to the preferential treatment at any point of time is an important factor in explaining changes at the margin, but it does not explain international trade. The patterns of trade follow established routes or links and the information flows that accompany these routes. Preferential tariff arrangements working against an established trade link will most definitely weaken that link in the short run, therefore, diminishing the volume of trade, but they will not break it completely. The actual breakage of the trade link is a long-term process and it will depend on the continuation of the preferential tariff arrangements working against it. The fact that the market shares of the Sino-Soviet bloc did not drop to zero in all importing countries after the implementation of the GSP and the Lomé, does not show any inconsistency in the results. It can be reasonably assumed that part of the market share was preserved through defensive pricing on the part of the Sino-Soviet exporters, since they were concerned with the acquisition of foreign exchange.[11]

The preferential arrangement will provide the beneficiary region with a tariff margin vis-à-vis other suppliers, therefore making this region more competitive. This is expected to weaken the trade links of those regions which show similarities in their export patterns and cost structure to the beneficiary region (trade diversion). The impact will not be so profound if the competing regions show substantial variation in the nature and quality of their export products.

The Central American region, the rest of the developing countries region, and to a leser degree the South American region, showed a substantial degree of similarity in their export pattern to that of the Lomé region. Although the similarity did not exist across all types of manufactures goods, it was, however, very important for certain commodity groups which made up the bulk of their exports. The fact that the EEC blocked off a part of its market for the Lomé exports did lead to a loss in the market share of the other competing sources. This loss is evident in Table 3. The Far East region was not affected by the reduced availability in the EEC import market mainly because its producers had a comparative advantage over other non-OECD producers and were, therefore, in a position to fill a substantial part of the market by displacing the exports of those producers. The loss was primarily shared by those exporters whose supply conditions and domestic rates of inflation negatively affected their export competitiveness.

Table 5 concentrates on the growth rates of the imports from Lomé by all importing countries using the 1974 ratio of Lomé imports to non—OECD imports as the base. All importing countries showed substantial rate of growth of manufactured imports from Lomé prior to 1974. The rates of growth of Japan exceeded those of the other three countries, while that of the EEC-6 is the lowest mainly because the EEC-6 was a major importer from Lomé under the Yaounde Convention and the Arusha Agreement, prior to the GSP implementation. After 1974, the EEC of both the Six and the Nine maintained high rates of import growth even though the growth rate declined. The growth rate of Japanese imports from Lomé, in the post-Lomé period was close to zero while that of the United States was negative; these data indicate the actual decline in the ratio. On the basis of the data contained in Tables 3 and 4, the Lomé Convention was essential to increasing the share of the Lomé region in the EEC markets after the decline in the pre-Lomé period. This increase was primarily accomplished through the quantitative restrictions imposed by the EEC and secondarily through the diversion of exports to the EEC and away from Japan and the United States. Although the actual Japanese and U.S. imports from Lomé increased, the increase was basically concentrated on certain resource-based commodity groups, which will be identified in the disaggregate results.

The impact of the quantitative restrictions of the EEC cannot be readily qualified, because the Lomé exporters were not in a position to take full advantage of their reserved part of the market. The utilization rate of the tariff quotas and tariff ceilings could serve as an indicator of the restrictiveness of the quantitative measures of the EEC, but only for individual commodity groups. An overall indicator cannot be established. The relative increase in the ratio of non-OECD imports to OECD imports for the EEC, Japan, and

Table 4. Analysis of Percentage Share of Imports by Region of Origin and Importing Region (1969-1978)

Year	*Sino-Soviet*	*Lomé*	*South America*	*Central America*	*Far East*	*Other Devel.*	*Total*
				EEC-6			
1969	23.16	5.59	5.30	3.40	34.07	28.47	100
1971	25.46	7.30	5.24	2.94	32.12	26.93	100
1974	26.29	4.27	7.11	2.16	39.50	20.66	100
1978	20.54	5.93	6.68	0.88	47.56	18.45	100
				EEC-9			
1969	26.79	10.98	4.15	3.55	36.65	17.86	100
1971	23.26	6.92	4.55	3.42	41.82	20.03	100
1974	24.23	4.72	6.24	1.99	45.59	17.23	100
1978	19.32	5.66	5.95	0.86	50.77	17.44	100
				United States			
1969	2.13	5.63	4.03	10.30	69.00	8.91	100
1971	1.54	5.04	4.91	10.13	71.82	6.56	100
1974	2.26	3.64	8.40	12.23	68.62	4.83	100
1978	3.07	2.96	6.23	9.62	73.36	4.75	100
				Japan			
1969	18.70	3.75	8.27	6.24	53.30	9.74	100
1971	16.51	6.14	4.16	2.65	62.01	8.51	100
1974	15.17	1.15	4.80	1.14	74.25	3.49	100
1978	10.83	1.18	2.41	1.50	79.45	4.62	100

Source: Tsanacas (1982), Statistical Appendix B, Tables B-3, B-5, B-11, and B-13.

Table 5. Growth Rates of Lomé Imports 1969-1971, 1971-1974, 1974-1978

Country	*Period*	*Lomé*
EEC-6	69-71	30.91
	71-74	70.96
	74-78	38.87
EEC-9	69-71	127.41
	71-74	46.61
	74-78	19.91
Japan	69-71	226.08
	71-74	433.91
	74-78	2.60
United States	69-71	54.67
	71-74	38.46
	74-78	-20.18

Source: Table 4.

the United States could serve as an approximation even though there is a differential degree of vulnerability in the manufacturing industries of the three countries. Generally, the trade policy of the United States is more liberal because of the U.S.' leadership position in international commerce. Table 6 shows the ratio of non-OECD imports to OECD imports and the growth rate of the ratio for all the importing countries. All countries show robust rates of increase of manufactured imports from the non-OECD sources. The rate of growth of the EEC is greater during the 1974-1978 period than during the 1971-1974 period while the growth rates of Japan and the United States greatly exceed those of the EEC for both of these periods.

The smaller increase registered by the EEC during the 1971-1974 period could be explained by the restrictiveness of the quantitative limitations, the rigid rules of origin, the strict process requirements, and the failure of the non-OECD exports to qualify for GSP preferential treatment mainly because of unfamiliarity with the scheme. The relaxation of the process requirements, the increased familiarity with the scheme, the cumulative origin requirements extended by the EEC, along with the implementation of the Lomé Convention were the main reasons for the increased rates of growth in non-OECD imports during the 1974-1978 period.

The tremendous increases in the Japanese ratios of non-OECD imports to OECD imports during the 1971-1974 and 1974-1978 periods are partially explained by the lower volume of Japanese non-OECD imports prior to 1971, the higher volume of Japanese direct investment in manufacturing and processing facilities, and, to a greater extent, by the implementation of the

Japanese GSP scheme. Interestingly enough, the major bulk of Japanese non-OECD imports originated in the Far East region which was the primary recipient of the Japanese direct investment. The increasing presence of Japanese multinationals in the Far East could very well explain the tremendous success of this region in capturing a large part of the U.S. and EEC import markets. The success is directly related to the diversified industrial base and the comparative cost advantage of the region. It is very logical to assume that the established trade links would generate additional links for products experiencing increases in international demand.

The geographic location was an additional factor affecting the market share of the Far East region, since the administration of the Japanese GSP scheme[12] best served those suppliers closer to the market. The domination of the Far East region in the Japanese import market is expected to continue in the future as the Japanese economy continues and completes its structural change, away from a low value-added component industry towards a higher value-added one, in its attempt to reduce the high dependency on foreign raw material.

The substantial increase in the U.S. imports of manufactures from the non-OECD sources especially during the 1974-1978 period (see Table 6), and the size of the commodity composition and the competitiveness effects, (see Table 3), clearly suggest a structural change in the import composition, along with a relative change in the market shares ofthe supplying non-OECD regions. It is not surprising that the substantial changes are occurring at this time given the implementation of the GSP scheme (1976) and the Lomé Convention (1975). The GSP tariff provided the non-OECD GSP beneficiaries with a preferential margin vis-à-vis OECD producers while it decreased the protection afforded to domestic producers by the same margin. The total impact of the GSP preferential trade arrangement which both liberalizes and distorts world trade, depends upon the relative magnitudes of trade diversion and trade creation. The data show that the total effect (sum of the trade creation and trade diversion) was quite substantial for the United States and it resulted in important substitutions among the supplying sources. This would indicate: (a) open and attractive U.S. markets; (b) severe vulnerability of the U.S. manufacturing industries to import penetration resulting from higher domestic labor costs and decreases in R&D intensity (Lowinger 1975); (c) the establishment of subsidiaries in non-OECD regions by U.S.-based multinationals seeking to reduce labor costs; (d) higher barriers to import penetration in alternative markets (EEC, Japan, and so forth) resulting in the redirection of imports to the United States; (e) pronounced and sustained export drives by non-OECD producers geared especially to the United States economy; and (f) new marketing linkages resulting in new export flows of nontraditional products, as the flow of information and the market familiarity improved.

A number of limitations, exclusions, and restriction incorporated in the U.S. GSP scheme did not allow for the full realization of the GSP benefits, therefore,

Table 6. Ratio of Non-OECD Imports to OECD Imports

Country	*1969*	*1971*	*1974*	*1978*
EEC-6	10.91	13.08	15.44	21.11
EEC-9	11.25	14.09	16.14	20.60
Japan	23.40	31.40	55.95	75.50
United States	36.17	47.73	74.07	104.67

Source: Tsanacas (1982), Statistical Appendix Table A-1.

resulting in a lower non-OECD market share, while certain other factors helped increase the share. Specifically, the United States excluded outright certain products from its GSP product list. Of these products, items such as clothing and textiles[13] represent the highest increase in LDC market penetration to the developed world. Certain countries were excluded outright from GSP treatment, while others were denied preferential access for various products under the "competitive need" criteria. Interestingly, there was no allowance for a growth factor in calculating the "competitive need" limit in 1978.[14] The improvement in the U.S.-USSR relations, the extension of the MFN clause to China, the opening of the U.S. markets to Chinese exports along with coproduction arrangements between U.S. firms and Soviet-bloc countries[15] were factors increasing the market share of the Sino-Soviet region and, therefore, the total non-OECD market share. The implementation of the Lomé Convention would increase the total non-OECD share in the United States depending on the volume and the types of restrictions imposed by the EEC in safeguarding a certain part of the markt for the Lomé producers.[16] These restrictions would redirect trade to the United States and away from the EEC markets. The change in GSP trade would not merely effect the change in the Lomé trade, but would exceed it, mainly because of the increased level of uncertainty of the EEC trade and liberal trade policy of the United States. The improvement in market familiarity resulting from traditional exports would most definitely lead to new export trade in nontraditional products and, therefore, result in a more beneficial GSP trade for the non-OECD regions.

It appears that the GSP was instrumental in increasing the U.S. import share of the non-OECD developing nations as a group. The same does not, however, hold true for the various regions as is evident in Table 3. The Far East region registered the largest gain and continued being the dominant source of U.S. manufactured imports. Attention should be focused on the decrease in the Far East share in the 1971-1974 period because such a decrease represented a shift to the EEC and Japanese markets and it was induced by the GSP implementation during that period. The large size of the commodity-composition effect provides strong indication of the diversification of the industrial base of this region and of its ability to switch the productive effort to those product groups which were not constrained by the competitive need criteria of the United States. In addition, it appears that the Far East producers of manufactured goods were able to take advantage of the reduced cost and product competitiveness of U.S. manufacturing firms by mounting sustained and sophisticated export drives especially in labor intensive, high-income elastic products. If these export drives were and still are of a cumulative nature; they improve market familiarity, increase routine and nonroutine flows of information, and facilitate financing arrangements, the Far East manufactured products will continue to displace manufactured products from other competing sources.

The other non-OECD regions were at a disadvantaged position, either because internal problems of factor rigidity in the export sector, soaring inflation rates, or high levels of domestic absorption prevented them from being competitive, or because of over-specialization in certain commodity groups which denied them preferential GSP tariff treatment on competitive need criteria grounds. This is apparent in the large values of commodity composition effect. Only the region covering the other developing countries experienced a positive commodity-composition effect because of oil-related products.

In conclusion, it should be pointed out that the United States excluded textiles and apparel items from GSP coverage which were of special interest to all the developing regions. The inclusion of these items in the U.S. GSP scheme would most definitely have changed the signs of the competitiveness residuals.

RESULTS ON DISAGGREGATE DATA

The decomposition of the aggregate results into the 27 three-digit SITC manufacturing commodity groups will provide valuable information as to their individual contribution in the change of the aggregate market share for the non—OECD exporting regions. The deviations from a constant norm at the commodity level are induced by a combination of market forces, commercial policies, and their impact on the cost and price competitiveness of each region for that specific commodity. The preferential tariff treatment under the GSP and the Lomé is not expected to have a profound effect on each and every commodity, since trade preferences are only one of several factors affecting trade patterns. The margin of preferences, equal to the MFN tariff in the industrialized nations, is expected to decrease the effective rate of protection[17] at the commodity level and to lead to the expansion of processing industries in developing nations. The comparative advantage and the diversification of the industrial base of each nation will indicate the relative importance of the commodities as sources of export earnings. The existence of traditionally-strong trade links between certain exporting regions and the corresponding

Table 7. Growth Rate in $\frac{\text{Non-OECD Imports}}{\text{OECD Imports}}$ Various Commodity Groups (1969-1971)

SITC Group	*EEC-6*	*EEC-9*	*United States*	*Japan*
512	0	- 4.93	- 6.86	+109.80
513	+178.18	+ 83.56	+ 33.48	- 61.98
532	- 24.63	- 25.32	+ 17.63	- 27.88
541	+ 13.54	- 8.34	+ 42.80	+237.44
551	- 4.80	+ 29.03	+ 40.85	- 8.71
561	+107.80	+ 98.74	- 5.76	+ 20.95
611	- 3.45	- 2.50	- 1.69	- 33.27
612	- 5.34	+ 4.00	+ 17.00	- 4.16
631	+ 38.66	+ 62.82	+2300.00	+538.92
632	+ 24.81	+ 26.65	+ 18.51	+ 81.56
651	- 6.76	- 10.42	- 44.01	+359.61
652	- 4.65	- 4.37	+ 30.21	+ 23.54
653	- 3.77	- 7.14	- 31.67	- 24.87
656	+ 9.76	- 11.19	+ 13.66	+ 45.22
657	+ 20.56	+ 1.09	+ 8.06	- 38.65
667	- 4.10	- 81.00	+ 6.91	+ 36.29
696	+ 52.63	+ 15.95	+ 38.48	+ 34.04
697	+ 80.25	+ 65.75	+ 21.68	+ 78.86
724	+ 56.36	+ 31.72	+ 47.50	+101.01
729	+ 8.88	+ 13.90	+ 51.43	+ 36.24
735	+ 44.64	+ 73.89	- 5.31	- 53.78
821	+ 40.95	+ 32.00	+ 1.01	+ 25.50
831	+ 29.23	+ 29.07	+ 13.18	+ 44.68
841	+ 40.86	+ 31.88	+ 95.48	+222.43
851	+ 6.96	+ 9.41	+ 95.83	+989.19
864	+ 37.12	+ 38.76	+ 118.69	+ 52.10
894	+ 15.67	+ 15.67	+ 52.04	+ 16.95
Percentage of commodities which increased	(70)	(67)	(78)	(72)

Source: Tsanacas (1981), Table 6-1.

OECD importers for certain types of manufactured goods, usually traded in large volumes, makes penetration by newly-establishing producers extremely difficult. These trade links are the result of past political and commercial affiliation and direct investment, and are expected to influence trade patterns even in the presence of preferential tariff treatment. It is apparent, therefore, that the acceptance of the hypothesis will not depend on every commodity group obeying the criteria.

Tables 7, 8, and 9 present substantial evidence of the ability of the non-OECD producers to penetrate the markets of developed nations following the

Table 8. Growth Rate in $\frac{\text{Non-OECD Imports}}{\text{OECD Imports}}$ Various Commodity Groups (1971-1974)

SITC Group	*EEC-6*	*EEC-9*	*United States*	*Japan*
512	- 13.45	- 27.29	- 51.51	+135.37
513	- 52.29	+ 0.75	- 14.56	+ 45.03
532	- 27.75	- 16.37	- 39.81	+723.10
541	- 1.60	- 2.50	- 56.61	+ 82.02
551	+ 50.47	+ 53.81	+ 74.50	+ 44.30
561	- 36.52	- 31.00	+ 38.38	- 10.09
611	+ 4.62	- 1.10	+ 75.28	- 23.42
612	+ 28.51	+ 10.20	+138.80	+252.19
631	+ 14.18	+ 15.28	+ 9.10	+ 92.31
632	+ 47.33	+ 43.67	+107.46	+ 8.18
651	+128.01	+103.28	+ 56.23	+ 47.27
652	+ 35.22	+ 2.59	+189.77	+ 59.29
653	+ 82.24	+ 68.37	+ 38.32	+ 23.62
656	+ 21.35	+ 70.14	+137.98	+212.75
657	- 14.13	- 12.19	+ 67.90	- 3.00
667	- 5.57	- 6.64	+ 50.47	+ 12.63
696	+ 85.34	+ 77.37	+ 74.78	+914.81
697	+ 30.83	+ 31.65	+158.21	+790.90
724	+133.13	+ 66.12	+174.14	+227.57
729	+122.95	+ 95.66	+144.77	+159.26
735	- 30.39	- 36.00	+ 41.15	- 72.09
821	+ 8.71	+ 9.09	+ 64.28	+117.43
831	+ 70.52	+ 54.99	+241.55	- 19.08
841	+ 76.46	+ 56.92	+ 38.74	- 32.77
851	+ 24.00	+ 3.61	+178.14	- 83.40
864	+ 35.01	+ 56.82	+209.18	+221.98
894	+ 36.74	+ 28.04	+ 65.19	+173.07
Percentage of commodities which increased	(71)	(71)	(90)	(75)

Source: Tsanacas (1982), Table 6-1.

reduction in the effective rate of protection and the granting of preferential access for their manufactured and semi-manufactured exports. The import penetration is no longer isolated to low-skilled labor-intensive production such as Apparel, Footwear, and Textiles, but is widespread to Electronics, Telecommunication, and Light Electrical Machinery. The new products are income and price elastic and depend primarily on international diffusion of technology, product cycle, establishment of subsidiaries by multinationals, and

Table 9. Growth Rate in $\frac{\text{Non-OECD Imports}}{\text{OECD Imports}}$ Various Commodity Groups (1974-1978)

SITC Group	*EEC-6*	*EEC-9*	*United States*	*Japan*
512	- 14.00	- 33.78	- 7.57	+ 19.63
513	- 16.60	- 34.14	- 3.21	- 3.90
532	- 10.90	+ 2.98	+ 3.56	- 42.61
541	- 14.55	- 33.95	- 37.78	+ 32.63
551	- 40.20	- 41.41	- 26.31	- 39.56
561	- 9.09	- 12.69	- 35.80	+ 9.67
611	- 5.33	- 3.59	+104.74	+ 89.61
612	+110.77	+116.95	+107.87	+ 37.11
631	+ 38.95	+ 16.53	+ 25.79	+869.76
632	+ 2.13	+ 9.92	+ 15.66	+ 56.26
651	+ 12.28	+ 8.84	+ 82.63	+366.92
652	- 37.59	- 28.28	+ 15.15	+153.24
653	+ 8.59	+ 2.60	- 48.97	+155.22
656	+ 16.36	- 28.80	+ 61.00	+ 11.96
657	+ 34.14	+ 32.95	+ 70.06	+386.73
667	+120.08	+140.22	+132.14	+ 42.56
696	+104.03	+ 24.56	+ 40.43	- 41.04
697	+ 34.25	+ 12.25	+ 60.67	- 14.37
724	+ 39.65	+ 41.52	- 30.30	+ 7.49
729	+ 78.71	+ 68.00	- 13.09	+ 7.52
735	+168.91	+111.11	+115.04	+ 0.30
821	+ 22.71	+ 20.23	+ 91.34	+298.26
831	+ 69.98	+ 77.96	+122.64	- 71.79
841	+ 4.62	+ 3.03	+173.15	+ 12.50
851	+ 19.42	+ 8.68	+106.95	+577.68
864	+497.32	+436.43	+342.15	+369.34
894	+ 33.08	+ 9.41	+ 88.56	+162.49
Percentage of commodities which increased	(70)	(70)	(70)	(78)

Source: Tsanacas (1982), Table 6-1.

also on the competitive edge extended to non-OECD producers through the GSP.

All four regions experienced large increases in import growth from the non-OECD regions indicating substantial trade creation and trade diversion effects[18] for all commodity groups with the exception of the SITC group 5, Chemicals. The United States experienced the largest increases, either because of the open and attractive U.S. markets, or because of the loss of competitiveness in the manufacturing industries. The Japanese growth rates reached very high levels during the 1971-1974 period, although not for all commodity groups, and continued in the same fashion during the 1974-1978 period. A low level of initial imports, in conjunction with the increasing presence of Japanese multinationals in the Far East could very well explain the tremendous growth rates. The EEC of the Six and the Nine experienced high rates of import growth from the non-OECD sources during all three periods, but more so, during the 1974-1978 period. There is substantial variation in the growth rates among the commodity groups for the different time periods. The growth rates of the chemicals (SITC-5) do, however, follow a negative pattern, especially in the aftermath of the OPEC crisis of 1974-1978. As a general rule, growth rates of the EEC are lower than those of the United States and Japan for both the 1971-1974, and the 1974-1978 time periods. Over 70% of the commodities of the sample experienced positive growth rates for the EEC during the 1971-1974 and 1974-1978 periods, while the figures are 90% and 70% for the United States and 75% and 78%, respectively for Japan.

The influx of manufactured imports from the non-OECD sources, forces fundamental adjustments in the labor markets of the developed world and increases the resistance to such imports, especially if the displacing source and the affected industry can be identified rather easily (Gray 1980). The severity of the burden imposed on the domestic labor market is likely to be the prime cause of the growth of protectionist sentiment (Walter 1972, pp. 23-34). The adjustment in commercial policy is carried out on individual commodity groups. If the policy results in the elimination of the preferential status granted under the GSP, it could lead to a decrease in the market share of the affected countries by making their exports less competitive vis-à-vis other developing countries.

Generally, the United States has been pursuing a more liberal trade policy mainly because of its leadership position in international commerce. Its markets have been open and attractive to exports from developing countries and these countries have enjoyed spectacular successes in the growth of the manufactured exports. On the other hand, the EEC governments and, to a somewhat lesser degree, the Japanese government have adopted restrictive trade policies through commodity reclassification and various nontariff measures, which make their markets less attractive by increasing the degree of uncertainty as to the tariff status of the various imported manufactured products. The impact of these restrictions has been absorbed mainly by the "weaker" developing country suppliers in the form of reduced market shares for the effected commodity groups. In this case, the "weaker" suppliers are the newly-established producers which lack the financial, technical, promotional, and marketing skills needed to penetrate a closed market, and the traditional produces which have been affected by higher costs and decreased competitiveness.

The import flows from region i to region j are a function of supply conditions in i, demand conditions in j, and trade resistance factors between i and j (Aitken

1973). The potential export supply of region i depends on: GNP, population, availability of productive factors and ability to develop these factors, inflow of technology, and the incorporation of this technology into the production technique. Any increases in the domestic level of absorption of exportables either through a higher GNP or through an input-output effect will effect the supply of exportables, while any increase in the Gross Domestic Product could stimulate exports through an increase in comparative advantage. In a similar way, the potential import demand for region j depends on: GNP, population, and the domestic level of production. The trade resistance factors will consist mainly of distance (as a proxy for the transport costs) and preferential tariff arrangements. Language and cultural barriers as well as political considerations will add considerably to these factors which are, however, expected to diminish once the initial trade flows are established, making additional trade flows more probable.

If more than two regions are considered, the possibility of substitution[19] between the sources of supply, or between the destination points, necessitates the use of relative prices in order to determine the direction and the volume of trade. Regions faced with rising export prices become less competitive and are forced to give up part of their market shares, while regions faced with rising prices in their import-competing industries are more vulnerable to import penetration.

Historical colonial ties are expected to not only decrease the trade resistance factors, since ex-colonies tend to follow earlier established trade patterns and linkages, but also to increase the intensity of the existing flows through the establishment and reinforcement of "mental maps" which increase the awareness of the decision makers as to characteristics of the potential trading partners and improve the communication and information flows. For individual commodity groups, it can be presumed that the resistance to trade will be least for those that form the bulk of world trade.

The presence of subsidiaries and/or affiliates of multinational corporations is important to the explanation of trade flows. The ability of the multinationals to concentrate groups of complementary factors at a point of geographic space quickly, to cooperate with local immobile resources dictates present and future trade patterns. The flow of routine and nonroutine specialized information between the head office and the subsidiaries opens up new trade and investment opportunities and revives old ones (Torquist 1977, p. 153). An improvement in the accuracy and an increase in the bulk of information will significantly enhance trade flows.

The imports from the various competing regions are, therefore, explained through the combination of demand and supply conditions and trade resistance factors. Under the CMS approach part of the change in the market share is explained through the world trade effect, the market effect and the commodity composition effect, and part is not explained through any of these effects and it is, therefore, captured in the competitiveness residual. The values taken by the residual for individual commodity groups are indicative of the increase or decrease in the market share of the region for that commodity group. Positive values indicate an increase, while negative values indicate a decrease.

Overall, it is expected that the regions receiving preferential treatment should be able to maintain their market shares. The failure to do so can be explained through any of three possibilities:

1. Small elasticity of substitution in the demand for imports.
2. The quantitative restrictions and limitations imposed by the importing countries along with the implementation of the Lomé Convention by the EEC offset the expansionary effects of the GSP preferential entry.
3. The exporting regions are facing an inelastic supply of exports, rising export prices, growth rates lower than the overall growth rate.

The possible explanations provided above are of varying degrees of importance depending on the importing region under consideration. All importing regions have shown a substantial elasticity of substitution in their demand for imports as evident by Tables 7, 8, and 9 even though it appears that the elasticity varies considerably among commodity groups. The quantitative restrictions of the EEC on GSP imports in the form of tariff quotes, tariff ceilings, maximum amounts, and member quota allocation (Murray 1977), as well as their commodity classification into sensitive, semi-sensitive, and nonsensitive and the changes in this classification are definitely more restrictive than the tariff ceilings and maximum amounts of Japan and the competitive need criteria of the United States. The effect of the EEC restrictions is expressed in the uncertainty element governing GSP trade and the possibility that the EEC importers were importing at the MFN tariff rate rather than the GSP tariff rate to safeguard against potential losses which would arise form a change in the tariff status of an imported commodity. In addition, the persistent underutilization of the quotas assigned to EEC members led to a further decrease in the GSP benefits. It is very probable that non-OECD suppliers facing such restrictions sought alternative market outlets, that is, Japanese and U.S. markets.

The EEC, through the implementation of its Lomé Convention, has discriminated in favor of the Lomé beneficiaries and against the other developing GSP beneficiaries. This discrimination is based on the ex-colonial status of many Lomé signatories and the continued reliance of the EEC on these countries both as suppliers of key raw material and as outlets for manufactured products (Coppens, Faber,and Lof 1977). The nature of the discrimination is in the form of no quantitative limitations or restrictions on Lomé imports along with a series of financial, technical, promotional, managerial, and production arrangements granted exclusively to the Lomé producers. The impact of the discrimination benefited the Lomé countries in a number of ways: It removed the uncertainty governing imports and increased the existing import flows, facilitated the establishment of new import flows, led to a systematic commitment of the resources and the productive effort by removing the risk that the effort will never succeed because of policy reversals. It is very possible that this commitment could generate dynamic elements in comparative advantage.

The short-term benefits of the Lomé Convention would be captured in the positive values of the competitiveness residuals, the reversal in the signs over the previous time period for the commodity groups previously imported by the EEC, and the establishment of new import flows for commodity groups which were not previously imported by the EEC from the Lomé region. In addition, a substantial level of Lomé exports would be diverted to the EEC away from Japan and the United States.

Certain exporting regions faced with severe problems of domestic inflation and an inability to switch to products experiencing increases in international demand because of key bottlenecks in the domestic supply, became less competitive and registered negative competitiveness residuals (Central America, South America). This assertion does not hold true for those commodity groups for which the region has demonstrated a substantial comparative advantage or has been a traditional well-established exporter. The inclusion of members of the group of NICs in the various regions helped the overall performance of that region because of the demonstrated ability of these countries to produce and export a wide range of manufactured goods. Most of the NICs are members of the Far East region and are, therefore, instrumental in the spectacular success of the region. Their success is attributable to a diversified industrial base, an influx of foreign technology and foreign subsidiaries, an educated, skilled, and motivated labor force, and an inherent ability to switch either to products experiencing increases in international demand, or to products facing relaxed barriers to entry in the markets of the developed countries.

Tables 11, 14, 15, 16, and 18 report the competitiveness residuals for each of the commodity groups of the sample, for each importing region by region of origin, for the three designated periods: 1969-1971 pre-GSP period, 1971-1974 post-GSP and pre-Lomé period, and 1974-1978 post-Lomé period. The signs and the values of the residuals confirm the expected results. To verify the findings, the chi-square values were calculated from the data in Statistical Appendix B of the author's dissertation and are reported in Table 10. The chi-square test involves a comparison of the expected frequencies with the observed or actual frequencies to determine whether the difference between the expected and the observed value is greater than might reasonably be anticipated to occur by chance (see Blalock 1960). The null hypothesis is set as follows: The market share of all the regions in the markets of the EEC-6, the EEC-9, the United

Table 10. X^2 Values for Import Patterns 1969-1978*

Commodity Group	*EEC-6*	*EEC-9*	*Japan*	*United States*
(512)	79.892**	157.496**	55.079**	36.549**
(513)	106.736**	128.506**	23.571	176.680**
(532)	1.002	1.603	4.322	0.318
(541)	28.830**	44.228**	42.559**	52.615**
(551)	30.245**	26.114**	3.552	14.652
(561)	21.765	27.484**	17.697	41.537**
(611)	29.647**	34.892**	3.213	15.686
(612)	3.373	3.165	1.880	8.781
(631)	85.888**	157.052**	71.622**	41.660**
(632)	15.444	15.200	2.158	14.590
(651)	126.831**	157.291**	30.569**	29.181**
(652)	82.686**	97.595**	36.363**	49.485**
(653)	26.052**	20.398	17.308	55.647**
(656)	19.529	17.987	6.180	6.837
(657)	59.103**	84.429	3.699	22.433
(667)	100.027**	287.274**	51.969**	88.853**
(696)	3.482	1.892	2.590	3.516
(697)	9.838	5.113	1.645	5.082
(724)	22.322	35.024**	5.801	151.774**
(729)	100.792**	73.305**	11.044	76.040**
(735)	98.216**	95.861**	99.295**	14.514
(821)	33.579**	26.172**	5.981	36.288**
(831)	46.900**	31.136**	1.662	44.308**
(841)	87.230**	83.183**	128.645**	202.338**
(851)	26.779**	43.478**	3.009	88.340**
(864)	55.893**	99.204**	4.734	21.326
(894)	21.239	11.792	1.727	37.989**

Notes: *df = 15. Critical value of X^2 at the 5% level of significance = 24.996.
**Denotes rejection of the hypothesis for the 15 degrees of freedom at the 5% level of significance.
Source: Tsanacas (1982), Statistical Appendix B.

States, and Japan remained constant over time; that is, the expected market shares did not deviate significantly from the observed ones. The critical value for the chi-square at the 5% level of significance for 15 degrees of freedom is equal to 24.996.

The null hypothesis will be rejected for those commodity groups whose calculated chi-square value exceeds the critical chi-square value. The rejection of the null hypothesis indicated that there is a statistically significant relationship, or that the market shares of the regions for the various commodity groups have changed over time.

The results indicate that there have been significant changes in the market shares of many commodity groups, especially those produced under similar cost structures in the Lomé and the non-Lomé developing regions. It was not expected that the market shares of all 27 commodity groups would undergo significant changes because preferential entry is only one factor affecting trade patterns. Further, the Lomé beneficiaries are not major producers of all manufactured products considered in this study due to lack of resource endowment and/or lack of required technical know-how. This latter point is essential in explaining the important variation in the number of commodity groups registering significant changes across the four importing regions; 18 for the EEC-6, 19 for the EEC-9, but 16 for the United States, and only eight for Japan. The Lomé Convention was implemented by the EEC only, and it appears responsible for the larger number of commodities undergoing significant structural changes. Thus substitution between sources indicates a substantial impact of Lomé on the GSP. The comparison of the numbers between Japan and the United States point to a differential GSP impact on their economies. The U.S. import market experienced a wider commodity change than the Japanese import market which could mean that the United States was either faced with more severe vulnerability of its manufacturing industries and/or its markets were more open and attractive to foreign imports.

The evidence in support of both hypotheses is sufficiently strong. The signs of the competitiveness residuals generally fall in line with the expected signs during the pre-GSP, post-GSP and pre-Lomé, and the post-Lomé time periods.

Table 11 reports the expected signs of the competitiveness residuals and the actual residuals of the Lomé region for the commodity groups of the sample. The percentages of statistically significant commodity groups confirming the expected sign are: 77% for the EEC-6, 68% for the EEC-9, 50% for the United States,[20] and 40% for Japan[21] for the 1969-1971 period. The high percentages recorded by the EEC-6 and the EEC-9 are attributed to the established trade links between the EEC and the ex-colonies, now members of Lomé. Imports from these countries, later Lomé signatories, were granted preferential entry under either the Arusha Agreement, the Yaounde Convention, or the British Commonwealth. The largest positive residuals are reported in Chemicals, Leather, and Veneers and Plywood, while the largest negative signs appear in SITC 667 (Pearls, Precious, and Semi-Precious Stones), SITC 729 (Other Electrical Machinery), and SITC 735 (Ships and Boats).

Japan is not a major importer from the Lomé region during this period as evident by the low and unimportant competitiveness residuals. The only two commodity groups worth mentioning are SITC 541 (Medicinal and Pharmaceutical Products) and SITC 735 (Ships and Boats) both registering positive competitiveness residuals. The United States is a larger importer from the Lomé region than Japan especially from the Caribbean members. The substantially large positive residual registered for SITC 541 (Medicinal and Pharmaceutical Products) is indicative of the presence of the subsidiaries of the U.S.-based pharmaceuticals in the Caribbean Islands while the negative values for SITC 631 (Veneers and Plywood), and SITC 841 (Clothing except Fur Clothing) point to a diversion of trade to the EEC. Overall, the commodity groups of importance to the United States are in Chemicals.

The 1971 implementation of a GSP scheme by the EEC-6 led to the erosion of the preferential status of the Lomé exporters which they enjoyed under the Yaounde Convention and the Arusha Agreement. Being faced with severe competition from other GSP preferred exporters the Lomé exporters were forced to give up part of their market shares as the EEC importers substituted freely between sources of supply. The wider product coverage under the GSP than under the other two preferential arrangements could have some positive effect on certain commodities which were not previously exported to the EEC under preferential terms. These commodity groups would probably register positive competitiveness residual signs contrary to the expected negative signs. The delay in the U.S. implementation of a GSP scheme during this period would divert trade to the EEC and Japan. The implementation of the Japanese GSP (August 1971) is expected to have only a minor impact on the Lome share of the Japanese market because of weak trade links between the two regions.

In the post-GSP period (1971-1974) 56% and 57% of the commodity groups registered the expected signs in the residuals for the Lomé, for the EEC-6, and for the EEC-9, respectively. This is clearly a decrease in the number of commodities obeying the hypothesis, which can, however, be explained as follows. The Lomé region was able to show positive residuals for Textiles, Fabrics, and Clothing commodity categories mainly because, under the LTA agreement, preferential entry to the EEC markets was limited to Colombia, Egypt, India, Jamaica, South Korea, Mexico, and Pakistan (see Table 11 SITC 651, SITC 652, SITC 653, and SITC 841). In addition, small yet positive residuals were for Lomé for: SITC 831 (Travel Goods and Handbags) and SITC 864 (Watches and Clocks), which were not previously exported to the EEC under preferential tariff arrangements. The SITC 611 (Leather) deserves special mention for the positive sign and the difference in size between the EEC-6 and the EEC-9. The small size of the residual for the EEC-9 shows the strong trade ties for leather between the United Kingdom and members of the South American region (Argentina, Brazil).

Overall, the Lomé exporters could not compete effectively with supplies from other developing regions without a preferential wedge vis-à-vis these suppliers and were forced to an important decline in their market share for a large number of manufactured commodities.

Japan continued to import a small volume of manufactured products from the Lomé region even during the 1971-1974 period. Over 80% of the statistically significant commodities "obey" the expected sign. The size of the residuals is, however, extremely low. The emergence of a trend for those commodities which

Table 11. Competitiveness Residuals for Lomé (Thousands U.S. $)

Period		*EEC-6*	*EEC-9*	*Japan*	*United States*
1969-1971	Expected	+	+	-	-
1971-1974	Signs	-	-	+	-
1974-1978		+	+	-	-
	SITC				
	512				
1969-1971		+ 6,646	+ 8,819	+ 1	- 1,270
1971-1974		- 9,279	- 4,734	+ 7	- 4,743
1974-1978		+ 818	+13,149	+ 934	- 628
	513				
1969-1971		+ 7,512	+19.811	+ 0	+ 3,292
1971-1974		-17,348	-25,775	+ 0	- 8,795
1974-1978		- 9,235	-23,642	+ 0	-31,019
	532				
1969-1971		- 191	- 307	- 2	- 33
1971-1974		+ 48	+ 54	- 100	- 11
1974-1978		- 122	+ 436	- 2	- 13
	541				
1969-1971		+ 7,793	+10,343	+ 1,787	+13,733
1971-1974		- 4,650	- 2,690	- 1,277	- 4,497
1974-1978		+ 1,233	+ 263	- 3,336	+ 412
	551				
1969-1971		+ 3,400	+ 3,406	+ 32	+ 280
19711974		- 2,021	- 3,167	+ 146	- 1,671
1974-1978		+ 1,619	+ 2,535	- 289	- 1,425

	561				
1969-1971		+ 807	+ 1,678	+ 541	- 1,785
1971-1974		- 511	- 492	- 335	- 2,470
1974-1978		- 3,492	- 4,140	- 538	+ 92
	611				
1969-1971		+ 1,248	+ 1,570	- 22	+ 215
1971-1974		+ 1,618	+ 78	+ 21	- 328
1974-1978		+ 5,232	+11,916	- 81	- 84
	612				
1969-1971		+ 4,426	+12,187	+ 2	-13,569
1971-1974		- 778	- 2,446	- 21	- 787
1974-1978		-22,531	-22,997	+ 2	- 1,051
	632				
1969-1971		- 171	- 299	- 32	- 117
1971-1974		- 249	- 142	- 178	- 258
1974-1978		- 186	- 526	- 125	- 120
	651				
1969-1971		+ 126	+ 171	+ 28	+ 0
1971-1974		+ 424	+ 584	+ 18	+ 2
1974-1978		+ 6,751	+13,488	+ 58	+ 7
	652				
1969-1971		- 263	- 322	0	+ 12
1971-1974		+ 5,338	+ 6,078	+ 208	+ 771
1974-1978		+ 9,133	+ 9,508	- 1,114	- 861
	653				
1969-1971		+ 54	+ 36	- 762	+ 141
1971-1974		+ 235	+ 406	+ 21	+ 115
1974-1978		+ 85	+ 15	- 80	- 245

(continued)

Table 11. *(continued)*

Period	SITC	*EEC-6*	*EEC-9*	*Japan*	*United States*
	656				
1969-1971		- 137	- 162	0	+ 6
1971-1974		- 299	- 142	+ 2	+ 24
1974-1978		+ 528	+ 940	- 5	- 32
	657				
1969-1971		- 271	- 282	0	+ 75
1971-1974		- 14	+ 16	- 8	- 92
1974-1978		+ 455	+ 499	+ 2	- 73
	667				
1969-1971		- 1,753	-28,091	+ 139	- 1,017
1971-1974		- 2,910	- 2,299	+ 1,061	+ 8,207
1974-1978		+72,608	+74,888	+ 1,171	+43,941
	696				
1969-1971		+ 2	+ 68	0	+ 4
1971-1974		- 2	- 76	0	- 3
1974-1978		+ 38	+ 16	0	- 7
	697				
1969-1971		+ 16	+ 24	0	+ 2
1971-1974		- 14	+ 9	+ 2	+ 2
1974-1978		+ 471	+ 453	- 5	- 6
	724				
1969-1971		- 460	- 820	0	- 372
1971-1974		- 633	- 3,162	0	- 744
1974-1978		+ 1,456	+ 954	- 2	- 148
	729				
1969-1971		- 4,436	- 6,250	+ 4	- 699
1971-1974		- 341	- 1,396	+ 265	- 1,170
1974-1978		+ 1,753	+ 4,599	- 842	- 5,889

	735				
1969-1971		- 3,784	- 2,606	+ 4,837	+ 31
1971-1974		- 2,781	- 3,579	- 359	- 36
1974-1978		+ 7,508	+ 6,873	-12,858	- 29
	821				
1969-1971		+ 212	+ 1,048	+ 2	+ 26
1971-1974		- 285	- 596	- 20	- 25
1974-1978		+ 1,066	+ 1,393	- 4	+ 26
	831				
1969-1971		+ 1	+ 24	+ 95	+ 304
1971-1974		+ 40	+ 28	- 141	- 395
1974-1978		+ 339	+ 327	- 4	+ 26
	841				
1969-1971		+ 199	- 852	0	- 6,191
1971-1974		+ 3,570	+ 4,145	+ 1	- 3,387
1974-1978		+22,494	+33,122	- 23	- 8,656
	851				
1969-1971		+ 46	+ 47	0	- 432
1971-1974		+ 158	+ 282	+ 7	- 357
1974-1978		+ 69	+ 999	+ 7	- 293
	864				
1969-1971		+ 5	+ 6	0	- 1
1971-1974		+ 6	+ 17	0	- 2
1974-1978		+ 533	+ 584	0	- 2
	894				
1969-1971		+ 45	+ 95	+ 2	+ 647
1971-1974		+ 35	+ 174	- 3	- 432
1974-1978		+ 829	+ 750	+ 2	- 3,303

Note: The competitive residuals were calculated by subtracting the expected imports from the adjusted imports, as explained in this paper, page 140, Step 4.
Source: Tsanacas (1982), Tables 6-3, 6-5, 6-11, and 6-13.

show positive competitiveness residuals for the EEC should be stressed, because it is expected to continue. These commodities either register a small value in the competitiveness residual or a negative sign, indicating a redirection of trade to the EEC.

The absence of a U.S. GSP scheme is clearly expressed in the negative competitiveness residuals of over 70% of the commodity groups. There are only a few commodity groups registering positive residuals. Most of these are in the Textiles and Fabrics categories. The only highlight for the Lomé region is SITC 667 (Pearls, Precious and Semi-Precious Stones), which registered the highest positive residual. The positive competitiveness residuals observed in the Chemicals category during the previous period are all negative during this period, perhaps because of the OPEC price increases in 1974.

The implementation of the Lomé Convention by the EEC, in the beginning of 1975, marks the reversal of the previous trend for the exports of the Lomé region by restoring the preferential wedge which the region enjoyed prior to the GSP. Almost 90% of the commodity groups show positive competitiveness residuals for both the EEC-6 and the EEC-9 confirming the expectations. The reversal in the trend must be attributed to the Lomé Convention, given the fact that the EEC was not increasing its overall imports from non-OECD sources during this period (see Table 9). Three commodity groups suffered substantial losses in market shares as evident by the large negative competitveness residuals. Two of these are oil-related: SITC 513 (Inorganic Chemicals) and SITC 561 (Manufactured Fertilizers), while the other one is resource-based SITC 631 (Veneers, Plywood Boards). Substantial gains are achieved in SITC 611 (Leather), SITC 667 (Pearls, Precious and Semi-Precious Stones), SITC 735 (Ships and Boats), and in all Textiles, Yarn and Clothing commodity groups.

The share of Lomé exports to Japan experienced an additional decrease in the post-Lomé period as exports were primarily directed to the EEC. Almost 70% of the statistically significant commodity groups met the expected sign criterion. Overall, only four commodity groups had positive residuals. The two worth mentioning are: SITC 512 (Organic Chemicals) and SITC 667 (Pearls, Precious and Semi-Precious Stones). It seems that both of these are tied to Japanese direct investment in the Caribbean and the African members of Lomé, respectively.

The similarities in the U.S. results to those of Japan are evident in Table 11. Almost 65% of the statistically significant commodities follow the negative expected sign even though the United States implemented the GSP scheme in 1976. Only five commodities have positive residuals. Of these, the only two of meaningful size are: SITC 541 (Medicinal and Pharmaceutical Products)—directly tied to U.S. subsidiaries in the Caribbean—and SITC 667 (Pearls, Precious and Semi-Precious Stones). The large negative values of the residuals are testimony to a redirection of a large volume of exports to the EEC.

Table 11 provides substantanial evidence of the importance of Lomé in reversing the downward trend of the market share of its beneficiaries in the EEC. The fact that the Lomé exports were more preferred while the exports of the other regions were discriminated against through a series of quantitative restrictions, maximum amounts, and limitations led to the substitution of their exports for Lomé exports in the EEC markets. These restrictions caused the substitution demand curve to shift in such a way as to limit and offset the GSP expansionary effect especially for commodities produced under similar conditions in Lomé and non-Lomé exporters. The improved market familiarity and the various types of assistance extended to the Lomé exporters by the EEC opened up new trade routes and strengthened existing ones. A large volume of non-Lomé exports were directed to other markets away from the EEC markets induced by higher levels of uncertainty. The United States and Japan received the largest volume of this redirected trade. This last assertion will become evident in the subsequent tables reporting the competitiveness residuals for the various regions.

Tables 12 and 13 report the imports from Lomé as a percent of impors from other non-OECD regions for 1974 and 1978 for a select group of commodities for the EEC-6 and the EEC-9, respectively. Based on the evidence from the tables, imports from the Lomé region increased faster than imports from the other regions for most of the reported commodities.

Tables 14 and 15 report the competitiveness residuals for South America and Central America, respectively. Both of these regions have experienced unique problems, political as well as economic, which have resulted in a substantial deterioration in their competitiveness. The political problems either in the form of revolutions or social and political unrest have made both regions unreliable sources of exports, while the economic problems expressed in the form of rampant inflation rates and reduced investment have increased their export prices in the world markets. In addition, the continuous readjustments in the exchange rates to resolve Balance of Payments problems have contributed to the diversion of importers to other markets. It seems that these regions were unable to recover from the supply shock of the 1974 OPEC price increases. The higher energy bills could very well have an important impact on their exports both in volume and prices. The higher prices for inputs would increase their export prices leading to a loss in competitiveness and a loss in market shares. It is, however, possible to observe increases in the market shares for certain commodities, since they are looking to finance the oil imports through higher volumes of exports. This is expected on exports of traditional nature for which the regions are established exporters. Brazil and Mexico, both members of the NIC group of countries are the only highlights of the two regions. Both countries have experienced substantial growth rates and have been the recipients of foreign direct investment by U.S. and Japanese firms, which resulted in increased exports of a wide variety. Their performance has

Table 12. Percentage Which Imports from Lomé Constitute of Imports from Non-OECD Regions for the EEC-6, Various Commodity Groups 1974 and 1978

Commodity Group	*Year*	*South America*	*Central America*	*Sino-Soviet*	*Far East*	*Other Developing*
(512)	1974	84.46	67.31	6.78	85.49	38.57
	1978	52.77	172.24	9.05	54.02	30.45
(541)	1974	130.95	276.28	74.90	154.02	276.23
	1978	184.39	274.76	90.20	221.33	171.84
(551)	1974	67.67	2667.44	56.35	84.08	89.28
	1978	146.74	535.79	156.02	61.27	103.83
(611)	1974	25.72	1075.60	173.55	12.91	87.70
	1978	31.29	1272.03	605.08	19.49	189.55
(651)	1974	2.71	15.87	8.63	3.09	5.58
	1978	10.53	183.33	60.14	22.66	44.59
(652)	1974	36.68	106.63	18.92	17.41	53.79
	1978	100.08	1163.10	52.79	30.93	103.36
(667)	1974	140.52	1498.94	57.77	25.15	27.30
	1978	634.75	25620.18	101.97	58.32	85.27
(735)	1974	402.08	212.50	10.55	89.91	109.45
	1978	98.44	187.64	26.57	176.82	1202.13
(841)	1974	39.20	188.64	2.72	1.20	2.86
	1978	78.65	762.55	10.45	3.53	10.15

[illegible] Percentage Which Imports from Lomé Constitute of Imports from Non-OECD Regions for the EEC-9, Various Commodity Groups 1974 and 1978

Commodity Group	*Year*	*South America*	*Central America*	*Sino-Soviet*	*Far East*	*Other Developing*
(512)	1974	144.61	67.88	10.52	96.65	53.40
	1978	52.77	172.74	9.05	54.02	30.45
(541)	1974	139.31	280.26	76.38	195.46	281.18
	1978	176.21	272.27	97.56	162.31	272.27
(551)	1974	58.74	727.86	48.39	72.98	94.77
	1978	125.37	277.54	150.95	60.18	119.96
(611)	1974	26.86	1292.50	194.85	12.09	97.79
	1978	40.22	1799.10	343.85	24.19	261.20
(651)	1974	2.92	17.52	9.12	2.21	5.61
	1978	16.85	198.60	128.41	33.59	52.55
(652)	1974	34.24	97.97	14.21	7.18	48.05
	1978	85.38	1226.85	41.46	11.94	77.95
(667)	1974	139.54	1498.02	57.49	25.07	26.99
	1978	63.75	24345.02	102.77	57.21	72.32
(735)	1974	342.98	203.90	10.52	77.21	97.27
	1978	105.62	205.44	19.52	151.36	280.10
(841)	1974	36.71	171.61	2.78	0.88	2.92
	1978	97.29	815.20	12.23	3.34	10.38

Source: Tsanacas (1982), Statistical Appendix B, Table B-5.

Table 14. Competitiveness Residuals for South America
(Thousands U.S. $)

Period		*EEC-6*	*EEC-9*	*Japan*	*United States*
1969-1971	Expected	+	+	-	+
1971-1974	Signs	+	+	+	-
1974-1978		-	-	+	+
	SITC				
	512				
1969-1971		+ 4,439	+ 7,627	+ 424	+ 1,508
1971-1974		- 5,225	- 5,039	+ 8,366	+ 6,384
1974-1978		+ 6,069	+ 6,381	-21,847	-10,810
	513				
1961-1971		+ 3,129	+ 2,661	- 267	+ 1,732
1971-1974		- 1,041	- 1,755	+ 50	+ 2,220
1974-1978		- 3,234	- 2	+ 1,048	- 3,880
	532				
1969-1971		+ 170	+ 297	+ 15	+ 28
1971-1974		- 147	+ 145	- 694	- 47
1974-1978		- 91	- 589	- 80	+ 35
	541				
1969-1971		+ 1,046	+ 1,217	+ 208	+ 2,758
1971-1974		- 228	- 3,655	- 422	- 635
1974-1978		- 1,924	- 2,198	+ 477	+ 190
	551				
1969-1971		+ 1,840	+ 1,638	- 42	+ 2,067
1971-1974		+ 1,154	+ 926	+ 537	- 795
1974-1978		- 1,924	- 4,017	- 70	- 4,866

1969-1971		- 99	- 705	- 313	+ 146
1971-1974		+ 123	- 84	+ 717	- 2,421
1974-1978		+ 701	+ 901	- 933	+ 483
	611				
1969-1971		- 2,154	- 139	+ 73	+ 2,802
1971-1974		+ 5,698	+ 8,599	+ 10	- 3,933
1974-1978		+ 8,288	+ 9,968	+ 223	+ 1,639
	612				
1969-1971		+ 111	+ 16	- 41	- 581
1971-1974		+ 58	+ 417	- 224	- 1,004
1974-1978		- 2,626	- 1,226	- 816	- 5,088
	631				
1969-1971		- 4,326	- 5,371	- 688	-13,432
1971-1974		- 6,570	- 9,713	+ 10	+ 1,475
1974-1978		- 4,853	- 2,518	+ 1,580	- 1,055
	632				
1969-1971		+ 441	+ 586	+ 1	- 189
1971-1974		+ 1,146	+ 1,916	+ 36	+ 1,446
1974-1978		- 2,201	- 2,767	- 102	- 3,983
	651				
1969-1971		+ 2,004	+ 2,541	+ 167	- 701
1971-1974		+20,772	+25,069	+ 1,039	- 71
1974-1978		+22,777	+31,091	- 2,105	+ 3,617
	652				
1969-1971		+ 1,041	+ 1,139	+ 26	+ 1,837
1971-1974		+12,921	+16,351	+ 710	- 1,405
1974-1978		- 4,507	- 6,281	- 4,096	+ 8,339
	653				
1969-1971		+ 24	+ 53	0	- 130
1971-1974		+ 1,437	+ 2,938	+ 532	+ 2,547
1974-1978		+ 2,074	+ 2,752	- 2,690	+ 4,541

(continued)

Table 14. (continued)

Period	SITC	EEC-6	EEC-9	Japan	United States
	656				
1969-1971		+ 632	+ 955	+ 1	+ 432
1971-1974		+ 4,346	+ 5,841	+ 62	+ 1,945
1974-1978		- 2,705	- 4,260	- 92	- 1,530
	657				
1969-1971		+ 40	+ 108	0	+ 260
1971-1974		+ 90	+ 83	+ 13	- 286
1974-1978		+ 130	- 88	- 68	+ 242
	667				
1969-1971		+ 1,889	- 5,213	+ 1,515	- 1,423
1971-1974		+ 1,745	- 2,488	+ 209	+ 2,192
1974-1978		-21,901	-25,124	-19,345	-13,240
	696				
1969-1971		+ 136	+ 222	0	- 56
1971-1974		- 99	- 24	+ 316	+ 140
1974-1978		- 906	- 595	- 569	- 870
	697				
1969-1971		+ 29	+ 38	+ 1	- 234
1971-1974		+ 101	+ 111	+ 17	+ 502
1974-1978		- 257	- 88	- 42	- 306
	724				
1969-1971		+ 453	+ 725	0	- 17
1971-1974		- 23	- 50	- 1	+29,731
1974-1978		+ 405	- 362	+ 238	-30,686
	729				
1969-1971		+ 629	+ 879	0	+ 684
1971-1974		+ 832	+ 807	+ 96	+11,572

1969-1971		+ 44	+ 62	- 6,587	+ 35
1971-1974		+ 479	+ 685	- 196	- 6
1974-1978		+14,030	+14,184	+ 3	+ 6,144
	821				
1969-1971		+ 553	+ 715	+ 6	+ 263
1971-1974		- 417	+ 562	+ 341	+ 2,444
1974-1978		- 1,548	- 4,639	- 2,197	- 5,449
	831				
1969-1971		+ 31	+ 42	- 6	+ 221
1971-1974		+ 2,182	+ 2,641	+ 13	+ 4,694
1974-1978		- 4,848	- 5,599	+ 123	- 5,794
	841				
1969-1971		+ 417	+ 634	+ 4	+ 7,693
1971-1974		+ 9,013	+11,858	+ 272	+17,029
1974-1978		+15,287	+13,608	- 153	- 2,985
	851				
1969-1971		- 95	- 38	+ 18	+12,466
1971-1974		+ 2,585	+ 5,370	+ 5	+18,207
1974-1978		+11,718	+17,632	- 220	-75,239
	864				
1969-1971		- 5	+ 46	0	- 65
1971-1974		+ 43	+ 195	+ 3	- 431
1974-1978		- 396	- 2,670	- 27	- 1,028
	894				
1969-1971		+ 22	+ 38	+ 9	+ 753
1971-1974		+ 222	+ 334	- 12	+ 1,439
1974-1978		- 142	- 76	+ 294	- 253

Note: The competitiveness residuals were calculated by subtracting the expected imports from the adjusted imports, as explained in this paper, page 140, step 4.
Source: Tsanacas (1982), Tables 6-3, 6-5, 6-11, 6-13.

been instrumental in preventing decreases in the market shares of the regions beyond those reported in Tables 14 and 15.

The EEC has traditionally imported a large volume of manufactured products from South America as evident by the large number of positive residuals during the 1969-1971 period. Over 75% of the commodity groups registered the expected positive sign for both the EEC-6 and the EEC-9 mainly because of strong trade ties and established trade patterns. The number of commodities registering positive residuals decreased steadily since 1971 as a result of the rapid deterioration in the international competitiveness of the region. Only seven commodity groups had positive residuals in the 1974-1978 period (see Table 14). Five groups represent traditional exports SITC 661 (Leather), SITC 651 (Textile Yarn), SITC 653 (Textile Fabrics), SITC 841 (Clothing), and SITC 851 (Footwear), while the other two are SITC 512 (Organic Chemicals) and SITC 735 (Ships and Boats). A quick reference to Tables 12 and 13 clearly indicates that the Lomé exports to the EEC increased faster than the South American exports for the same commodity groups with the exception of SITC 512 and SITC 735. Over 60% of the commodity groups "obey" the sign criterion for the 1971-1974 and 1974-1978 periods for both the original and the enlarged EEC.

Japan is not a major importer of South American manufactures. The gains which were observed during the 1971-1974 period, 21 commodity groups reporting a positive sign for the residuals, disappeared during the next period as the competitiveness of the region deteriorated drastically. Only seven commodity groups reported positive residuals, the largest gains appearing in SITC 513 (Inorganic Chemicals) and SITC 631 (Veneers, Plywood Boards, and so forth). The other commodity groups experienced a decrease in market share, having been replaced by Far East manufactures in the Japanese market.

The expected signs find little support from the data for South America. Only a little over 30% of the commodity groups followed the expected positive sign indicating that the region was unable to capitalize on the Japanese GSP scheme. The fact that South America continued to export certain commodities to the EEC indicates the presence of strong trade patterns even in the presence of the Lomé provisions.

The United States has paid close attention to the South American region and it has initiated massive economic programs to aid its economies. Large volume of direct investment by U.S. multinationals have been located in this region with partial success as demonstrated by the large number of positive residuals especially during the 1969-1971 period. Over 70% of the commodity groups meet the expected sign. The delay in the implementation of the U.S. GSP scheme created a diversion of certain exports to EEC and Japanese markets in the 1971-1974 period. The United States did, however, increased its imports from the region for such SITC groups as: 724 (Telecommunications Apparatus), 729 (Other Electrical Machinery), 841 (Clothing except Fur

Clothing), and 851 (Footwear). The increase in these commodity groups reflects the interests of the U.S. multinationals in the region (Bergsten, Horst, and Moran 1978). During the 1974-1978 period, the implementation of the U.S. GSP scheme should have led either to an increase in the market share for a large number of commodity groups, or, at least, to an increase in the market shares of those commodity groups which experienced an increase during the previous period. The preferential advantage under the GSP was, however, nullified by: (a) internal problems of political unrest (making the region an unreliable source of exports); (b) rampant inflation which decreased the GSP preferential advantage; (c) the exclusion of Ecuador and Venezuela from GSP coverage under the Green Amendment; (d) the exclusion of Footwear and Textiles from GSP coverage; and (e) the restrictive nature of the U.S. competitive-neec criteria particularly for imports originating in Chile, Peru, Brazil, and Argentina.

A wide variety of products registered negative signs in the competitiveness residuals contrary to the expected positive signs. Only 38% of the products "obey" the expected sign. Surprisingly, Textile items showed positive signs in the residuals, although excluded from the U.S. GSP scheme (see Table 14). The possibility that the South American Textile items were diverted to the U.S. markets from the EEC markets carries a lot of weight, especially since these items were produced and exported by Lomé producers and the EEC had reserved a substantial part of its market for these producers.

The position of Central America in the EEC markets has shown persistent deterioration since the implementation of Lomé in 1975 for all commodity groups with minor exceptions in the SITC categories: 541, 551, 735, and 851 (see Table 15). The region is not a major exporter to the EEC even though Mexico has substantial trade ties with the Community. Mexico, as a major oil exporter and as a member of the NIC's group, is responsible for the positive residuals in most of the commodity groups. The similarities in the export production of the rest of the Central American economies to the economies of signatories of Lomé is a tremendous disadvantage for the region, since the EEC markets are very restrictive. There are no persisitent and sustained export drives to break into the European markets preferring instead the open and attractive U.S. markets. Over 65% of the commodity groups followed the expected signs for the residuals for the EEC-6 and the EEC-9.

Japan is a minor trading partner of Central America. Scattered signs of new trade being established are evident in Table 15, mainly because of an increased volume of Japanese direct investment in the region. The geographic location, the political and economic turmoil and the overall instability of the region are huge barriers to any significant trade links with Japan. Encouraging results were observed only in SITC 512, SITC 724, and SITC 735. The importance of Mexico should be stated explicitly since it represents the highlight of the region. Only 43% of the commodity groups registered the expected positive

Table 15. Competitiveness Residuals for Central America (Thousands U.S. $)

Period		*EEC-6*	*EEC-9*	*Japan*	*United States*
1969-1971	Expected Signs	-	-	-	+
1971-1974		+	+	+	-
1974-1978		-	-	+	+
	SITC				
	512				
1969-1971		- 94896	-11,816	- 493	- 663
1971-1974		- 3,596	-28,458	- 2,704	- 6,873
1974-1978		- 5,291	-10,429	+ 3,081	+ 253
	513				
1969-1971		- 2,488	- 5,975	- 681	- 4,723
1971-1974		+ 1,830	+ 1,944	- 613	- 53
1974-1978		- 8,706	- 7,427	- 629	+23,908
	532				
1961-1971		0	0	0	0
1971-1974		0	+ 2	0	+ 30
1974-1978		0	- 4	0	+ 33
	541				
1969-1971		- 7,560	-12,686	- 1,654	-16,179
1971-1974		+ 787	+ 1,479	- 879	+ 1,902
1974-1978		+ 468	+ 260	- 326	- 2,562
	551				
1969-1971		- 531	- 1,289	+ 27	- 713
1971-1974		- 272	- 68	- 20	- 1,500
1974-1978		+ 1,124	+ 2,401	+ 252	+ 5,086
	561				
1969-1971		- 1	- 2	0	+ 412
1971-1974		+ 3	+ 6	0	- 4,722
1974-1978		+ 4,808	+ 5,082	0	- 7,792

	611				
1969-1971		+ 49	+ 65	- 110	- 539
1971-1974		- 464	- 393	- 319	- 221
1974-1978		+ 37	+ 316	- 256	+ 930
	612				
1969-1971		+ 16	+ 21	0	+ 539
1971-1974		- 6	+ 11	- 1	- 2,121
1974-1978		+ 40	- 15	- 6	+ 836
	631				
1969-1971		+ 41	+ 52	0	+ 5,982
1971-1974		- 29	+ 78	+ 1	- 234
1974-1978		- 71	- 297	0	+ 5,489
	632				
1969-1971		+ 57	+ 296	+ 3	- 453
1971-1974		- 100	- 58	+ 88	- 4,741
1974-1978		- 284	- 337	+ 65	+ 636
	651				
1969-1971		- 371	- 460	0	- 1,961
1971-1974		+ 3,618	+ 4,220	+ 805	+ 905
1974-1978		- 7,131	- 2,235	- 6,862	+ 1,648
	652				
1969-1971		+ 193	+ 296	+ 104	+ 1,240
1971-1974		+ 4,625	+ 5,850	+ 163	+ 4,268
1974-1978		- 9,939	- 8,579	- 6,330	- 7,205
	653				
1969-1971		+ 80	+ 100	0	+ 6
1971-1974		+ 54	+ 180	+ 178	+ 1,425
1974-1978		- 442	- 654	- 1,045	- 818
	656				
1969-1971		+ 222	+ 288	+ 8	+ 156
1971-1974		- 350	- 200	- 65	+ 1,102
1974-1978		- 293	- 334	+ 172	+ 2,238

(continued)

Table 15. (continued)

Period	SITC	*EEC-6*	*EEC-9*	*Japan*	*United States*
	657				
1969-1971		- 1	+ 7	+ 5	+ 89
1971-1974		- 31	- 24	- 9	+ 10
1974-1978		- 8	- 8	- 16	- 530
	667				
1969-1971		+ 175	+ 3,030	- 2,084	+ 36
1971-1974		+ 221	- 3,337	- 1,889	- 265
1974-1978		- 3,463	- 3,845	+ 1,551	+ 170
	696				
1969-1971		+ 1	+ 6	0	- 180
1971-1974		+ 3	+ 4	0	- 12
1974-1978		- 16	- 29	0	- 12
	697				
1961-1971		- 8	- 8	+ 2	+ 169
1971-1974		+ 3	+ 22	- 21	+ 512
1974-1978		- 6	- 49	+ 17	- 3,836
	724				
1961-1971		- 149	- 21	0	+13,156
1971-1974		+ 18	- 230	- 1	- 4,763
1974-1978		+ 229	+ 524	+ 3,358	- 8,978
	729				
1969-1971		+ 3,351	+ 4,269	+ 1	- 1,175
1971-1974		- 3,469	- 3,014	+ 1,043	+ 4,397
1974-1978		-13,883	-13,121	- 3,114	-75,985
	735				
1969-1971		+12,819	+15,690	+ 354	+ 346
1971-1974		- 8,476	-10,030	- 40	- 316

	821				
1969-1971		+ 109	+ 75	+ 3	+ 138
1971-1974		- 150	- 64	- 43	- 398
1974-1978		- 7	- 77	- 104	-10,856
	831				
1969-1971		- 18	- 21	- 5	+ 311
1971-1974		+ 28	+ 36	+ 4	+ 2,173
1974-1978		- 128	- 126	+ 58	- 6,601
	841				
1969-1971		- 189	- 327	- 76	+ 1,562
1971-1974		+ 1,881	+ 2,202	+ 54	- 9,719
1974-1978		- 2,505	- 1,482	- 55	+75,909
	851				
1969-1971		- 29	- 36	0	- 3,202
1971-1974		- 11	0	0	- 4,513
1974-1978		+ 1,703	+ 1,852	+ 35	-16,603
	864				
1969-1971		+ 3	+ 4	0	+ 3
1971-1974		+ 10	+ 14	+ 1	+ 1,787
1974-1978		- 188	+ 86	+ 175	- 9,410
	894				
1969-1971		+ 82	+ 110	+ 36	- 3,092
1971-1974		+ 25	+ 152	- 53	- 4,286
1974-1978		- 169	- 280	+ 41	-23,602

Note: The competititveness residuals were calculated by subtracting the expected imports from the adjusted imports, as explained in this paper, page 140, step 4.
Source: Tsanacas (1982), Tables 6-3, 6-5, 6-11, and 6-13.

sign in 1974-1978 down from the over 50% during the previous two periods 1969-1971 and 1971-1974.

The Central American region had been the recipient of economic aid and assistance from the United States because of its strategic location and the continuous Cuban involvement. Up to 1974, the region was consistently increasing its share of the U.S. markets for a wide variety of products, even though the United States delayed its GSP scheme. Table 15 testifies to this fact as well as to the difficulty in establishing an expected sign for the 1971-1974 period. The evidence does, however, point to a persistent and rather substantial decline in the share of many commodity groups since 1974. This decline was due to a series of political and economic factors: political unrest, loss of competitiveness, decreased reliability in filling export orders, and high domestic inflation rates. The implementation of the U.S. GSP scheme in 1976 did little to the export position of the region thanks to the severity of the U.S. competitive-need criteria. The competitive-need limitation (see pages 130-133) was instrumental in denying GSP coverage on imports from this region—Panama and Nicaragua 82.1%, Guyana 81.8%, Dominican Republic 74.7%, and Mexico 43.3% (see UNCTAD TD/B/C.5/71, 1981). The lower transportation cost advantage was nullified by the imposition of the MFN tariff on certain exports exceeding the limit and higher costs associated with small-scale production. The substantial volume of GSP trade, deemed preferential access under the competitive-need limitation, provides strong indication of (a) pressing need for diversification of the industrial base; (b) need to grant cumulative origin status to Central American countries; and (c) need for exporters to seek alternate markets in Europe and Japan.

The overall market share of the region is rescued somewhat by the improved and expanding U.S.-Mexico trade ties. This trade, initiated by cheaper labor costs, was later extended from assembly-type plants towards the manufacturing of components. "Border"-type industries, such as leather, electrical machinery, and telecommunications along with twin textile plants, helped increase the U.S. imports from Mexico, overcoming the denial of preferential entry on over 60 manufactured products. Further, the discovery of vast oil reserves provided a tremendous boost to the petrochemical and fertilizer industries.

Commodity groups "obeying" the expected sign and registering large positive residuals were: SITC 513 (Inorganic Chemicals), SITC 551 (Essential Oils and Perfumes), SITC 631 (Veneers, Plywood Boards), SITC 651 (Textile Yarn), SITC 656 (Articles of Textile Material), and SITC 841 (Clothing except Fur Clothing). The Clothing Category represented the largest increase. The biggest disappointments were in SITC 729 (Electrical Machinery), followed by SITC 894 (Permulators, Toys, Games), SITC 851 (Footwear), SITC 821 (Furniture), and other commodity groups. It is very possible that the recession in the United States in the aftermath of the OPEC price hikes in 1974 had an impact in these mainly income-elastic commodity groups.

The region, consisting of other developing countries, is a major trading partner of the EEC mainly because of: (a) geographic location; (b) prior trade ties to the EEC through a series of preferential arrangements (Morocco, Algeria, Tunisia, Egypt, Lebanon, Malta, and Cyprus); and (c) heavy reliance of the EEC for oil and oil-related products (Saudi Arabia, Indian Ocean Arab States, Iran, Libya). In addition, Israel and Yugoslavia, both members of this region, are essential suppliers of manufactured exports to the EEC; having established a diverse industrial base. The region ranked second to the Far East in control of market share for the EEC-6 and third for the EEC-9 during the post-GSP, pre-Lomé period. Although the rank was preserved for the EEC-9 during the post-Lomé period 1974-1978, it was not preserved for the EEC-6 (see Table 4).

The competitiveness residuals for the region labelled "other developing countries" are reported in Table 16. The percentage of commodity groups registering the expected sign for the residuals was high during the 1969-1971 period for both the EEC-6 and the EEC-9. The lower percentage in 1971-1974 is attributed to the failure of many countries' members of this region to be signatories of the LTA agreements, therefore, not qualifying for GSP coverage for Textiles.

The commodity groups which posted substantial gains in market shares (large positive residuals) during the 1974-1978 period were oil-related: SITC 512 and SITC 513 (Organic and Inorganic Chemicals), and SITC 561 (Manufactured Fertilizers). An important gain in SITC 841 (Clothing) was observed for the EEC-9 only, indicating strong United Kingdom preferences for clothing imports from this region. Overall, however, the similarities in the export patterns between the countries of this region and the country signatories of Lomé induced a substantial loss in market shares for a large number of commodity groups. The observed decreases are attributable to the loss and/or the sharing of previous preferential advantage with other exporters and to the quantitative limitations imposed by the EEC on certain products, especially products originating in Yugoslavia. The limitations had a large effect on SITC 611 (Leather), SITC 821 (Furniture), and SITC 851 (Footwear). The large positive residual registered in SITC 612 (Manufactures of Leather) is explained by the restrictive nature of the limitation on leather, forcing a switch towards the production and export of these products.

The importance of Israel as a supplier of pharmaceuticals is reflected in the positive residual for SITC 541 (Medicinal and Pharmaceutical Products). The SITC 894 (Permulators, Toys, Games) although not statistically significant under this study, could be an important category in the future, especially if the quantitative limitations on other manufactures continues.

The share of the Japanese import market controlled by the region consisting of the rest of the developing countries showed somewhat of an improvement in the 1974-1978 period after continuous deteriorations during the previous

Table 16. Competitiveness Residuals for Other Developing Countries (Thousands U.S. $)

Period		*EEC-6*	*EEC-9*	*Japan*	*United States*
1969-1971	Expected	+	+	+	+
1971-1974	Signs	+	+	+	-
1974-1978		-	-	+	+
	SITC				
	512				
1969-1971		- 424	- 4,478	+ 483	- 172
1971-1974		+ 5,936	+10,828	- 1,612	- 1,112
1974-1978		+ 7,079	+ 8,827	+ 893	+ 3,596
	513				
1969-1971		- 3,482	- 6,015	- 507	- 287
1971-1974		+10,037	+16,661	+ 834	+ 4,574
1974-1978		+18,916	+22,005	- 92	- 3,142
	532				
1969-1971		+ 6	+ 7	0	+ 1
1971-1974		+ 11	+ 15	+ 808	+ 8
1974-1978		- 50	- 72	- 70	- 9
	541				
1969-1971		- 97	+ 113	+ 443	- 250
1971-1974		+ 465	+ 556	- 521	+ 332
1974-1978		+ 3,283	+ 4,051	- 1,191	+ 557
	551				
1969-1971		- 4,131	+ 337	+ 17	- 147
1971-1974		- 1,332	+ 1,689	- 19	- 19
1974-1978		+ 694	+ 633	+ 37	- 553
	561				
1969-1971		+ 6,560	- 9,483	+ 326	+ 1,228
1971-1974		- 910	- 1,073	- 1,389	- 1,240
1974-1978		+ 1,290	+ 7,094	+ 849	+ 4,675

	611				
1969-1971		+ 2,728	+ 3,750	- 6	- 292
1971-1974		- 4,992	- 4,302	- 1	+ 634
1974-1978		- 4,692	- 5,613	0	- 3,814
	612				
1969-1971		- 250	- 102	+ 2	- 8
1971-1974		- 652	- 1,531	- 47	- 122
1974-1978		+ 5,088	+ 5,142	+ 2	- 463
	631				
1969-1971		+ 241	- 6,248	- 3,059	- 563
1971-1974		+ 840	- 500	- 21	+ 34
1974-1978		- 2,348	- 6,722	- 1	- 129
	632				
1969-1971		- 2,038	- 2,093	- 16	- 290
1971-1974		- 1,980	- 1,263	- 5	- 592
1974-1978		- 2,664	- 2,513	- 20	- 1,3887
	651				
1969-1971		- 8,647	-10,857	- 272	- 2,587
1971-1974		-12,644	-15,301	+ 344	- 2,136
1974-1978		- 8,498	- 1,953	- 837	- 231
	652				
1969-1971		- 5,063	- 5,474	- 36	- 478
1971-1974		-14,255	- 9,356	- 171	- 4,919
1974-1978		+ 1,799	+ 4,245	- 976	- 2,792
	653				
1969-1971		+ 475	+ 173	+ 1,013	+ 5,738
1971-1974		- 6,380	- 5,640	- 35	- 3,196
1974-1978		- 3,112	- 5,059	- 220	- 647
	656				
1969-1971		- 914	- 1,088	- 36	- 103
1971-1974		- 356	+ 746	- 33	+ 16
1974-1978		- 42	+ 1,251	+ 27	+ 331

(continued)

Table 16. (continued)

Period	SITC	*EEC-6*	*EEC-9*	*Japan*	*United States*
	657				
1969-1971		- 2,057	+15,730	+ 24	- 344
1971-1974		-16,270	-16,555	- 53	- 2,377
1974-1978		-18,996	-30,319	+ 222	- 9,111
	667				
1969-1971		- 793	+21,213	- 445	- 943
1971-1974		- 106	+ 3,009	- 794	-10,592
1974-1978		-63,338	-50,334	- 2,858	-40,106
	696				
1969-1971		- 36	+ 49	0	+ 10
1971-1974		- 26	- 67	- 5	- 89
1974-1978		+ 22	+ 135	0	+ 18
	697				
1969-1971		+ 23	+ 273	+ 3	- 384
1971-1974		- 352	- 268	+ 4	+ 11
1974-1978		- 4,605	- 886	- 38	- 1,595
	724				
1969-1971		+ 392	- 997	- 1	- 6,483
1971-1974		- 2,489	- 3,138	+ 1	- 9,970
1974-1978		- 9,210	- 447	- 4	+ 1,105
	729				
1969-1971		+ 293	- 1,165	- 36	- 192
1971-1974		- 1,861	- 4,264	- 13	- 567
1974-1978		+ 2,922	-15,213	- 26	+ 2,298
	735				
1969-1971		+ 4,980	+ 6,234	- 26	+ 43
1971-1974		- 1,556	- 1,911	+ 117	- 31
1974-1978		- 6,308	+ 91	+ 642	- 267

	821				
1969-1971		- 2,769	- 2,763	- 7	- 1,291
1971-1974		- 4,628	- 3,178	+ 98	- 4,371
1974-1978		-14,176	-34,628	+ 1,198	-13,118
	831				
1969-1971		- 1,507	- 1,531	+ 15	+ 1,764
1971-1974		- 1,020	- 223	- 156	+ 2,036
1974-1978		-17,028	- 9,941	- 136	-18,676
	841				
1969-1971		- 605	+ 4,143	+ 2,289	- 2,364
1971-1974		-19,234	- 2,414	- 8,564	- 7,416
1974-1978		-38,609	+22,402	- 668	-33,669
	851				
1969-1971		- 392	- 251	- 40	+ 452
1971-1974		- 2,515	- 21	- 29	- 689
1974-1978		- 5,980	+ 1,369	+ 283	+27,846
	864				
1969-1971		- 17	+ 27	0	+ 29
1971-1974		+ 26	+ 29	0	+ 309
1974-1978		- 1,180	- 1,513	- 3	- 5,053
	894				
1969-1971		+ 229	+ 651	- 28	+ 1,088
1971-1974		- 968	- 1,174	- 1	- 9
1974-1978		+ 2,286	+ 4,208	+ 81	- 680

Note: The competitiveness residuals were calculated by subtracting the expected imports from the adjusted imports, as explained in this paper, page 140, step 4.
Source: Tsanacas (1982), Tables 6-3, 6-5, 6-11, and 6-13.

two periods (see Table 16). The improvement is attributable to gains in Chemicals, Fertilizers, Ships and Boats, Furniture, and Footwear. Losses were observed in Pharmaceuticals and in Precious, Semi-Precious Stones, while the rest of the commodity groups underwent minor changes. The gains were tied to the Japanese direct investment in the region and, in the case of SITC 821 (Furniture) and SITC 851 (Footwear), to the quantitative restrictions imposed by the EEC on imports from Yugoslavia. The region was not in a position to compete effectively with the Far East producers which were the major suppliers to Japan and its exports were displaced. The percent of commodities "obeying" the expected sign was a rather disappointing 30% for both the 1971-1974 and the 1974-1978 time periods.

There are three groupings of commodities observed in the U.S. import analysis of the region covering the other developing countries (see Table 16). Group 1 consists of commodities whose market share increased (positive residuals): SITC 512, SITC 541, SITC 561, SITC 724, SITC 729, and SITC 851. The increases in the market shares range from 4% for Footwear to 25% for Manufactured Fertilizers. The prominent commodities of this group are Organic Chemicals, Manufactured Fertilizers, and Footwear. The increases in the first two, are the results of the oil-processing and refining facilities established by the U.S. oil companies in the region, while the increase in Footwear is attributed to the higher imports from Yugoslavia which displaced the higher-priced imports from South America. This redirection of Yugoslavian trade to the United States was most definitely tied to the EEC restrictions. The increases in Telecommunications and Electrical Machinery were the results of the close U.S. trade ties with Israel. Group 2 consists of those commodities which failed to increase their share of the U.S. market (negative residuals): SITC 657, SITC 667, SITC 821, SITC 831, and SITC 841. The losses range from 7% for Pearls, Precious, and Semi-Precious Stones to 16% for Floor Coverings. The decreases in this group were not only evidence of the sheer dynamism of the Far East producers, their competitive edge, their ability to penetrate and capture large shares of the U.S. markets, but also the shortcomings of the U.S. GSP. The competitive-need limitation had a substantial impact on Furniture and Handbags (SITC 821 and 831) while the exclusion of Clothing from GSP coverage impacted on SITC 841. The decrease in SITC 667 (Pearls, Semi-Precious, and Precious Stones) was caused by lower imports from Israel which is one of the premier exporters of worked stones in the world. The fact that the Lomé region increased its share of the U.S. market during the same period suggests the possibility that the U.S. importers preferred unfinished and unworked stones, especially since there was a tremendous price increase in 1978. Group 3 consists of commodities which experienced only minor variations. These commodities were not produced competitively by the countries of the region and/or did not qualify for preferential tariff treatment.

The collective impact of the three groups of commodity categories, mentioned above, left the overall position of the region almost unchanged in 1978 which indicates that the gainers offset the losers. The expected signs were confirmed by over 75% of the commodities during the 1971-1974 period, but only by 40% during the 1974-1978 period for the reasons mentioned above in the explanation for Group 2.

The predominant position of the Far East region in the international markets for manufactures is evident by the fact that the region increased its share of the markets for all importing regions during all the time period with the exception of the U.S. market during the 1971-1974 period. The region has captured over 50% of the aggregate non-OECD import market for the EEC of 9 (50.77), Japan (79.45), and the United States (73.63), and approaches that figure for the EEC of 6 (47.56).

The diversified industrial base, the ability to adapt foreign technology to the production process and to penetrate foreign markets have extended this region a cost competitiveness which not only surpassed that of other developing regions, but also challenged that of established OECD producers. Table 16 provides evidence of that superiority in the form of positive residuals for a large number of commodity groups. The numbers for the various importing regions and sub-periods are shown below.

	1969-1971	*1971-1974*	*1974-1978*
EEC-6	15	19	18
EEC-9	15	18	17
Japan	20	15	22
United States	13	15	19

Although there is no uniformity, it appears that the Far East performance in the Chemicals lagged behind the performance of other commodity groups, mainly because of the lack of the resource base to produce these products. The largest commodity residuals appeared in the commodity groups covered under the 7 and 8 one-digit SITC classification, while, in the 6 SITC one-digit classification groups, a substantial diversion is observed depending on the importing region. The observed residuals for the EEC-6 fluctuated between a high plus 69,953 for Clothing items (SITC 841)[22] to a low negative 33,206 for Veneers and Plywood (SITC 631). For items produced competitively by producers of Lomé signatory countries and by producers of Far East GSP beneficiaries, the Lomé producers outperformed the Far East producers: SITC 541, SITC 611, SITC 651, SITC 652, SITC 667, and SITC 735 (see Tables 12 and 13). This observation has to be attributed to the restrictive nature of the quantitative limitations imposed by the EEC, given that the Far East

Table 17. Competitiveness Residuals for the Far East
(Thousands U.S. $)

Period		*EEC-6*	*EEC-9*	*Japan*	*United States*
1969-1971	Expected	+	+	+	+
1971-1974	Signs	+	+	+	-
1974-1978		+	+	+	+
	SITC				
	512				
1969-1971		+ 1,291	+ 1,138	- 200	- 19
1971-1974		+ 1,405	+ 4,459	+ 1,154	+ 6,976
1974-1978		+ 5,845	+ 7,908	+23,200	+ 6,057
	513				
1969-1971		- 70	- 91	+ 311	- 13
1971-1974		- 236	+ 342	+ 454	+ 633
1974-1978		- 114	+ 442	+ 1,859	+ 1,241
	532				
1969-1971		- 3	- 18	- 11	+ 6
1971-1974		0	- 22	- 46	- 6
1974-1978		+ 176	+ 356	+ 275	+ 36
	541				
1969-1971		- 870	- 147	+ 134	+ 6
1971-1974		+ 1,069	+ 962	+ 5,367	+ 1,167
1974-1978		- 1,755	+ 1,794	+11,604	+ 1,538
	551				
1969-1971		- 998	- 585	+ 311	- 1,726
1971-1974		+ 2,117	+ 2,467	- 978	+ 2,465
1974-1978		+ 5,082	+ 6,155	+ 1,549	+ 1,464
	561				
1969-1971		+ 6	- 7	+ 14	0
1971-1974		- 7	+ 66	+ 7	+ 322
1974-1978		0	- 69	+ 3,234	- 317

	611				
1969-1971		- 2,793	- 7,118	+ 35	- 1,677
1971-1974		- 675	- 2,601	+ 284	+ 4,082
1974-1978		- 3,941	-16,491	- 236	+ 719
	612				
1969-1971		+ 139	+ 99	- 37	+ 65
1971-1974		+ 373	+ 736	- 119	+ 1,337
1974-1978		- 1,531	- 2,710	+ 1,267	+ 4,741
	631				
1969-1971		+ 2,215	+21,091	+ 4,294	+ 22,222
1971-1974		+ 6,051	+17,221	- 1,909	- 922
1974-1978		-33,206	+50,537	- 1,412	- 3,503
	632				
1969-1971		+ 1,161	+ 1,635	+ 190	+ 1,177
1971-1974		+ 2,129	+ 1,537	+ 471	+ 4,126
1974-1978		+ 5,351	+ 9,247	+ 602	+ 5,290
	651				
1969-1971		+ 5,156	+ 5,470	+ 4,855	+ 4,945
1971-1974		- 5,367	- 6,288	- 3,202	+ 1,441
1974-1978		-12,294	-33,205	+27,114	- 6,314
	652				
1969-1971		+ 4,753	+ 7,014	- 107	- 2,517
1971-1974		-11,965	-29,595	- 5,092	- 9,427
1974-1978		+ 9,719	+24,221	+ 401	- 20
	653				
1969-1971		+ 1,011	+ 1,153	+ 4	- 6,293
1971-1974		+ 8,392	+ 6,817	- 826	- 1,617
1974-1978		+ 6,226	- 21	+13,780	- 6,482
	656				
1969-1971		- 1,100	- 1,632	+ 238	- 340
1971-1974		- 2,989	- 8,441	+ 7,253	- 2,613
1974-1978		+17,577	-15,606	- 2,637	- 2,999

(*continued*)

Table 17. (continued)

Period	SITC	*EEC-6*	*EEC-9*	*Japan*	*United States*
	657				
1969-1971		+ 2,632	+ 2,285	- 428	- 107
1971-1974		+12,267	+13,027	- 204	+ 2,475
1974-1978		+31,187	-51,499	+ 7,511	+ 2,169
	667				
1969-1971		- 3,749	+30,419	+ 429	+ 2,989
1971-1974		- 5,638	- 7,264	+ 127	+ 5,892
1974-1978		-10,354	-17,647	+18,078	+ 22,126
	696				
1969-1971		+ 25	- 347	+ 29	+ 199
1971-1974		+ 372	+ 479	+ 65	+ 5
1974-1978		+ 1,534	+ 1,087	+ 631	+ 1,182
	697				
1969-1971		- 189	+ 264	+ 40	+ 598
1971-1974		+ 1,148	+ 1,346	+ 344	- 630
1974-1978		+ 8,796	+ 5,271	+ 360	+ 5,205
	724				
1969-1971		+ 325	+ 4,924	+ 140	- 6,184
1971-1974		+11,569	+15,468	- 151	- 13,303
1971-1978		+ 7,367	+ 7,865	- 2,649	+ 38,494
	729				
1969-1971		+ 1,770	+ 6,072	+ 132	+ 1,358
1971-1974		+17,949	+21,301	- 797	- 15,539
1974-1978		+19,881	+14,608	+ 4,659	-147,256
	735				
1969-1971		+ 201	- 150	- 708	- 454
1971-1974		+ 1,903	+ 2,309	+ 297	+ 384
1974-1978		- 316	- 2,893	- 810	- 4,045

	821				
1969-1971		- 116	- 52	+ 61	+ 934
1971-1974		+ 722	+ 713	+ 2,327	+ 2,781
1974-1978		+11,667	+15,834	+ 1,643	+ 30,572
	831				
1969-1971		+ 1,388	+ 1,856	- 125	- 2,592
1971-1974		+ 855	+ 692	+ 291	- 8,519
1974-1978		+27,691	+28,239	+ 132	+ 31,870
	841				
1969-1971		-25,916	-40,518	+ 2,957	- 380
1971-1974		+26,470	- 5,275	+27,566	- 3,824
1974-1978		+69,953	- 4,418	+37,610	- 76,559
	851				
1969-1971		- 27	- 2,652	+ 1,137	- 2,863
1971-1974		+ 433	- 7,799	- 328	- 12,658
1974-1978		+ 5,641	+ 6,266	+ 2,725	+ 63,966
	864				
1969-1971		+ 376	+ 441	+ 199	+ 37
1971-1974		+ 1,253	+ 2,254	- 77	- 1,677
1974-1978		+37,169	+64,084	+ 820	+ 15,274
	894				
1969-1971		- 792	- 2,101	+ 208	+ 1,307
1971-1974		+ 4,171	+ 4,047	+ 19	+ 2,911
1974-1978		+17,040	+11,291	+ 991	+ 29,346

Note: The competitiveness residuals were calculated by subtracting the expected imports from the adjusted imports, as explained in this paper, page 140, Step 4.
Source: Tsanacas (1982), Tables 6-3, 6-5, 6-11, and 6-13.

was successfully increasing its share of these commodities in other markets. For certain other commodity groups for which the Lomé beneficiaries registered positive residuals, the residuals registered by the Far East in the U.S. and the Japanese markets exceeded those of the EEC which is evidence of some Far East export diversion away from the EEC and towards alternative markets: SITC 724, SITC 729, SITC 894 (see Table 17).

The enlargement of the EEC to include the United Kingdom led to somewhat different results as compared to the results for the original EEC mainly because of the Commonwealth ties between Far East members and the United Kingdom. Although in some commodity groups, the enlarged market led to higher competitive residuals: SITC 652, SITC 821, SITC 831, and SITC 864; in other commodity groups the signs of the residuals were different: SITC 631, SITC 653, SITC 656, SITC 657, and SITC 841. These differences have to be attributed, either to stronger trade links between the United Kingdom and the Far East region, especially for Veneers and Plywood (SITC 631), or to increased and sustained efforts by Far East exporters to penetrate the markets of other EEC members. In reference to the latter, it should be stressed that: (a) not all members of the Far East were granted GSP treatment; and (b) the commonwealth tariff rates were phased out over a three-year span during which the United Kingdom was to harmonize its external tariffs to those of the other EEC members. The possibility that the Far East exportes shifted their products to the markets of other EEC members explains the differences in the signs of the residuals.

The evidence indicates that the Far East region has been successful in penetrating the EEC markets, but not to the same extent that it penetrated the Japanese and the U.S. markets. The relaxation of the process requirements and the more liberal rules of origin, instituted by the EEC in 1974 (see UNCTAD, TD/B/C.5/23, 1974), brought substantial benefits to the Far East region during the 1974-1978 period, even though the consistent reclassification of the products as sensitive and semi-sensitive and the resulting quantitative limitations were neutralized by the market familiarity and the ability of the Far East exporters to interpret these limitations better than other non-OECD exporters could. It must be pointed out that four nations of the Far East (Hong Kong, Korea, Singapore, and Taiwan) were members of the group of Newly Industrializing Countries and, as such, they did have a comparative advantage over other countries in cost competitiveness and product competitiveness as well as in market familiarity. These elements of comparative advantage were beneficial to the region not only in fulfilling the EEC quotas and ceilings much faster than other regions, but also in enabling the producers to switch their efforts to products faced with less restrictions and more open markets.

The percentage of commodity groups residuals "obeying" and confirming the expected signs increased steadily from the 1969-1971 period for the EEC-6 and the EEC-9. Over 70% of the commodity groups registered the expected positive residuals during the 1971-1974 period. The percentage decreased to 60 during the 1974-1978 period following the implementation of the Lomé Convention and the readjustment in the EEC import markets to safeguard a segment for Lomé exports.

The dominant position of the Far East developing countries in the Japanese market has been shown in Table 4. The domination, and the commodity groups responsible for it, is confirmed by the positive residuals of over 65% of the commodity groups in Table 17. The liberalization of Japanese trade after the isolation in the 1960s; the numerous revaluation of the yen and the implementation of a GSP scheme in 1971 have spurred a substantial increase in the imports of manufactured goods. This increase, which started in 1970, continued into 1978 mainly because it involved imports at low manufacturing stages and products of high income and price elasticity of demand. Further, the structural changes that took place in the Japanese economy induced by higher energy costs, land scarcity, higher domestic wages, increased public awareness to pollution, and the loss of the competitive position against low-wage neighbors mainly in labor-intensive production changed the composition of Japan's imports. The economy switched away from low value-added component production and towards a higher value-added production. As a result, more light manufactures and textiles of a labor-intensive, low-skill type were imported.

The data indicate that the biggest beneficiary of the expanded import trade was the Far East region. The high concentration ratio of Japanese imports in favor of the Far East, initially observed in 1971, increased through 1974 and 1978 even for those commodity groups for which the non-OECD to OECD imports declined during the same periods. The explanation for this concentration, which approached one for many products, is directly tied to the comparative advantage of the producers, the Japanese direct investment in the region, especially in manufacturing (Tsurumi 1977; Sekiguchi 1979), and to the preferential edge under the GSP. In particular, the administration of the scheme through ceilings and maximum amounts and the monitoring of these restrictions, either through daily and monthly control (90% of GSP trade) or prior allotment (10% of GSP trade), reinforced the already advantageous competitive position of the Far East exporters by decreasing the level of uncertainty regarding the tariff status of the imported commodities.

The examination of the various commodity groups at the peak of domination, the 1974-1978 periods, reveals that the Far East had negative competitiveness residuals for five groups only: SITC 611 (Leather), SITC 631 (Veneers, Plywood Boards), SITC 656 (Made-Up Articles of Textile Materials), SITC 724 (Telecommunications Apparatus), and SITC 735 (Ships and Boats). It seems that the flexible administration scheme, introduced in 1974, and the singling out of the Republic of Korea, in applying the maximum amount limitation, were responsible for the negative residuals for at least two of these commodity groups, SITC 656 and SITC 724.

The rest of the commodity groups registered positive residuals ranging from high 37,610 for SITC 841 (Clothing Items) to low 132 for SITC 831 (Travel Goods and Handbags). Large residuals were observed in SITC 512 (Organic Chemicals), SITC 651 (Textile Yarn and Thread), SITC 541 (Medicinal and Pharmaceutical Products), SITC 667 (Pearls, Precious, and Semi-Precious Stones), and SITC 653 (Textile Fabrics, Woven). Most of these products have high income and price elasticities of demand. It is expected that Japan will continue to increase its imports for these products as the domestic industry switches to high value-added production and the level of income increases. There is little indication, if any, to suggest that the Far East region is not going to capture the biggest share of this increased volume of imports.

The United States has been visibly more receptive to exports of manufactured products by non-OECD developing countries than other developed countries. This suggests that the United States was either faced with more vulnerability of its manufacturing industries and/or its markets were more open and attractive to foreign imports (Gray 1982). The Far East developing countries have been able to establishing strong trade ties with the United States and they have come to control a large share of the U.S. import market for manufactures. Evidence of the aggregate share was presented in Table 4. Although the share decreased slightly during the 1971-1974 period, it rebounded during the 1974-1978 period, accounting for three-quarters of total U.S. imports from non-OECD sources. The main reasons for the decline were the implementations of a GSP scheme by the EEC and Japan in 1971 and the delay in implementing such a scheme by the United States. The implementation of the U.S. GSP scheme in 1976 was responsible for the increase in the share of the Far East region by intensifying and strengthening established trade links for most, but not all, commodity groups.

An important variation in the degree of domination of the Far East exporters was observed throughout the commodity sample. For certain commodity groups, the degree of domination exceeded the aggregate, while for others, it was even higher than that of OECD exporters. The only major one-digit SITC commodity category trailing all others was probably Chemicals, induced by a limited resource base. Certain provisions of the U.S. GSP scheme has a substantial impact on the market of the Far East region for certain commodities and they prevented the region from registering even higher concentration ratios. These provisions range from an outright exclusion of certain commodity groups such as Clothing, Watches, and Footwear from GSP coverage, to the value-added requirement of 35% and, finally, to the competitive-need limitation. Under the value-added requirement, the value of imported materials and components cannot exceed 35% of the export value of the final product. Under the competitive-need limitation, the MFN tariff rate would apply instead of the GSP preferential tariff rate if annual U.S. imports of a product exceeded either: (1) 50% of total U.S. imports; or (2) $25 million annually ($33.4 million in 1978 as a result of a growth factor).

The value-added requirement and the competitive-need limitation accounted for the denial of preferential access for $2.8 billion of import trade in 1978. Preferential access was denied on 45 products from Hong Kong, 28 products from the Republic of Korea, 20 products from India, and 13 products from the Phillipines (see UNCTAD TD/B/C.5/74, 1981). In terms of aggregate figures, 34% of imports from Malaysia, Thailand, and the Phillipines were denied preferential access solely on the base of the $25 million competitive-need limitation which was not allowed a growth factor in 1978.

The cost and price competitiveness and the reliability of the Far East region in fulfilling import orders did overcome the disadvantage associated with the competitive-need limitation and the imposition of the MFN tariff. The data do not allow any disaggregation to estimate the exact impact of the competitive-need limitation but, it can be reasonably assumed that certain commodity groups would have shown larger increases in the absence of such a limitation. An indirect method of indicating the impact was provided through the examination of the performance of the same commodities in the EEC and the Japanese markets.

Table 17 reports the expected signs and the actual values for the competitiveness residuals for the Far East region. The percentage of commodity groups confirming the expected sign increased in every time period and it was close to 60% in 1978. The limitations and exclusions of the U.S. GSP scheme prevented an even higher percentage of confirmation of the expected signs.

The commodity groups mostly affected the provisions of the U.S. GSP are: SITC 729 (Electrical Machinery), SITC 841 (Clothing except Fur Clothing), SITC 651 (Textile Yarn), SITC 653 (Textile Fabrics, Woven), and SITC 656 (Made-Up Articles of Textile Material). The Electrical Machinery category registered the highest negative residuals for the United States, yet it was positive for the other three importers. The value-added requirement and the competitive-need limitation are responsible for the poor performance. The other commodity groups, mentioned above, registered negative residuals since they were excluded from GSP coverage.

Impressive gains were shown for the rest of the commodity groups especially SITC 724 (Telecommunications Apparatus), SITC 821 (Furniture), SITC 831 (Travel Goods and Handbags), SITC 851 (Footwear), SITC 864 (Watches and Clocks), and SITC 894 (Permulators, Toys, Games). Two commodity groups are of special interest, Footwear and Watches, since they were in the list of commodities excluded from GSP coverage. Both of these groups registered positive residuals. The residual for Footwear was higher for the United States than the other markets indicating perhaps: (1) a large displacement of imports from other sources; (2) an increased demand for Footwear in the United States;

Table 18. Competitiveness Residuals for the Sino-Soviet Bloc
(Thousands U.S. $)

Period		*EEC-6*	*EEC-9*	*Japan*	*United States*
1969-1971	Expected	+	+	-	-
1971-1974	Signs	-	-	-	+
1974-1978		-	-	-	-
	SITC				
	512				
1969-1971		- 2,460	- 1,280	- 215	+ 616
1971-1974		+10,768	+23,042	- 5,209	- 630
1974-1978		-14,503	-25,812	- 6,257	+ 1,541
	513				
1961-1971		- 2,460	-10,387	+ 1,145	+ 5
1971-1974		+ 6,292	+ 8,585	+ 1,319	+ 1,429
1974-1978		+ 2,376	+ 8,644	- 2,187	+12,905
	532				
1969-1971		+ 20	+ 24	- 2	0
1974-1974		+ 88	+ 97	+ 31	+ 5
1974-1978		- 95	- 127	- 122	- 16
	541				
1969-1971		- 311	+ 1,162	- 914	- 568
1971-1974		+ 2,560	+ 3,351	- 2,269	+ 1,735
1974-1978		- 1,291	- 4,168	- 7,225	- 131
	551				
1969-1971		- 1,573	- 4,677	- 346	+ 240
1971-1974		+ 354	+ 1,535	+ 335	+ 1,521
1974-1978		- 5,227	- 7,694	- 2,478	+ 276
	561				
1969-1971		- 7,273	-10,444	- 567	0
1971-1974		+ 1,307	+ 1,582	+ 1,001	+ 1,076
1974-1978		- 3,298	- 8,863	- 2,612	+ 2,862

1969-1971		+ 927	+ 1,881	+ 32	- 508
1971-1974		- 1,777	- 1,372	+ 4	- 231
1974-1978		- 4,134	- 122	- 121	+ 616
	612				
1969-1971		- 21	- 33	0	0
1971-1974		+ 222	+ 361	- 21	- 33
1974-1978		- 1,380	- 1,586	- 17	- 16
	631				
1961-1971		- 2,595	-21,705	- 549	- 637
1971-1974		+ 488	- 4,632	+ 1,504	+ 436
1974-1978		- 3,402	-17,975	- 164	+ 266
	632				
1969-1971		+ 596	+ 104	- 147	- 123
1971-1974		- 946	- 1,990	- 407	+ 13
1974-1978		- 14	- 3,098	- 417	- 426
	651				
1969-1971		+ 1,761	+ 3,139	- 4,777	+ 306
1971-1974		- 6,790	- 8,280	+ 996	- 140
1974-1978		- 3,737	- 7,170	-17,250	+ 1,276
	652				
1969-1971		- 655	- 2,643	0	- 478
1971-1974		+ 3,340	+10,662	+ 3,843	+10,718
1974-1978		-10,179	-23,111	-12,124	+ 2,555
	653				
1969-1971		- 1,643	- 1,509	- 253	+ 538
1971-1974		- 3,736	- 4,701	+ 133	+ 727
1974-1978		- 4,649	+ 3,003	- 9,737	+ 3,655
	656				
1969-1971		+ 1,299	+ 1,645	- 214	- 149
1971-1974		- 347	+ 2,202	- 7,218	- 472
1974-1978		-15,054	-13,194	+ 2,540	+ 1,995

(continued)

Table 18. (continued)

Period	SITC	*EEC-6*	*EEC-9*	*Japan*	*United States*
	657				
1969-1971		- 343	-17,833	+ 399	+ 8
1971-1974		+ 3,962	+ 3,452	+ 262	- 271
1974-1978		-12,500	-21,568	- 7,647	+ 7,303
	667				
1969-1971		+ 4,246	-31,752	+ 323	+ 362
1971-1974		+10,188	+11,390	+ 1,293	- 5,432
1974-1978		+26,449	+22,069	+ 1,414	-12,888
	696				
1969-1971		- 126	+ 2	- 29	- 23
1971-1974		- 248	- 313	- 376	- 40
1974-1978		- 672	- 612	- 62	- 309
	697				
1969-1971		+ 128	- 574	- 44	- 151
1971-1974		- 885	- 1,217	- 566	- 298
1974-1978		- 4,398	- 4,699	- 291	+ 540
	724				
1969-1971		- 560	- 3,808	- 139	- 88
1971-1974		- 8,431	- 8,886	+ 150	- 927
1974-1978		- 141	- 3,572	- 942	+ 247
	729				
1969-1971		- 1,605	- 3,803	- 100	+ 34
1971-1974		-13,109	-13,431	- 594	+ 1,151
1974-1978		- 8,081	- 4,573	- 457	+ 1,559
	735				
1969-1971		-14,260	-19,398	+ 717	0
1971-1974		+10,432	+12,530	+ 183	+ 4
1974-1978		-19,432	-16,051	- 2,799	- 15

	821				
1969-1971		+ 2,011	+ 978	- 60	- 69
1971-1974		+ 4,759	+ 2,565	- 2,705	- 426
1974-1978		+ 2,986	- 2,069	- 530	- 1,172
	831				
1969-1971		+ 106	- 380	+ 26	- 8
1971-1974		- 2,055	- 3,171	- 10	+ 13
1974-1978		- 6,,025	- 4,570	- 116	- 132
	841				
1969-1971		+23,115	+36,929	- 5,174	- 284
1971-1974		-21,688	-10,489	-19,322	+ 7,316
1974-1978		-67,876	-63,063	-36,740	+46,110
	851				
1969-1971		+ 501	+ 2,929	- 1,114	- 6,417
1971-1974		- 648	+ 2,177	+ 348	+ 26
1974-1978		+13,095	-28,114	- 2,756	+ 367
	864				
1969-1971		- 361	- 524	- 199	- 2
1971-1974		- 1,339	+ 2,505	+ 73	+ 16
1974-1978		-35,938	-60,570	- 936	+ 219
	894				
1969-1971		+ 416	+ 1,209	- 226	- 697
1971-1974		- 3,487	- 3,532	+ 49	+ 367
1974-1978		-19,835	-15,876	- 1,314	- 1,480

Note: The competitiveness residuals were calculated by subtracting the expected imports from the adjusted imports, as explained in this paper, page 140, step 4.
Source: Tsanacas (1982), Tables 6-3, 6-5, 6-11, and 6-13.

and/or (3) closed EEC markets diverting exports to the United States. The same arguments could apply to Watches and Clocks, except the value of the residuals is higher in the EEC than in the United States.

The positive values of the competitiveness residuals are testimony to the diversified industrial base of the Far East region and its ability to switch to products facing open and unrestricted foreign markets. The presence and the importance of subsidiaries of Japanese-based multinationals in the Far East was essential to the overall performance of the region because the products of these subsidiaries did not only satisfy the Japanese home market, but were also available for exportation to other markets.

There is no doubt that the GSP brought substantial benefits to developing countries of the Far East, especially to the ones which are members of the NIC group. The implementation of the Lomé Convention has made GSP more beneficial to these countries by diverting trade from the closed and safeguarded EEC markets to the open and attractive U.S. markets. A study by Bowen and Pelzman in 1980 reported an overall deterioration of the U.S. competitiveness in manufacturing indicating that the markets were susceptible to a large degree of import penetration from sophisticiated and sustained export drives from established Far East exporters.

The implementation of the GSP and the Lomé Convention forced fundamental changes in the market share of the Sino-Soviet bloc. The European members of the Bloc have been major trading partners of the EEC taking full advantage of their geographic location. Imports from the Sino-Soviet bloc, with the exception of Rumanian imports, were discriminated against, having been imported under full tariff rates and duties. The Bloc was, however, competitive in world markets because of its industrial base and its peculiar structure of market prices. The market prices were not market prices in the traditional sense, because they did not reflect true opportunity costs. Market prices in such cases do adjust to safeguard market shares, especially if these markets are important sources of hard currency. The implementation of the EEC's GSP scheme did, in fact, threaten such established market shares by increasing the competitive edge of the exporters of developing countries vis-à-vis the Bloc countries.

The expected signs and the actual values of the competitiveness residuals for the Sino-Soviet Bloc are reported in Table 18. The percentage of commodity groups confirming the expected signs for the residuals increased steadily since the 1969-1971 period for the EEC-6, the EEC-9, and for Japan but not for the United States. Over 80% of the residuals "obeyed" the expected sign for the three importing regions in 1978, while the figure was slightly over 30% for the United States.

The negative values taken by the residuals indicate that the impact of GSP and the Lomé Convention on the market shares of the Sino-Soviet Bloc was substantial. The competitive edge of the developing countries, via the elimination or reduction of the tariff rates, had an immediate impact on the share of the Bloc for certain commodity groups and a delayed impact on other commodity groups affected immediately were commodities produced competitively by developing countries: Clothing and Textile Items, Leather Goods, Small Electrical Machinery, and Watches. As the developing countries intensified and diversified their production efforts to take full advantage of their GSP benefits, the Sino-Soviet Bloc experienced further decreases in the share of commodities which were not affected immediately; certain Chemicals and Textile Items. The implementation of the Lomé Convention forced additional declines in the Sino-Soviet share of the EEC markets by discriminating further against their exports. The commodity groups posting negative residuals after the implementation of the Lomé Convention were: SITC 541 (Medicinal and Pharmaceutical Products), SITC 551 (Essential Oils and Perfumes), SITC 561 (Manufactured Fertilizers), SITC 652 (Cotton Fabrics, Woven), SITC 656 (Made-Up Articles of Textile Material), and SITC 657 (Floor Coverings).

The trade diversion resulted in a decrease of the Sino-Soviet share of the EEC market for all but three commodity groups: Inorganic Chemicals, Furniture, and Pearls, Precious, and Semi-Precious Stones. The Bloc continued to increase its market share for Inorganic Chemicals as well as for Furniture mainly because of the East-West coproduction arrangements for the development of natural resources. For both of these commodity groups the Western firms were usually in charge of marketing and merchandising the final product. Pearls, Precious, and Semi-Precious Stones have always been in great demand by the West and they have been traditionally steady sources of foreign exchange for the Communist Bloc.

Overall, the implementation of the GSP decreased the competitiveness of the Sino-Soviet Bloc by increasing the preferential tariff margin of the developing countries. In addition, the Lomé Convention intensified the deterioration by diverting trade to its signatories and away from Eastern countries. No data were available as to any export price adjustment by the governments of the Bloc to affect losses in competitiveness. If such adjustments did take place, they served as a buffer against larger losses than those reported in the data. Evidence does, however, exist for the imposition of the MFN tariff rate on Rumanian exports of Organic Chemicals. The Newly Industrializing Countries were the major displacing force of the Sino-Soviet exports to the EEC, although the Lomé region did share in this displacement, especially for Textiles. Further displacement is very probable, especially if certain EEC quantitative restrictions on imports from developing countries are relaxed, enabling these countries to take full advantage of their preferential positions.

The Sino-Soviet Bloc ranked second to the Far East as a supplier of manufactured goods to Japan. The ranking was preserved after the implementation of a GSP scheme by Japan, but there was a 65% decrease in the aggregate share. The contribution of the various commodity groups to this decrease was expressed in the negative values taken by the competitiveness residuals (see Table 18). The decreases were spread over the whole range of the commodities making up the sample, with the exception of SITC 656 (Made-Up Articles of Textile Material) and SITC 667 (Pearls, Precious and Semi-Precious Stones). The largest import displacement was observed in the Textiles and Clothing commodity groups even though mainland China expanded its exports to Japan for these commodities. The major displacing source was the Far East developing countries, which controlled 80% of the Japanese market.

The U.S. trade policy with the Communist Bloc is heavily influenced by detente between the United States and the Soviet Union. Any improvements in the relations between the two superpowers is expected to increase their trade flows and, therefore, the market share of the Soviet Bloc. The same reasoning most definitely applies with reference to the United States-mainland China relations.

Generally the Sino-Soviet Bloc increased its overall share of the U.S. market at a time when its share was decreasing in other markets (see Table 4). Although the Sino-Soviet exports were least preferred, certain commodity groups posted important gains as indicated by the positive residuals in Table 18. The increases in Chemimcals, both Organic and Inorganic, have to be attributed to the large and increasing number of production sharing/coproduction agreements between Western firms and the Communist States. The number of industrial cooperation agreements especially in Chemicals and Petrochemicals increased from 600 in 1973 to over 1600 in 1976 (McMillan 1977). The usual form of payment is in kind or in the form of the product produced under the coproduction agreement. Since the Western firm is responsible for marketing the product, exports would increase. The increases in the Textiles, Fabrics, and Clothing Items were directly related to the normalization of the United States-China relations and the lifting of the trade embargo under the Nixon and Ford administrations. The extension of a MFN clause to mainland China would have a tremendous impact on the market shares of the abovementioned commodities.

In concluding, it should be stressed that the lack and/or inadequacy of quality control, design, serviceability, and financing of Soviet exports, along with a bias against trade or a policy of trade aversion have been instrumental in diminishing trade flows between the Soviet Bloc and the United States. There is strong indication of expanded trade flows between the United States and China especially in labor-intensive products and light manufactures. The need of the Sino-Soviet Bloc to finance imports of capital goods and technology from the West could very well lead to essential changes in marketing and merchandising practices and to sustained and prolonged export drives to penetrate and control Western markets.

SUMMARY AND CONCLUSION

The impact of the Lomé Convention on the Generalized System of Preferences was examined under the two hypotheses set forward in the introduction of the paper. The values and the signs of the competitiveness residuals obtained under the CMS model provide sufficiently strong evidence for the acceptance of both hypotheses. The Lomé Convention has been instrumental in reviving and strengthening the shares of its members in the EEC markets by restoring and reinforcing the preferential commercial treatment which was eroded by the EEC GSP implementation. By blocking off a part of its import market for its long-time associates through a series of quantitative limitations, and by increasing the uncertainty as to the tariff status of the various commodity groups through reclassifications, the EEC has discriminated against the non-Lomé developing nations and has forced these nations to seek alternate market outlets in Japan and the United States. The lower growth rates in the EEC imports from the non-Lomé developing nations, for a substantial number of commodities, indicate a drastic reduction in the effects of the GSP in the European Economic Community.

The reduction has basically afffected those regions which have exhibited similarities in their export patterns to those of the Lomé region or have been unable to switch their productive efforts to products sold in open and attractive markets. The data indicate that the Far East region was least affected by the implementation of the Lomé Convention. The effect on the other regions displayed a substantial degree of variation. The spectacular success of the Far East countries in the Japanese and the U.S. markets is testimony of the diversification of their economies, the attractiveness of these markets and, indirectly, of the restrictive nature of the EEC markets. The diversion of Lomé exports away from the United States and Japan, and to the unrestricted European markets, created additional market outlets for the exports of non-Lomé nations. These nations were able to achieve higher benefits under the GSP, especially for competitively-produced exportables.

Although the paper has analyzed the short-term effects of the Lomé Convention, it is very reasonable to assume that these effects will increase in the future as the cooperation, coproduction, and financial aspects of this Convention take control asnd improve the export possibilities of its beneficiaries. In all, the Generalized System of Preferences can be considered a weak version of the Lomé Convention, because this Convention contains all the elements that a truly Generalized System of Zero-Tariff Preferences should contain.

APPENDIX: LIST OF DEVELOPING COUNTRIES AND TERRITORIES SIGNATORIES OF THE LOMÉ CONVENTION

Bahamas	Malagasy Republic
Barbados	Malawi
Botswana	Mali
Burundi	Mauritania
Cameroon	Mauritius
Central African Republic	Niger
Chad	Nigeria
Congo, People's Republic of	Portuguese Guinea
Dahomey	Rwanda
Equatorial Guinea	Senegal
Ethiopia	Sierra Leon
Fiji	Somalia
Gabon	Sudan
Gambia	Swaziland
Ghana	Tanzania
Grenada	Togo
Guinea	Tonga
Guyana	Trinidad and Tobago
Ivory Coast	Uganda
Jamaica	Upper Volta
Kenya	Western Samoa
Lesotho	Zaire
Liberia	Zambia

Source: Council Regulation No. 1213/75, *Official Journal of the European Communities* 18, No. L. 124 (May 15, 1975).

NOTES

1. For an explanation of the ceiling allocation of the EEC, see UNCTAD documents TD/B/C.5/3 (1971), TD/B/C.5/23 (1974), and TD/B/C.5/48 (1977).
2. For an explanation of the U.S. competitiven need criterion, see UNCTAD documents TD/B/GSP/USA/1 (1976), TD/B/C.5/30, Add. 4, 14 (1977), and TD/B/C.5/74 (1981).
3. There is annual growth factor attached to the $25 million limit depending on the growth rate of the U.S. GNP. The figure was $37.3 million in 1978.
4. The regional groupings receive cumulative origin in the EEC are: the Association of South East Asian Nations, the Central American Common Market and the Andean Group.
5. This analysis was adapted from Flanders (1963).
6. There is an extensive discussion in the literature as to the usefulness and appropriateness of the concept of the elasticity of substitution both in general and in its application to studies of demand for imports. Specifically see, Morrissett (1953), Tinbergen (1946), and Polak (1950). In general, the objections raised to the use of the concept of the elasticity of substitution apply least to the present situation.
7. For the conversion UNCTAD/ST/STAT/SERM/35 Rev. 1, was used.

8. The detailed data have not been included here. They can be found in Tsanacas (1982). The "raw data" consist of dollar value of imports for each commodity group by point of origin. Unless it is otherwise stated, all the tables and references to data are taken from the material to be found in the Statistical Appendices.

9. This clearly implies different trade patterns for the United Kingdom, Denmark, and Eire.

10. India does not meet the growth dimension part of this criterion, because its export share has not doubled since 1963.

11. Market prices in the Sino-Soviet Bloc are not prices in the traditional sense, because they do not reflect scarcity. They are merely accounting units and as such they can be adjusted to maintain a constant flow of foreign exchange.

12. Over 90% of the Japanese GSP trade is administered on a daily and/or monthly basis.

13. The heavy reliance of U.S. apparel firms on production sharing with twin plants in Mexico and other nations will explain the high volume of U.S. imports.

14. Interestingly, in 1978, there was no allowance for the growth factor holding the imports to 1977 level. See UNCTAD Document TD/B/C.5/71 (1981).

15. The number of industrial cooperation agreements increased from 600 in 1973 to over 1800 in 1976. Most of these agreements cover raw material resources (petrochemical, timber, chemicals). See McMillan (1977).

16. The part of the EEC markets which was reserved for the Lomé exporters was established irrespective of whether these exporters were able to occupy it or not.

17. The effective rate of protection on products in advanced stages of processing are much higher than the nominal tariff rates. For more information in calculating the effective rate see Balassa (1967).

18. For the calculation of the two effects turn to Baldwin and Murray (1977) or Balassa (1967).

19. For a detailed explanation of the Elasticity of Substitution in International Trade see Kubinski (1954) and Polak (1951).

20. The sign of the most residuals for the United States is expected to be negative for the following two reasons: geographic location and colonial ties of EEC markets with ACP nations. Positive signs are expected for commodities imported from the Caribbean members of the Lomé Convention because of the presence of subsidiaries of U.S. multinationals.

21. Most of the competitiveness residuals are extremely low in value to be of any significance; further, many commodity groups not exported to Japan would have a zero competitiveness residual.

22. Many members of the Far East region were signatories of the Arrangement Regarding International Trade in Textiles which superceded the expired LTA in 1974; Afghanistan, Bangladesh, India, Indonesia, South Korea, Malaysia, Pakistan, Phillipines, and Thailand. This arrangement covered man-made fabrics as well.

REFERENCES

Aitken, N.D. (1973). "The Effects of the E.E.C. and E.F.T.A. on European Trade." *American Economic Review* (December).

Balassa, B. (1967). "Trade Creation, Trade Diversion in the E.E.C." *Economic Journal* (March).

———. (1967). "The Impact of the Industrial Countries Tariff Structure on the Imports of Manufactures from Less Developed Areas." *Economica* (November).

Baldwin, R.F. and T. Murray. (1977). "MFN Tariff Reductions and Developing Country Trade Benefits Under the GSP." *Economic Journal* (March).

Bergsten, C.F., T. Horst, and H.T. Moran. (1978). *American Multinationals and American Interests.* Washington, DC: The Brookings Institute.

Blalock, H.M., Jr. (1960). *Social Statistics.* 2nd ed. New York: McGraw-Hill.

Bowen, H. and J. Plezman. (1980). "A Constant Market Share Analysis of U.S. Export Growth." Economic Discussion Paper 10. U.S. Department of Labor, Bureau of International Labor Affairs.

Coppens, Faber, and Lof. (1977). "European Community's Security of Supply with Raw Materials and the Interests of Developing Countries: The Need for a Cooperative Strategy." *The Lomé Convention and a New International Economic Order,* edited by A. Von Geusau. Leydan: A.W. Sijthoff.

European Community. (1975). Official Journal 18 Vol. 124 Council Regulation No. 1213/75.

Flanders, J.M. (1963). "The Effects of Devaluation on Exports—A Case Study United Kingdom 1949-1954." *Bulletin of the Oxford University Institute of Statistics,* XXV.

Frans, A.M. (1977). *The Lomé Convention and a New International Economic Order,* edited by Alting Von Geausau. Leydan: A.W. Sijthoff.

Gray, H. (1980). "The New International Economic Order: A Constructive Alternative." *Foreign Trade Review* (April-June).

———. (1982). "The U.S. Share of NIC Export Growth." Unpublished paper, Rutgers University.

Krueger, A.O. (1980). "The Newly Industrializing Countries, Experience and Lessons." Congressional Research Services. An International Economic Agenda, Major Issues for the 97th Congress (November).

Kubinski, Z.M. (1954). "Measurements of Elasticity of Substitution on International Trade." *South African Journal of Economics.*

Leamer, E. and R. Stern. (1970). *Quantitative International Economics.* Boston, MA: Allyn and Bacon.

Lowinger, T.C. (1975). "The Technology Factor and the Explanation of the Export Performance of the U.S. Manufacturing Industry." *Economic Inquiry* (June).

McMillan, C.H. (1977). "East-West Industrial Cooperation." United States Congress Joint Economic Committee, "East European Economics Post Helsinki: A Compendium of Papers." Washington, DC: Government Printing Office.

Meade, J.E. (1955). *The Theory of Customs Union.* Amsterdam: North Holland Publishing Co.

Morrissett, I. (1953). "Some Recent Uses of Elasticity of Substitution—A Survey." *Econometrics* (January).

Murray, T. (1977). *Trade Preferences for Developing Countries.* London: Macmillan.

Polak, J.J. (1950). "Note on Measurement of Elasticity of Substitution in International Trade." *Review of Economics and Stastistics* (February).

———. (1951). "Measurements of Elasticity of Substitution in International Trade." *Review of Economic Statistics* 32(1).

Richard, J.D. (1971). "Constant Market Shares Analysis of Export Growth." *Journal of International Economics* 1.

Sekiguchi, S. (1979). *Japanese Direct Foreign Investment.* Monclair, NJ: Allanheld, Osmun and Co.

Tinbergen, J. (1946). "Some Measurements of Elasticities of Substitution." *Review of Economic Statistics* (February).

Torquist, G. (1977). "Comment." In B. Ohlin, B. P.-O. Hesselborn, and P.M. Wijkam (eds.), *The International Allocation of Economic Activity Proceedings of a Nobel Symposium Held at Stockholm.* New York: Holmes and Meier.

Tsanacas, D.P. (1982). "The Impact of the Lomé Convention on the Generalized System of Preferences." Unpublished Ph.D. Thesis, Rutgers University.

Tsurumi, Y. (1977). *Multinational Management Business Strategy and Government Policy.* Cambridge, MA: Ballinger.

UNCTAD (1971). "BTN and SITC Commodity Classification." Document ST/STAT/SERM/35, Rev. 1: Geneva.

———. (1973). "Operation and Effects of the Generalized System of Preferences of the European Economic Community." Document TD/B/C.5/3: Geneva.

———. (1974, 1977). "Operation and Effects of the Generalized System of Preferences of the European Economic Community." Documents TD/B/C.5/23, TD/B/C.5/48: Geneva.

———. (1976, 1977). "Operation and Effects of the Generalized System of Preferences of the United States." Documents TD/B/GSP/USA/1, TD/B/C.5/30, Add. 4, 14: Geneva.

———. (1981). "Differential Treatment in the Contest of the Generalized System of Preferences." Documents TD/B/C.5/71, TD/B/C.5/74: Geneva.

Viner, J. (1950). *The Customs Union Issue*. New York: Carnegie Endowment for International Peace.

Walter, I. (1972). "How Trade Policy is Made: A Politico-Economic System." In R.G. Hawkins and I. Walter (eds.), *The United States and International Markets*. Lexington, MA: Lexington Books.

TRADE POLICY OPTIONS IN THE DESIGN OF DEVELOPMENT STRATEGIES

George N. Yannopoulos

INTRODUCTION

The place of trade policy in the design of development strategies has been extensively debated over the past two decades. This debate has been carried out in terms of the merits and disadvantages of two trade policy options, namely the option of import substitution pursued within the framework of an inwards-looking trade and development strategy and the option of export orientation followed within the framework of an outwards-looking trade and development strategy. The relative merits of each of these two trade policy options depend on the extent to which they enable developing countries to attain a desired level of industrialization with the minimum cost in real resources. In this paper, it is argued that the trade policy options available in the formulation of a development strategy are not exhausted by these two polar cases. Between the inwards-looking and the outwards-looking options there are intermediate choices. These intermediate choices are characterized by different degrees of selectivity in their outwards orientation. Selectivity can be either geographical or sectoral.

Research in International Business and Finance, vol. 7, pages 209-223.

ISBN: 0-89232-906-8

This paper discusses the range of available options in trade policy matters in the design of development strategies and examines the principles that influence the choice among these options. The next two sections critically summarize the current state of the debate. The subsequent section provides a simple taxonomic scheme illustrating the rante of available options and discusses the general principles determining the choice among them. The final section examines in more detail the choice among two basic schemes of selective outwards-oriented trade and development strategies, that is, the option of self-reliance and the alternative of preferential trading with economically more advanced economies.

THE ROLE OF EXTERNAL TRADE IN THE DESIGN OF DEVELOPMENT STRATEGIES

The role of trade in fostering economic development is not a subject new to economics. It has attracted the attention of the classical economists right from the formative years of the discipline of political economy (Kravis 1970). The observation of Mill (1965, collected works) that "the opening of foreign trade . . . sometimes works as a sort of industrial revolution in a country whose resources were previously undeveloped" is very indicative of the views of the classical economists on the link between international trade and growth. Interest in the subject has been recently renewed with export-led growth becoming the dominant (and some will say the fashionable) theme of the development literature. What is new in the current debate among the development and international economists is the focus on trade policy choices and, in particular, the detailed examination of the relative effectiveness of alternative trade strategies in accelerating the development of the less-developed economies (for the early firing shots in the contemporary debate on the subject, see Streeten [1973]).

Two policy choices have become the subject of passionate advocacy and empirical scrutiny. A third policy choice has recently been articulated by Adelman (1984)—the agricultural demand-led industrialization strategy, ADLI, for short. However, this policy option is offered as an alternative to the two major policy options only when countries "are not anticipating a sufficiently rapidly expanding growth in world demand for their nontraditional exports," that is, under conditions of export pessimism. Thus, under more general assumptions, the two fundamental policy options offered to developing economies for the design of their development strategies continue to be the alternatives of inwards-looking (or oriented) and outwards-looking (or oriented) development (or industrialization) strategies—ILDS and OLDS, for short. Development strategies are classified as outwards-or inwards-oriented on the basis of the relative importance they attach to incentives to exports and to import substitution (Balassa 1982). Although there is now general agreement on this terminology, there appears, nevertheless, to be no general agreement on the constituent elements and the basic features of each of these development strategies.

Take, for example, the case of the outwards-oriented development strategy. One tendency among its supporters is to make it equivalent to a free trade policy of nondiscrimination and nonintervention (Henderson 1982). Another group of advocates defines an OLDS as a set of policies characterized by relatively uniform incentives for export and domestic sales accompanied by measures for the maintenance of realistic exchange rates. Adopting this approach, Balassa (1975) denies that an OLDS involves discrimination in favor of exports and against import substitution. The strategy simply consists of the removal of three types of disincentives: (1) disincentives against exports and in favor of domestic sales within industries, (2) discriminatory measures in favor of import-competing over export industries. First, Balassa (1983) goes as far as to argue that, provided an OLDS consists of the removal of these types of disincentives, then it will also encourage efficient import substitution provided that appropriate domestic measures are pursued. Second, import substitution, through the pursuit of an OLDS, can occur in products which tend to suffer discrimination under the tariff structures built up under more traditional ILDS. Finally, Krueger (1978) and McAleese (1978) regard an OLDS as a set of policies involving measures of positive discrimination for the promotion of exports (along with appropriate exchange rate policies), provided such measures are in favor of a general bias toward exports in the aggregate rather than selectively introduced in favor of specific export items. Thus, for these writers, an OLDS is essentially an export promotion strategy. The bias in favor of exports in advocated not because exports are virtuous or growth is of necessity export-led (indeed Krueger [1981] emphatically states that the primary sources of growth are fundamentally internal) but rather for the impact it exerts on the structure of incentives. An exports promotion development strategy forces fovernments to reduce price-distorting measures and controls and to respond to international market changes flexibly and timely. The main advantage of a development strategy with positive discrimination in favor of exports is in terms of the constraints it imposes on governments and firms through the discipline of the international market. These constraints on the behavior of economic agents minimize the costs of intervention, facilitate adjustment to change, and guide the owners of factors of production to channel their resources to activities where the country possesses comparative advantages. Therefore, the rationale for an export promotion development strategy can be explained in terms of the externality effects of an expanding export sector. These externality effects include more appropriate incentives for technological improvements and better management practices, greater capacity utilization, scale economies, learning effects of higher output rates, and similar. The externalities of export expansion are reflected in higher marginal factor productivities of the export sector (Feder 1982). These productivity gains explain the higher growth rates of countries following an OLDS (Balassa 1978; Tyler 1981; Kavoussi 1984). The grwoth gains of this type of OLDS induce governments to further remove distortive measures both in the product and in the factor markets in attempts to promote more rapid growth. This gives rise to a cumulative process of more rapid growth and new sources of comparative advantages (Chenery 1980). Another advantage claimed for this type of OLDS is its higher employment growth as exportables from developing countries, particularly to industrialized nations, are labor and predominantly low-skill intensive (Krueger 1983).

Those viewing both the analysis of the merits of an OLDS and the empirical evidence on its impact on growth with scepticism have argued that the strategy is unsustainable on export pessimism grounds. It is difficult to support export pessimism arguments, particularly in the light of the evidence on the emergence of a second generation of successful Third World exporters (Havrylyshin and Alikhani 1982) and of the growing import penetration of developed countries' markets of manufacturers by exporters from the developing countries despite the rise of neoprotectionism (Hughes and Krueger 1984).

IDEAL VERSUS REALISTIC OPTIONS IN THE DESIGN OF DEVELOPMENT STRATEGIES

The polarization of discussion between inwards-looking and outwards-looking development strategies oversimplifies and misrepresents the real choices policymakers are faced in designing appropriate strategies for the promotion of economic growth. The discussion in the literature on the costs and benefits of each of these development strategies makes the implicit assumption that economic welfare is evaluated in terms of individual consumption of goods and services and ignores the fact that collective consumption of goods may also exert an impact on economic welfare. Such a collective consumption good, from which the population in developing countries derives economic welfare and has a positive preference for its provision, is the level of industrial production or more accurately the proportion of the gross national product derived from industrial activities. The implications of the existence of a preference for industrial production have been well examined in the literature on customs unions (Johnson 1965; Cooper and Massell 1965) but have been ignored in the literature on development strategies. When the level of industrial production is regarded as a kind of collective consumption good then a community may be prepared to pay the sacrifice entailed in attaining a given degree of industrialization. Given the preference for industrialization, the sacrifice a community will be prepared to pay for attaining a certain level of industrial production depends on what Cooper and Massell (1965) called the marginal cost of industry. This marginal cost of industry is defined as the amount by which the average cost of producing the industry's output exceeds the cost of a comparable import. Another interpretation put forward by Gray (1986) is that industrial production is often regarded as an intermediate target for the attainment of another collective good, namely the preservation of the democratic form of government.

The implication of a preference for industrial production, for our discussion on the choice of development strategies, is clear. The policymaker may be faced with a situation where, under an ILDS, the cost of supporting a given level of industrial production becomes prohibitive through time but, at the same time, the consequence for opting for an outwards-oriented industrialization strategy is to accept a level of industrialization below that preferred by the community. This may arise if the community preferences are such that the preferred level of industrial production that maximizes community welfare is larger than the one that would result from the pursuit of an outwards-oriented development strategy that entails a unilateral reduction of the level of protection vis-à-vis the rest of the world. Under these conditions, the policymaker will have to look for intermediate strategies. The existence of intermediate strategies has more or less been ignored with the exception of a brief reference to them by Streeten (1982). Streeten has indeed emphasized that not all options open to policymakers are exhausted by the contrast between outward-looking and inwards-oriented strategies and pointed out to the possible superiority of selective strategies of looking outwards. However, he did not discuss systematically either the range of options available or the factors determining the choice among these options.

There is an additional factor that strengthens the view that the polarization of the discussion that has taken place in the literature misrepresents the real choices available to policymakers in industrializing countries. For the real choice open to policy makers is not to move from an import substitution policy to a fully-fledged outwards-looking strategy. Rather, it is the selection of a set of measures that progressively eliminate the costs of protection associated with the pursuit of inwards-looking strategies in the past while keeping to an economically and politically acceptable level the costs of adjustment associated with trade liberalization and allowing time to local firms to acquire export marketing experience without full exposure to international competition. The resource reallocation required with the shift from an ILDS to an OLDS is not costless. These costs of adjustment cannot be ignored by policymakers who have to compare them to the costs of protection before they decide on the desirable degree of opening of their economy to international competition. The costs of adjustment become more difficult to handle the longer an ILDS has been in existence. Protection under an ILDS gives rise to rent-seeking lobbies that put up strong political pressures to resist and buffer change (Findlay and

Wellisz 1984). Given this framework, within which choices have to be made, the issue is the selection of transition paths from ILDS to OLDS—not an outright move from one strategy to another. Again, Krueger (1984) did spot the issue but her discussion of the choice of transition paths is short and only in very general terms. The question of intermediate development strategies and the choice of transition paths are taken up in the next section.

THE RANGE OF AVAILABLE OPTIONS

Between an ILDS involving protection of import substitution industries from all sources of international competition and an OLDS that involves the unilateral reduction of the tariff and nontariff barriers vis-à-vis the rest of the world, there exists a continuum of intermediate options available to policymakers for the promotion of industrialization and the acceleration of economic development. These intermediate policy options can be defined in terms of the degree of selectivity they adopt in the application of the trade policy instruments they employ. Trade policy instruments can be applied selectively by differentiating either among countries or among products, or among countries and products. Trade and development strategies that are selective between countries (i.e., geographically-selective strategies) involve the elimination of the discriminatory arrangements of an ILDS vis-à-vis a limited number of countries either developed or developing.

A geographically-selective OLDS can be implemented in practice through the participation of the developing country in a customs union, a free trade area, or a common market. Trade and development strategies that are sectorally selective involve the removal of the discriminatory arrangements of an ILDS with respect to specific sectors or product groups. Table 1 presents a classificatory scheme that distinguishes six different categories of trade and development strategies in terms of country and product coverage of the trade policy measures utilized.

The simple classificatory scheme of Table 1 illustrates the range of realistic options available to policymakers in the design of their trade and development strategies. On the basis of this classificatory scheme, one can define six major options open to policymakers. A global OLDS (left hand side of row one) involves the elimination of the three types of disincentives identified by Balassa without discriminating between exports and imports either in terms of their country or in terms of their industry of destination and origin. Whilst, from a cosmopolitan point of view, it offers the higher welfare, it is unlikely to meet the national industrialization objectives of the developing countries and can give rise to serious adjustment costs. Geographically-selective OLDS offer the advantage of reciprocal concessions from the partners in the preferential trading area. This will tend to reduce the adjustment costs of the change from

Table 1. Characteristics of Alternative Trade and Development Strategies

Country Coverage	Product Coverage: All Products	Product Coverage: Selected Products
1. World	Global OLDS	Product Selective OLDS
2. Developed Economies (all or selected countries)	Comprehensive Preferential Trading Arrangements	Limited Preferential Trading Arrangements
3. Developing Economies (all or selected countries)	Self-reliance strategies (global or regional)	Limited strategies of self-reliance

an inwards to an outwards-looking development strategy. Further, selectivity through limited country or product coverage by reducing the costs of resource reallocation creates conditions for easier political acceptability of the change in policy. In particular, selectivity with respect to products may lead to Preferential Trade Arrangements (PTAs) specifically designed to maximize trade diversion.

A geographically-selective OLDS is described in the classificatory scheme of Table 1 (left side of row 2) as a comprehensive PTA in order to emphasize first, that it is not limited to a few products, and second, that it involves reciprocity. A PTA with nonreciprocity acts as an incentive to export expansion but does not restructure the system of incentives in the way suggested by the advocates of OLDS. Indeed, it can be argued that it is precisely this limitation of the nonreciprocal PTAs (e.g., the GSP) that partly explains why a number of beneficiary countries (particularly those with low industrial capacity) have not been able to fully take advantage of the export opportunities created from the improved access to donor countries' markets. It follows that it is only PTAs with the characteristics of a customs union or a free trade area that can be used as vehicles for the pursuit of a selective OLDS.

Having pointed out the range of trade policy options available in the design of trade and development strategies, let us now turn to the factors determining the choice of the appropriate option. In the next section, we discuss the factors determining the choice between a global and a geographically selective OLDS without inquiring whether this selectivity should favor partners from the developed or the developing world. This last issue is taken up in the last section of this paper.

However, PTAs are also linked to another objective, that is, to influence the level of foreign direct investment channelled to the preference-receiving regions and, through this, the level of industrialization. The links between PTAs and foreign investment are explored in detail in Yannopoulos (1987).

GLOBAL VERSUS SELECTIVE OLDS

A selective OLDS may offer four distinct advantages. It offers, first, opportunities for "market swapping" in the sense that the reciprocal concessions expected from the partner countries generate additional benefits in terms of the sharing in the savings of tariffs and transportation costs economized through the redirection of trade flows (Wonnacott and Wonnacott 1981). A global OLDS does not ensure that third countries will reduce tariffs and other impediments to the exports of the country adopting an OLDS. Comprehensive PTAs enable all participating countries to share in the resulting savings in tariffs and transportation costs.

Second, a selective OLDS enables a developing country to attain a level of industrial production higher than the level attainable under a global OLDS at a cost in national income foregone much lower than that incurred when import substitution policies are pursued in the context of an ILDS. A selective OLDS, involving the pooling of markets with a limited number of partners in the framework of a PTA, enables all countries involved to attain the combined industrial output level at a lower cost in terms of income foregone because of the economies of specialization made possible through the pooling of markets. Comprehensive PTAs can act as instruments for the promotion of a more rational pattern of import substitution while, at the same time, offering several of the benefits of outwards-orientation such as operating established production units closer to their optimum size, setting up of new units that would have been uneconomic to operate under a nationalist-based ILDS, and the like.

When countries have a preference for industrial production and, hence, the level of industrialization attained has the properties of a public consumption good, global OLDS will yield suboptimal solutions in the sense that they fail to maximize the community's combined utility from the consumption of private and public consumption goods. The implications of a preference for industrial production for trade policies can be illustrated by using the diagrammatic device developed by Cooper and Massel (1965). In Diagram 1 curves S_X and S_Y represent the "supply of industry" curves in X and Y, respectively. The supply of industry curves show the variations of the excess cost of industry (over the cost of a comparable import) with the level of industrial output in each country.

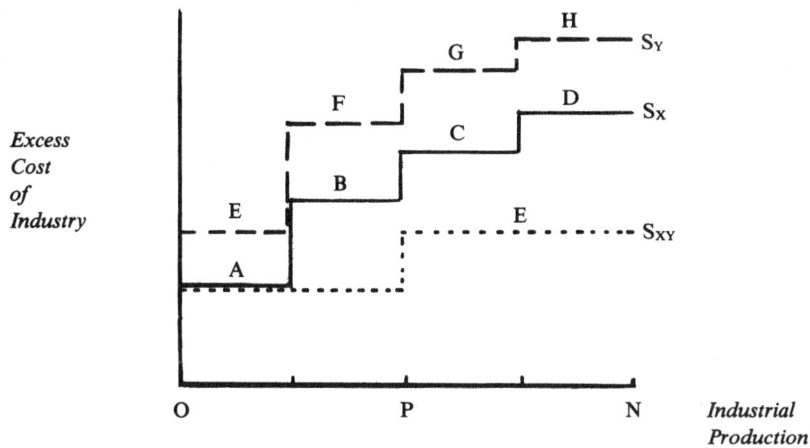

Diagram 1.

Assume, now, that the size of the preferred industrial output in both countries is OP. If each country pursues its own independent development strategy, it will employ the appropriate trade policy instruments to ensure that it attains its preferred level of industrial production (OP). The income foregone associated with this policy can be measured by the area below the supply of industry curve. Under these assumptions, country X will produce goods A and B, and country Y will produce goods E and F.

Now, if both countries decide to pool their markets together through a comprehensive PTA, their combined supply of industry curve will be represented by the dotted line in Diagram 1 (S_{XY}). The combined output of industrial goods will be the same as before but sacrifice, in terms of income foregone, wil now be much lower. This reduction in the excess cost of industry is made possible through the specialization encouraged from the PTA; as it can be seen from the diagram, country X specializes in the production of product A doubling the size of the output it produced before whilst country Y specializes in the production of E also doubling its previously attained level of output.

It is clear from the situation depicted in Diagram 1 that a global OLDS would have resulted in the attainment of a level of industrial production below the level preferred by the community. Additionally, a selective OLDS is preferable to an ILDS from another point of view. In a dynamic sense, curves S_X and S_Y will be subject to upwards displacements through time as the deleterious effects of lack of competition and distorted incentives structures, associated with import substitution policies, produce their cost-raising effects. In contrast, curve S_{XY} is expected to shift downwards as the intensified competition within the larger market further improves the efficiency of production.

A third advantage of a selective OLDS is the 'training ground' argument. A selective OLDS provides the training ground to enable inexperienced producers to acquire the expertise of export marketing techniques without exposing themselves to the head-on competition of the international market (Michalopoulos 1975). As marketing knowledge and marketing skills are scarce resources in developing countries, this is a critical contribution that a selective OLDS can make to development.

Finally, a fourth advantage of a selective OLDS is its flexibility in reducing the political resistance to the transition from an ILDS toward more outward-looking strategies. Its advantages, in this respect, are that by properly selecting partners and/or products, it can generate a concentration of benefits to particular groups of firms, workers or local authorities which then acquire the incentive to lobby effectively against the protectionist measures of ILDS. Transition away from ILDS entails adjustment costs that give rise to adjustment resistance by the groups affected. The more concentrated the adversely-affected groups are, in comparison with the groups benefiting from the change in the system of incentives, the more difficult it becomes to implement the transition away from ILDS. A selective OLDS offers opportunities for reversing the pattern of the distribution of the resulting costs and benefits.

Going back to Diagram 1, one can see that if the (discounted) adjustment costs from shifting production from good B to expanded output for A exceed the (discounted) savings in resource costs resulting from specialization, then resistance to the pooling of markets will be strong—and it will be stronger the more concentrated the adjustment costs are in certain localities or groups.

The flexibility possessed by selective OLDS in creating effective interest group backing for the transition in policy may sometimes act to the detriment of the rest of the world as when products to exchange preferences are selected with a view to minimize the trade creation effects of preferential trading and expand its trade diversion effects. This danger is more serious in limited PTAs (RHS of row 2 and 3 in Table 1). This is why selectivity, with respect to products, can lead to a new bias of the incentive system with very few benefits of outwards-orientation.

Notwithstanding the above comments on product selective OLDS, the discussion up to this point focussed primarily on the factors that influence the choice between a global OLDS and a geographically-selective OLDS, without discussing whether the particular group of countries selected to exchange preferences affect the net outcome. This issue must now be examined in order to establish whether a selective OLDS, favoring other developing countries, that is, a strategy of self-reliance, offers more net advantages in comparison to a selective OLDS favoring industrialized or generally industrially more developed economies. This last option is often referred in literature as "integration among unequals" and has been criticized implicitly by the followers of the dependency school of development. Our analysis in the next section shows that this option should not be rejected in principle, as it may offer, under certain conditions, a more efficient alternative of reaching certain industrialization goals.

INTEGRATION AMONG UNEQUALS OR SELF-RELIANCE?

The choice between a selective OLDS, involving partners from the industrialized world, and a selective OLDS, involving partners from the developing world (self-reliance), is not as easy as it is often made to look. Some economists believe that the "psychological" benefits from reduced "dependence" are so important in the case of self-reliance schemes that such schemes are superior to any preferential trading arrangement with advanced industrialized economies (Yeats 1981; Kaplinsky 1984). On economic grounds, the question of the choice between the two must surely be made in terms of the reduction of the marginal or excess cost of industry that each option offers. As most developing countries tend to be higher cost producers, the downward shift of the supply of industry curve may be more limited when a country tries to pool markets with other developing countries than with more developed partners.

Diagram 2 illustrates the supply of industry curves of three countries: A, B, and C. Country B is the more economically advanced of the three. Country A is a middle-level developing economy whilst country C is the least developed of the three. Country A wishes to bring down its excess cost of industry given its preferred level of industrial production (ON). If it negotiates a preferential trading agreement with the developed economy, country B, the new joint supply of industry curve will be $S_{(AB)}$ in Diagram 2A. On the assumption that the preferred level of industrial production is ON in both countries, the preferential trade arrangement enables the two countries to attain that level at the lower excess cost of industry shown by dotted line $S_{(AB)}$. This is achieved through specialization. Country A is now producing only product X and exchanges it on preferential terms with its partner B which specializes in F.

Now take the same country—country A—and find what will happen if it negotiates a preferential trading arrangement with the other developing country—country C. Country C is a higher cost producer relative to B. Through specialization, the preferred level of industrial production can still be reached at a lower excess cost of industry compared with the individual supply of industry curves of the two partners. Notice, however, that the joint supply of

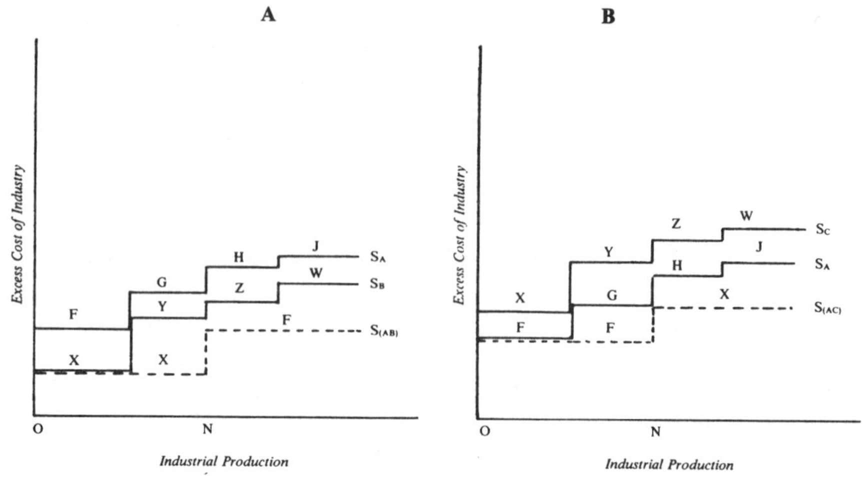

Diagram 2.

industry curve $S_{(AC)}$ lies at a level higher than that of the joint supply of industry curve $S_{(AB)}$ and the pattern of specialization is reversed. Surely if A is faced with the choice of pursuing a selective OLDS with either partner B or C, it will be to its advantage to choose B.

The choice may not however be as straightforward as indicated by Diagram 2. In the case described, the two partners share equally in the distribution of the benefits from specialization. It is conceivable that if B is more efficient than A in every line of production (i.e., if the supply of industry curve in A lies above that of B at every point) the joint supply of industry curve will consist of products manufactured from locations in B, leaving no industrial output for production in A. But as Cooper and Massell have suggested, this situation can be rectified with the adoption of an appropriate tariff structure (Cooper and Massell 1965).

There are additional advantages of preferential trade arrangements with more advanced partners than the option of self-reliance. First, as the markets of the industrialized countries are the key markets for the nontraditional exports of the developing countries, a preferential trade arrangement with these countries remove the uncertainty of export pessimism that often acts as a restraint in stimulating export production in the developing economies. Second, the markets of these countries may act as better "incubators" in assisting developing countries' producers to acquire the marketing experience in exporets that they lack. The markets of the industrialized partners are likely to be sophisticated enough to act as useful "incubator markets" while the preferential arrangement offers them breathing space by reducing the strength of international competition within the preferential trade area. One can recall the case of the preferential agreements of the EEC with a number of Mediterranean countries in agricultural products (both processed and unprocessed) to see the relevance of this point.

CONCLUSIONS

Let us now recapitulate the argument advanced so far. We started from a position where the costs of continuing an ILDS are fully recognized but the level of industrial production is regarded as a collective consumption good. Under these conditions, the appropriate development strategy is selective rather than global outwards-looking. Further, we argued that, under special conditions regarding the shape and the position of the individual supply of industry curves, selectivity in the form of preferential trading arrangements with partners from the industrialized world may bring more advantages in the sense of larger reductions in the excess cost of industry for reaching the preferred level of industrial output. This must not be regarded as universally valid as the specific conditions affecting the marginal, or excess cost of industry, will vary from case to case.

This discussion is useful in the sense that it provides the rationale for explaining, in the tradition of positive economics, the preference of many semi-industrialized and less-developed economies from the Mediterranean region and elsewhere in adopting trade and development strategies involving selective orientation toward more advanced, industrialized, countries and, in particular, the countries of the EEC and EFTA. It further helps to understand the many difficulties that self-reliance schemes have been facing in practice.

The taxonomic scheme presented here although not exhaustive, nevertheless provides a useful framework in examining the development strategy options open to policymakers. Its usefulness is in highlighting the existence of a number of intermediate OLDS that have been neglected in the literature—a literature polarized for many years now between the two extreme cases of ILDS and OLDS.

REFERENCES

Adelman, I. (1984). "Beyond Export-Led Growth." *World Development* 12(9):937-949.

Balassa, B. (1975). Reforming the System of Incentives in Developing Countries." *World Development* 3(June).

———. (1978). "Exports and Economic Growth: Further Evidence." *Journal of Development Economics* (June):181-189.

———. (1982). *Development Strategies in Semi-Industrial Economies.* Baltimore/London: The Johns Hopkins Press.

———. (1983). "Outwards Versus Inwards Orientation Once Again." *The World Economy* 6(2):215-218.

Chenery, H. (1980). "Interactions Between Industrialisation and Exports."*American Economic Review* 70 (2):281-287.

Cooper, C.A. and B.F. Massell (1965). "Toward a General Theory of Customs Unions for Developing Countries." *Journal of Political Economy* 73:461-476.

Feder, G. (1982). "On Exports and Economic Growth." *Journal of Development Economics* 12:59-73.

Findlay, R. and S. Wellisz. (1984). "Toward a Model of Endogenous Rent-Seeking." Chapter 6 in D.C. Collander (ed.), *Neoclassical Political Economy: The Analysis of Rent-Seeking and DUP Activities.* Cambridge, MA: Ballinger.

Gray, H.P. (1986). "Protection in a Democracy: A Conversation with H. Peter Gray and R. Licklider." *Eastern Economic Journal* 12 (2): 89-93.

Havrylyshin, O. and I. Alikhani. (1982). "Is There Cause for Export Optimism? An Inquiry into the Existence of a Second Generation of Successful Exporters." *Weltwirtschaftliches Archiv* 188 (4).

Henderson, P.D. (1982). "Trade Policies and 'Strategies': Case for a Liberal Approach." *The World Economy* (3):291-303.

Hughes, H. and A.O. Krueger. (1984). "Effect of Protection in Developed Countries on Developing Countries Exports of Manufactures." Pp. 389-418 in R.E. Baldwin and A.O. Krueger (eds.), *The Structure and Evolution of Recent US Trade Policy.* Chicago: University of Chicago Press.

Johnson, H.G. (1965). "An Economic Theory of Protection, Tariff Bargaining and the Formation of Customs Unions." *Journal of Political Economy* 73:256-283.

Kaplinsky, R. (1984). "The International Context for Industrialisation in the Coming Decade." *Journal of Development Studies:* 75-97.

Kravis, I.B. (1970). "Trade as a Handmaiden of Growth: Similarities Between the Nineteenth and Twentieth Centuries." *Economic Journal* 80:850-872.

Kavoussi, P.M. (1984). "Export Expansion and Economic Growth: Further Empirical Evidence." *Journal of Development Economics* 14:241-250.

Krueger, A.O. (1978). *Foreign Trade Regimes and Economic Development: Liberalisation Attempts and Consequences.* Cambridge, MA: National Bureau of Economic Research.

———. 1981. "Loans to Assist the Transition to Outwards Oriented Policies." *The World Economy* 3:461-476.

———. (1983). *Trade and Employment in Developing Countries: vol. 3: Synthesis.* Chicago/London: University of Chicago Press.

———. (1984). "Trade Policies in Developing Countries." Chapter 11 in R.W. Jones and P.B. Kenen (eds.) *Handbook of International Economics.* New York/Amsterdam: Elsevier.

McAleese, D. (1978). "Outwards Looking Policies, Manufactured Exports and Economic Growth: The Irish Experience." Pp. 313-351 in M.J. Artis and A.R. Nobay (eds.), *Contemporary Economic Analysis.* London: Croom Helm.

Michalopoulos, C. (1975). Expanding Trade Among Developing Countries: The Role of Limited Preferential Arrangements." *Journal of Common Market Studies.* (March): 308-318.

Mill, J.S. (1965). *Collected Works.* London: University of Toronto Press and Routledge & Kegan Paul.

Streeten, P. (ed.) (1973). *Trade Policies for Development.* London: Macmillan.

———. (1982). "A Cool Look at Outwards Looking Strategies." *The World Economy* 5 (2):159-169.

Tyler, W.J. (1981). "Growth and Export Expansion in Developing Countries: Some Empirical Evidence." *Journal of Development Economics* 9:121-130.

Wonnacott, P. and R. Wonnacott. (1981). "Is Unilateral Tariff Reduction Preferable to a Customs Union? The Curious Case of the Missing Tariffs." *American Economic Review* 71:704-714.

Yannopoulos, G.N. (1987). "European Community Tariff Preferences and Foreign Direct Investment." *Banca Nationale del Lauozo Quarterly Review* 160 (March):93-109.

Yeats, A.J. (1981). *Trade and Development Policies: Leading Issues for the 1980s.* London: Macmillan.

PART IV

INTERNATIONAL TRADE NEGOTIATIONS

THE ROLE OF DEBT AND THE MACROECONOMY IN THE URUGUAY ROUND:

THE CASE OF LATIN AMERICA

Julio Nogués

Trade liberalization leading to increased competition around the globe is one of the most, if not the most, important policy for enhancing growth prospects. The goal of the Uruguay Round of Multilateral Trade Negotiations (MTNs) is precisely to liberalize trade policies. In this round, the role of developing countries will be an important determinant of the outcome of the negotiations. There are two major factors determining the extent of developing countries' participation; their attitude and the degree to which these economies are positioned to support far-reaching trade liberalization measures.

Although the willingness to negotiate actively varies from country to country, the attitude of developing countries in this round is more positive than has hitherto been the case. For example, by early 1988 they have tabled numerous proposals for trade liberalization of industrial countries barriers. However, there are serious doubts that they are well-positioned to sustain their own trade liberalization. One of the major lessons that has been drawn from numerous trade liberalization attempts is that if the macroeconomy is unstable

Research in International Business and Finance, vol. 7, pages 227-241.

ISBN: 0-89232-906-8

and/or domestic, financial, and labor markets are seriously affected by policy-induced rigidities, liberalization measures are likely to be followed by reversals.

Many developing countries are facing serious macroeconomic problems of both domestic and external origin. On the domestic side, the major issues probably stem from the size and degree of inefficiency of public sectors as well as from policy-induced rigidities in important markets. On the external side, the growing protectionist policies of major country markets, wide swings in international interest rates, historically low terms of trade, unstable commodity markets, uncertainties associated with debt negotiations, and restricted access to financial resources also place serious obstacles before trade liberalizaiton processes.

Amelioration of some of these external problems including protectionist measures to LDCs exports, unstable commodity markets, and low terms of trade will be determined by the etent to which industrial countries open their markets. But success of the Uruguay Round will also be determined by the extent to which developing countries also liberalize their trade regimes.

In this regard, the important remaining difficulty that developing countries face when attempting to stabilize their macroeconomies is debt. The notion which I want to stress is that for many countries, the sheer size of the debt plus other characteristics of the debt-negotiating process place serious obstacles before the attainment of macroeconomic stabilization targets. And, in a situation of economic crisis characterized by an absence of relative macro-stability and access to financial capital, it will remain extremely difficult to sustain far-reaching trade liberalization measures. Although the analysis will use, as an example, some indebted Latin Americna countries, the arguments and conclusions are of a more general nature.

The second section of this paper discusses some aspects of the role that the Uruguay Round plays for developing countries, followed by a presentation of some lessons regarding the importance that macroeconomic policies have for sustaining trade liberalization policies. The fourth section argues that although some trade liberalization programs have been implemented since the debt crisis erupted, by and large the trade regimes of Latin American countries remain inward-oriented. I present some statistical evidence to show that this situation is harming the growth and employment prospects of these economies and also as well, their ability to generate surpluses and to service their debts. The fifth section emphasizes that uncertainties and macroeconomic problems, which are partly related to debt service and debt negotiations, represent a barrier to macroeconomic stabilization, and, therefore, to the introduction and sustainability of a trade liberalization program. In this sense, the debt problems might become an important determinant of the degree of success of the Uruguay Round. Finally, I give some concluding comments.

IMPORTANCE OF LIBERALIZING TRADE IN THE URUGUAY ROUND

Even though a majority of developing countries are signatories to the GATT, so far, during the post-World War II era, and with few exceptions, they have not participated actively in the MTNs. The belief that inward-oriented trade policies were appropriate for achieving social and economic development goals has been a major force behind their attitude. This attitude has been reinforced by the fact that the GATT has provided developing countries with a special and prefernetial treatment which, in fact, gave them freedom to introduce or retain significant protectionist measures.[1] But attitudes and ideas have been changing. For one thing, the import-substitution strategy no longer provides significant growth opportunities to developing countries. In fact, an important number of LDCs—including, in Latin America, Argentina, Bolivia, Chile, Colombia, Costa Rica, Haiti, Mexico, Panama, and Uruguay—have realized this and have been introducing unilateral liberalization measures.

The Uruguay Round provides an opportunity for strengthening and continuing these reforms. Liberalization of trade through MTNs implies significant benefits. First, for any country, the gains from trade liberalization increase as other countries also reduce their trade barriers. For developing countries, this might be particularly important. It has been suggested that much of the discriminatory trade policies of industrial against developing countries could be attributed to a lack of participation of the latter group of countries in the previous MTNs (Finger 1977). For example, the escalation of industrial countries' tariff barriers discriminate against developing countries (Finger and Olechowski 1986). Also, since the end of the Tokyo Round, the extent of nontariff barriers of industrial countries has been growing and, in some products such as textiles and agriculture, fall heavily on developing countries and particularly on indebted countries (Nogués, Olechowski, and Winters 1986). The loss to developing countries arising from these barriers are enormous (the 1986 World Development Report measures some cases of agricultural protection). If developing countries do not participate in the Uruguay Round, it is unlikely that the more discriminatory barriers, which their exports face in industrial countries, will be dismantled.

A second major advantage of liberalizing trade through MTNs is that the political pressures on the trade-policy decision process is more balanced than when trade is liberalized unilaterally. In the MTNs, the opposition by import-competing interests to trade liberalization is compensated by the active participation of export groups who take into consideration the greater access to foreign markets. This political consideration could be of great importance, particularly in developing countries with a strong and powerful elite of protected entrepreneurs.

Another characteristic of the MTNs, which could be used in favor of improved macroeconomic policies, is the binding of import barriers. In principle, a country that has bound its trade barriers cannot increase its protection level without facing the threat of retaliation from other countries. Hopefully, this characteristic would be used by policymakers in developing countries to replace trade policy as an instrument of balance of payments adjustment by other, more appropriate, policies.

Perhaps it is the perception of these gains which has recently prompted a number of developing countries to position themselves to participate actively in the Uruguay Round. For example, during the last couple of years and with the purpose of participating in this round, the following countries have requested—and, in some cases, already obtained—accession to the GATT: Algeria, Bulgaria, Costa Rica, El Salvador, Guatemala, Honduras, Mexico, and Tunisia. China has also requested resumption of its status as a contracting party to GATT. In many cases, these countries have (or will) reduce and bind import barriers. Developing countries have also tabled numerous proposals for trade liberalization.

But even if, for political and eocnomic considerations, it were easier to liberalize trade when other countries liberalize, the fact remains that individual countries need to sustain their liberalizaiton process with relatively stable macroeconomic policies. The growth of protectionist policies in industrial countries, during the 1980s, is a clear and painful example of how trade policies can be abused when macroeconomic disequilibrium grows. The next section will review research results on the link between trade policies and the macroeconomy in developing countries.

MACROEOCNOMIC POLICIES, TRADE LIBERALIZATION ATTEMPTS AND INDEBTED COUNTRIES

From Liberalization to Import Compression: The Case of Latin America

During the late 1970s and early 1980s, several Latin American countries, including Argentina, Chile, Peru and Uruguay, introduced *unilateral* trade liberalization policies. Unfortunately, from an economic perspective, some of these were ill-conceived programs. In part, the unsoundness of these programs can be attributed, in many cases, to the fact that the driving force behind the shift to more open trade policies was not so much the objective of increasing the efficiency and international competitiveness of these economies, but the notion that import and exchange rate policies could be used as anti-inflationary instruments.[2]

Because at that time several of these Latin American countries were following expansionary fiscal policies, inflation remained high (Table 1) and the attempt

Table 1. Annual Change in Consumer Price Indices
1977-1986
(percent)

Year	*Argentina*	*Chile*	*Mexico*	*Peru*	*Uruguay*
1977	176.1	91.9	29.0	38.1	58.2
1978	175.5	40.1	17.5	57.8	44.5
1979	159.5	33.4	18.2	66.7	66.8
1980	100.8	35.1	26.4	59.2	63.5
1981	104.5	19.7	27.9	75.4	34.0
1982	164.8	9.9	58.9	64.4	19.0
1983	343.8	27.3	101.8	111.2	49.2
1984	626.7	19.9	65.5	110.2	55.3
1985	672.1	30.7	57.7	163.4	72.2
1986	90.1	19.5	86.2	77.9	76.4

Source: *International Finance Statistics Yearbook* (1986).

Table 2. Real Exchange Rates Indexes, 1978-1986*

Year	*Argentina*	*Chile*	*Mexico*	*Peru*	*Uruguay*
1978	54	85	84	88	72
1979	77	86	89	90	79
1980	100	100	100	100	100
1981	91	118	114	119	112
1982	51	106	81	122	118
1983	43	87	72	115	72
1984	50	85	84	115	69
1985	44	69	86	94	67
1986	44	58	60	106	66

Note: * The real exchange rate is the inverse of the nominal exchange rate times the ratio of the wholesale price index of the trading partner to the domestic wholesale price index. Thus, a decline (increase) is a real depreciation (appreciation). The index is weighted and the weights are given by the value of trade with the main trading partners.

Source: Laird and Nogués (1988), Table 2.

to use the exchange rate as an anti-inflation instrument led to an important appreciation in real exchange rates. For example, Table 2 shows that, between 1978 and 1980, the rate of appreciation was 52% and 23% in Argentina and Chile, respectively. In Mexico and Peru, although the rate of apreciation was smaller it continued until 1981, and in Uruguay until 1982.

The inconsistencies of these policy packages were such that they generated much uncertainty—for example, uncertainty on the time path of expected real devaluation and interest rates—leading, in some cases, to unprecedented amounts of capital flight (Dornbusch 1985).

Episodes of expansionary fiscal policies and currency overvaluation have been historically common among Latin American countries. Traditionally, periods of currency overvaluation lasted until foreign exchange reserves were depleted. When this occurred, countries implemented a traditional IMF recipe of devaluing while, at the same time, attempting to restore fiscal balance.

This time, the expansionary Latin American policies of the late 1970s and very early 1980s confronted a new international environment; one whose major characteristic was an unprecedented high mobility of capital flows. Policymakers took advantage of the easy access to financial resources for sustaining inappropriate economic policies and macroeconomic disequilibria. Table 3 shows that by 1981—just before the debt crisis appeared—the total external debt of Latin American countries had grown to U.S.$295 billion; up from U.S.$162 billion in 1978.

Clearly, during these years, the process by which banks made their lending decisions contained flaws; their massive lending to countries with overvalued currencies and unsustainable macroeconomic disequilibria permitted these policies to continue far longer than otherwise and, in the end, made them unable to service the interest payments on the loans they received (Fischer 1987).

This point can be made more explicit by using the case of Argentina as an example. Between 1978 and 1981, the foreign debt of this country grew by U.S.$22 billion. As said, this lending took place while the domestic currency was grossly overvalued, and the trade balance was shifting from a surplus of U.S.$2.9 billion, in 1978, to a deficit of U.S.$1.4 billion, in 1980.

It is, I think, clear, with the macroeconomic policies of those years, that Argentina would have soon entered a balance of payment crisis. In the absence of foreign loans, Argentina would have been forced to take corrective actions sooner. In this event, the debt problem would have been less serious and the adjustment less painful.

When, in mid-1982, banks decided to stop lending to what already were highly-indebted countries, they also requested them to comply with their debt-service obligations. The indebted countries were suddenly facing a crisis. The likelihood that a crisis will lead to the introduction of harmful economic policies is high. In the short run, and amidst a panic situation, the only way by which countries could hope to service their debts was by reducing imports as much as possible. Although almost all countries devalued, input compression was also implemented by raising tariffs, and, most importantly, by introducing across-the-board import licensing. In Argentina and Mexico, these latter measures were introduced in late 1982. While Chile avoided introducing licensing measures, it raised its uniform tariff rates from 10% to 35% and, in addition, initiated more than 100 countervailing duty actions, particularly against imports from neighboring countries. Peru raised its tariff rates in 1984

Table 3. Debt and Debt Service Ratios of Some Latin American Countries 1980-1985 (billions of U.S. $)

Year	*1980*	*1981*	*1982*	*1983*	*1984*	*1985*
Total External Debt						
Argentina	27.2	35.7	43.6	45.1	46.8	48.4
Chile	12.1	15.7	17.3	18.2	20.0	20.2
Mexico	57.5	78.3	86.1	93.0	97.4	97.4
Peru	10.0	10.3	12.3	12.4	13.1	13.7
Uruguay	1.7	2.2	2.6	3.3	3.3	3.9
Latin America and the Caribbean	242.4	295.3	331.5	354.8	372.4	383.9
Total External Debt as a Percentage of GNP						
Argentina	51.1	65.6	79.9	75.5	64.4	79.9
Chile	45.5	50.3	77.9	100.4	115.1	142.2
Mexico	31.9	34.0	55.5	69.8	60.4	58.3
Peru	53.8	47.9	58.6	75.0	74.6	88.2
Uruguay	16.5	19.3	29.2	64.9	68.5	83.2
Latin America and the Caribbean	35.3	37.8	47.5	59.7	60.5	62.3
Public Debt Service as a Percentage of Exports of Goods and Services						
Argentina	17.7	18.2	23.9	25.0	25.9	41.7
Chile	21.9	29.6	20.0	18.3	26.2	26.2
Mexico	32.1	28.1	34.2	40.0	34.9	36.9
Peru	31.2	44.8	36.6	19.3	14.6	7.9
Uruguay	12.4	10.0	13.4	20.6	29.8	30.6
Latin America and the Caribbean	21.6	21.8	26.4	25.4	23.8	26.2
Private Debt Service as a Percentage of Exports of Goods and Services						
Argentina	n.a.	n.a.	n.a.	n.a.	n.a.	n.a.
Chile	16.0	27.8	42.1	29.4	26.0	17.9
Mexico	5.9	6.9	10.4	5.4	14.3	11.3
Peru	5.7	7.2	7.9	9.2	9.7	8.2
Uruguay	3.4	3.6	14.5	2.9	2.6	5.9
Latin America and the Caribbean	9.1	10.6	13.3	9.3	9.4	7.4

Note: n.a. = Not available.
Source: *World Debt Tables* (The World Bank 1986).

and introduced across-the-board licensing in 1985. Finally, Uruguay was an exception in that it avoided introducing across-the-board import licensing measures, but continued with its program of tariff reductions.

These measures had a drastic short-run impact on imports. Table 4 shows that the decline started in 1982-1983. Between 1981 and 1983, imports declined in U.S. dollar value by 51% in Argentina, 56% in Chile, 64% in Mexico,

Table 4. Trade Flows of Latin American Countries
(millions of U.S. $)

	Argentina			*Chile*			*Mexico*			*Peru*			*Uruguay*			*LAC**		
Year	*Exports*	*Imports*	*Trade Balance*	*Exports*	*Imports*	*Trade Balance*	*Exports*	*Imports*	*Trade Balance*	*Exports*	*Imports*	*Trade Balance*	*Exports*	*Imports*	*Trade Balance*	*Exports*	*Imports*	*Trade Balance*
1978	6401	3488	2913	2460	2886	-426	6246	7992	-1745	1941	1601	340	686	710	- 24	n.a.	n.a.	n.a.
1979	7810	6028	1782	3835	4190	-355	9301	12131	-2830	3491	1951	1540	788	1166	-378	n.a.	n.a.	n.a.
1980	8021	9394	-1373	4705	5469	-764	16066	18896	-2830	3898	3062	837	1059	1668	-610	89100	90500	-1400
1981	9143	8431	712	3836	6513	-2677	19938	24037	-4099	3249	3802	-553	1230	1592	-362	95900	97600	-1700
1982	7623	4859	2764	3706	3643	63	21230	14435	6795	3293	3721	-428	1256	1038	218	87400	78300	9100
1983	7835	4119	3716	3831	2845	986	22312	8550	13762	3015	2722	293	1156	740	417	87500	56000	31500
1984	8100	4118	3982	3650	3357	293	24196	11255	12941	3147	2140	1007	925	733	191	97500	58800	38700
1985	8396	3519	4877	3743	2954	789	21867	13460	8407	2967	1868	1098	854	675	178	91900	57600	34300
1986	6987	4392	2595	4199	3099	1100	16031	11432	4599	2509	2525	-16	1088	791	297	n.a.	n.a.	n.a.

Notes: n.a. = Not available.
* Latin American and the Caribbean data obtained from CEPAL (1987).
Source: International Finance Statistics, Lines 77aad & 77abd (Merchandise Exports & Imports), and CEPAL (1987).

Table 5. Capital Flows in Latin America
1978-1986
(in billions of U.S. $)

	Capital	*Capital*	*Net Transfer*
1978	26.2	10.2	16.0
1979	29.1	13.6	15.5
1980	29.4	17.9	11.5
1981	37.5	27.1	10.4
1982	20.0	38.7	-18.7
1983	3.2	34.3	-31.2
1984	9.2	36.2	-27.0
1985	2.4	35.1	-32.9
1986*	8.5	30.7	-22.2

Note: * Preliminary 1987.
Source: CEPAL (1987), Table 8.

28% in Peru, and 54% in Uruguay.[3] Import contraction has been the most important policy adjustment allowing indebted countries to transfer huge financial surpluses abroad. Table 5 shows that between 1979 and 1981 Latin American countries received a net resource inflow of U.S.$37.2 billion. In contrast, during the next three years, the net resource outflow was twice as large. In order to effect this transfer, Latin American imports declinedby more than a third; from U.S.$91 billion, in 1980, to U.S.$58 billion, in 1985.

This is a recent and painful example of how trade liberalization policies can be reversed when macroeconomic disequilibriums are permitted to grow and foreign financing is abruptly eliminated. Unfortunately, examples of this policy behavior are not restricted to Latin America.

The Lessons from Other Experiences

The post-World War II experience with unilateral trade liberalization programs in 19 LDCs including Argentina, Brazil, Chile, Colombia, Greece, Indonesia, Korea, New Zealand, Pakistan, Peru, Philippines, Portugal, Singapore, Spain, Sri Lanka, Turkey, Uruguay, and Yugoslavia is being documented in an ongoing multicountry-research project sponsored by the World Bank. In a recent paper, the directors of this project discussed the role that the macroeconomy has played in trade liberalization attempts. They conclude that a "significant deficit involving a substantial loss of foreign exchange reserves, is most likely to abort a liberalization attempt."[4] Drawing on these and other experiences, the 1987 World Development Report has recently concluded that "It is virtually impossible to sustain trade reforms in an economy facing a stabilization crisis" (World Bank 1987).

Thus, the accumulated evidence not only on Latin American countries but also on other numerous trade liberalization attempts, strongly suggests that relative stability and appropriate macroeconomic policies are of paramount importance for sustaining them.

Theory predicts that import contraction effected through protectionist trade policies will entail long-run costs in the form of reduced employment and growth and, therefore, on the ability of economies to service debt. Unfortunately, some of the available figures show that, in fact, these costs are being materialized. I turn now to a brief analysis of these dynamic considerations.

TRADE BARRIERS AS AN IMPEDIMENT TO GROWTH, EMPLOYMENT, AND DEBT SERVICE

Theory and empirical research have shed light on the social costs of protectionist regimes. This research suggests that protected economies:

- Are more likely to develop oligopolistic and monopolistic market structures;
- Fail to reap the benefits of economies of scale;
- Redistribute income from the society at large—including foregone fiscal revenues—to the protected entrepreneurs. This is particularly serious when protection is implemented through direct import controls, as is the case in a number of Latin American countries;
- Fail to induce entrepreneurs to strive for maintaining high efficiency standards;
- Fail to generate sufficient employment opportunities. This occurs not only because protection tends to be higher for relatively capital-intensive industries, but also because other distortions in factor markets induce the adoption of capital-intensive techniques (Krueger 1983).

Although there are other negative consequences associated with protected economies, these have often been used to explain why protection not only results in static welfare losses, but also tends to harm long-run growth performance.[5]

Table 6 shows that, in recent years, the growth and employment performance of Latin-American countries has, in fact, worsened significantly. Per capita-income levels have been declining steadily and, in some cases, such as Argentina, have reached alarming proportions. This decline in living standards cannot be attributed entirely to the resource misallocation which has been triggered by the protectionist policies and the consequent import contraction. Other factors have also contributed. Of major importance has been the decline

Table 6. Real Per Capita Income and Unemployment Rates

Country	*Accumulated Change (1981-1986) in Per Capita Income (%)*	*Rate of Urban Unemployment (%)*	
		1980	*1986**
Argentina	-15.3	2.3	4.6
Chile	-5.9	11.8	13.1
Mexico	-10.2	4.5	4.8
Peru	-8.1	10.9	8.2
Uruguay	-13.6	7.4	10.7

Note: * Preliminary.
Source: CEPAL (1987). Per capita income (Table 3) and unemployment rates (Table 4).

in terms of trade and investment levels—in particular, public investment—which has taken place as the government budgets have had to make room for the interest payments on the public-sector debts.

Finally, the available evidence suggests that, for several indebted countries, it is becoming more difficult to maintain high trade surplus. For example, Table 4 shows that vis-à-vis the peak trade surplus of the 1980s, the reduction of this surplus during 1986 has been the following: Argentina 35%, Mexico 67%, Peru more than 100%, and Uruguay 24%. Chile, in contrast, is the only country in our sample that, until 1986, shows a positive trend in its trade balance surplus. Nevertheless, for the region as a whole, the bad news outweighs the good. For Latin America and the Caribbean, CEPAL (1987) estimates that, for 1986, the trade surplus was U.S.$18.7 billion; a reduction of almost half the 1985 level.

While the case for trade liberalization appears to be strong, unfortunately, a majority of highly-indebted countries appear to have great difficulties in both stabilizing and introducing appropriate longer-run macroeconomic policies. In this regard, the next section will discuss the difficulties that a high-debt service creates.

DEBT SERVICE AS A DETERMINANT OF MACROECONOMIC STABILITY

In principle, there is always a policy package which, if implemented, can stabilize the price level and the macroeconomy. There are problems not only in finding the policy package that would minimize the social costs during the transition period, but also and most importantly, is the ability of a country's leadership to convince the citizens of the need to go through a period of hardship in order to improve long-run income prospects.

Unfortunately, the available evidence suggests that, in spite of the hardships already suffered by people of indebted countries, the stabilization and liberalization policies introduced thus far have not prevented the debt problem from getting worse. In Latin America, between 1980 and 1985, the external debt to GDP ratio increased by 59% (Table 3).

In what follows, I want to emphasize that a high and growing debt also implies growing difficulties in managing the macroeconomy. There are several ways by which the debt and the debt negotiations have an impact on the macroeconomy.

First, there is the sheer size of the numbers. In Table 3, debt to GDP ratios go from 66% in Venezuela to 142% in Chile. Multiply this by the interest rate and you get an idea of the relative magnitudes of the resource transfers which would be needed for servicing the debt. Thus, fluctuations in international interest rates put severe strains on macro-management and tend to further destabilize the macroeconomy of indebted countries. Just to give a quantiative idea, a one-percentage point higher interest rate implies that Latin American countries have to generate close to US$4 billion more in additional foreign exchange revenues in order to meet interest payment obligations. Interest rate fluctuations are associated with the macroeconomic imbalances of industrial countries and, in indebted countries, they generate serious final problems.

Second, some dimensions of debt negotiations and their outcome, including those referring to spread and grace periods, are contingent on relative bargaining power, which, in turn, is determined at least in part by the circumstances—often unpredictable—surrounding a specific negotiation. Here, the scenario is constantly changing. For example, it took Mexico several months to complete what, in 1987, was labelled the most favorable debt negotiation for a developing country. Argentina has recently signed a similar deal. But in this case, the Mexico precedent and the 1987 unilateral action of Brazil to suspend its debt-service payments were major factors in enhancing Argentina's negotiating power and arriving at a fast agreement. Unpredictable events such as these are important determinants of the outcome of the negotiations. This adds another dimension of uncertainty to the management of the macroeconomy.

Third, each of these complex negotiations in itself must follow a number of steps whose timing and outcome cannot be predicted a priori. For example, a typical debt negotiation goes through the following steps: (1) an economic program with the IMF must be agreed; (2) this program must be accepted by the commercial banks; (3) the major commercial banks must then align the smaller banks and ensure that they will put up the money; and (4) the banks usually request the countries to negotiate a sectorial or structural adjustment loan with the World Bank and obtain agreement from the Paris Club to defer official debt service. When all of these steps have been completed, the IMF program finally goes forward. This complex debt-negotiating procedure adds another dimensions of uncertainty to the indebted countries.[6]

Fourth, the uncertainties generated by the debt and the debt-negotiating process become a major determinant of expectations in the indebted country.

As the negotiations become lengthy and uncertain and debt ratios worsen, the country will be perceived as being riskier. This leads savers to demand a higher-risk premium which in turn will result in a higher real interest rate with all the social costs that this might imply.[7]

Finally, even if the debt-negotiating process could become more predictable a heavily-indebted country will remain an uncertain place for private investment. This is simply because one never knows how the tax incidence and tax structure (and relative private profitability of different investments) might shift over time as resources need to be generated in order to service the debt. This, in turn, increases the ex ante uncertainties regarding the profitability of investing in indebted countries.

CONCLUDING COMMENTS

The stakes for the world economy of an active participation of developing countries in the MTNs are important. If these countries liberalize, they will gain by:

- improving the allocation of their resources;
- increasing their international competitive edge; and
- improving their growth and employment prospects.

For industrial countries, trade liberalization of developing countries is also important. The gains for their economies stem mainly from:

- greater access to the markets of LDCs; and
- improved capacity of LDCs to generate foreign exchange earnings and service their debts.

Thus, the success of the MTNs will be determined, in part, by the extent to which developing countries are committed to trade liberalization and take an active participative role. In this regard, the post-World War II experience shows that the ability of developing countries to introduce significant trade liberalization measures is constrained by the extent to which their accompanying policies can sustain an open-trade regime. In particular, an abundant experience has shown that an unstable macroeconomy, resulting in a balance of payments crisis, plus restricted access to international financial resources have been major determinants of reversals of trade liberalization policies.

Unfortunately, the macroeconomy of an important number of indebted countries poses serious doubts regarding the extent to which they can sustain open-trade regimes. In spite of the stabilization measures that have been introduced in recent years, inflation rates of some indebted countries remain high. Also, per capita incomes have been declining and debt ratios have continued to increase. If the recent past is of any use for predicting the near future, then I must conclude that the prospects for per capita-income growth and debt service of Latin American countries are poor.

While there is little doubt that indebted countries can introduce more stringent stabilization and restructuring measures, the purpose of this paper has been to stress that, because of several factors including the magnitude of the debt, the short-run and uncertain nature of the debt-negotiating process, and the limited access to international financial resources, the goal of stabilizing the macroeconomy remains extremely difficult for these countries to achieve.

Highly-indebted developing countries enter the Uruguay Round with this trade-debt gridlock. Such a gridlock will affect the nature and extent of the concessions that they will be able to offer. Thus, from a trade liberalization perspective—which, in my view, should be the driving goal for enhancing growth prospects—it makes sense to ease the uncertainties and macroeconomic problems associated with the high debt-service payments of indebted countries. One of the worst scenarios that could occur if developing countries faced foreign exchange shortages and lack of access to financial resources is for them to have to resort again to trade policy as an instrument of balance of payments adjustment. Avoiding this and creating a scenario that would allow developing countries to introduce far-reaching and long-lasting trade liberalization measures during the Uruguay Round is in the interest of the international trade and financial community.

NOTES

The World Bank does not accept responsibility for the views expressed herein which are those of the author and should not be attributed to the World Bank or to its affiliated organizations.

1. See Hudec (1987) for a history of how the special and differential treatment has been introduced to the GATT.

2. See, for example, Nogués (1986a) on Argentina; Nogués (1986b) on Peru and Corbo; and de Melo and Tybout (1986) on Argentina, Chile, and Uruguay.

3. In Peru, import-licensing measures were extended significantly in 1985. During this year, and in relation to 1981, imports declined by 51%. Income contraction also played an important role, particularly in 1983, when climatic conditions were extremely adverse.

4. Choksi, Michaely, and Papageorgiou (1986). These authors report that this situation has been encountered in several countries including Argentina, Brazil, Chile, Indonesia, Korea, Pakistan, Peru, Phillippines, Portugal, and Spain.

5. See also the *1987 World Development Report* for an analysis of 41 developing countries where it is shown that in terms of per capita-income growth the most outward-oriented and inward-oriented economies have been the best and worst performers, respectively.

6. Problems get compounded when IMF targets cannot be achieved and countries must request a waiver or renegotiate a new economic program. In these cases, several of the debt-negotiating procedures have to be repeated before the money is forthcoming.

7. This occurs in countries where, because of the crowding-out effect, real interest rates are already quite high.

REFERENCES

Choksi, A., M. Michaely, and D. Papageorgiou. (1986). "The Phasing of a Trade Liberalization Policy." *World Bank CPD Discussion Paper No. 42.*

Comisión Económica de America Latina (CEPAL). (June 1987). *Recent Economic Development in Latin America and the Caribbean.* Santiago: CEPAL.

Corbo, V., J. deMelo, and J. Tybout. (1986). "What Went Wrong with the Recent Reforms in the Southern Cone?" *Economic Development and Cultural Change* 34, 3(April): 607-640.

Dornbusch, R. (1985). "External Debt, Budget Deficits and Disequilibrium Exchange Rates." In J. Smith and J. Cuddington (eds.), *International Debt and the Developing Countries.* The World Bank.

Finger, J.M. (1977). "Trade Liberalization: A Public Choice Perspective." In R. Amascher, R.G. Haberler, and T. Williet (eds.), *Challenges to a Liberal-International Econoimc Order.*

Finger, J.M. and A. Olechowski. (1986). "Trade Barriers: Who Does What to Whom?" Mimeo. Washington, DC: The World Bank.

Fischer, S. (1987). "Sharing the Burden of the International Debt Crisis." *American Economic Review* (May).

Hudec, R. (1987). "Developing Countries in the GATT Legal System." *Thames Essays.* Trade Policy Research Centre.

Krueger, A.O. (1983). *Trade and Employment in Development Countries.* Chicago: The University of Chicago Press.

Laird, S. and J.Nogués. (1989). "Trade Policies and the Debt Crisis." *The World Bank Economic Review* (May).

Nogués, J. (1986b). "An Historical Perspective of Peru Trade Liberalization Attempt." *World Bank DRD Discussion Paper No. 51.*

Nogués, J., A. Olechowski, and L.A. Winters. (1986). "The Extent of Nontariff Barriers to Industrial Countries' Imports." *The World Bank Economic Review* 1.

Patterson, E. and G. Patterson. (1987). "Objectives of the New GATT Round." In J.M. Finger and A. Olechowski (eds.), *A Handbook for the Uruguay Round.* Washington, DC: The World Bank.

World Bank. (1986). *World Debt Tables.* Washington, DC: The World Bank.

________. (1986). *World Development Report, 1986.* Washington, DC: The World Bank

________. (1987). *World Development Report, 1987.* Washington, DC: The World Bank.

RAMIE:

THE OPENING AND CONTROLLING OF A LOOPHOLE IN THE MULTIFIBRE ARRANGEMENT

Brenda A. Brockman

There has been a long history of protection in the textile and clothing industries. This protection has taken the form of either voluntary export restraints, tariffs, or quotas. Since 1974, textile and apparel trade has been regulated by the International Agreement Regarding Trade in Textiles, usually known as the Multifibre Arrangement (MFA). The MFA provides a legal framework for the restriction of apparel and textile product trade among nations when domestic textile and apparel industries are disrupted by imports of cotton, wool, and man-made fiber products. The three goals of the MFA include the liberalization of trade, economic development, and the movement of less competitive industries into more productive enterprises.

The Multifibre Arrangement has been renewed three times since 1974. Each renewal has seen the institution of various changes, while maintaining the original purpose—the limitation of market disrupting exports. The most recent version of the MFA, negotiated in July 1986, extended the agreement to limit those vegetable fibers which compete with cotton, wool, and man-made fiber goods.

Research in International Business and Finance, vol. 7, pages 243-254.

ISBN: 0-89232-906-8

The goods most affected by the extended MFA coverage are garments made with more than 50% of ramie, jute, or linen. Since 1981, several Asian countries have begun to process large amounts of ramie, a vegetable fiber similar to cotton. Ramie is blended with cotton, or man-made fibers to produce such apparel as sweaters, slacks, and shirts. If ramie made up the majority of the value of a garment, the garment could be exported without being subject to the quota guidelines established by the MFA. This situation existed until 1986 when the MFA was renegotiated.

This paper examines the effectiveness and evolution of the MFA with the development of ramie production. The first section summarizes the main features of the MFA, followed by a presentation of the background on ramie and an examination of the loophole in the MFA which encouraged the development of ramie and other similar fibers. The concluding section details the changes brought about by the fourth version of the MFA and assesses the long-term effect of ramie on international trade in apparel.

BACKGROUND

The motivations for the MFA are found in the import statistics of many industrialized nations. Since 1972, the Asian countries of Hong Kong, Korea, Taiwan, and the People's Republic of China have become major producers of the world's textiles and apparel. These countries now account for a large percentage of the world's apparel production and exports. The primary importers of these goods are the large industrialized countries such as the members of the European Economic Community and the United States. The United States also supports a well-developed textile and apparel industry of its own.

Countries, such as the United States, with relatively active textile industries were concerned that lesser-developed countries, which were able to produce comparable textiles and apparel at lower costs, would significantly increase their exports of these goods. In time, these exports would overwhelm the older textile and apparel industries which were unable to compete with the lower-cost industries and so would be forced into extinction. This adjustment would cost the industrialized countries a great deal of revenue and many jobs unless all of the displaced workers could be productively employed.

The primary provisions of the MFA are concerned with the limitation of high levels of textile and apparel exports. The 12 articles of the MFA establish a framework for appropriate quotas and for the monitoring of the quota system.

The core of the MFA is found in Articles 3 and 4. These articles state that if a country felt that its market was being disrupted, it could issue a "call" which would require the exporting country to negotiate limits on its exports. If these negotiations did not resolve the problem within 60 days, the importing country could then set temporary quotas equal to the export level for the previous 12-month period.

Annex A of the MFA establishes the criteria by which a situation of market disruption will be judged. These criteria include product turnover, market share, profits, export performance, industry employment, volume of disruptive and other imports, production, utilization of capacity, productivity, and industry investment. The MFA states that textile and apparel market disruption is present when there is "a sharp and substantial increase or imminent increase of imports of particular products from particular sources (U.S. Department of State 1974) or when these products are offered at prices which are substantially below those prevailing for similar goods of comparable quality in the market of the importing country.

The second annex of the MFA, Annex B, is important to those producers interested in expanding the amount of their exports. This annex establishes a built-in growth mechanism which requires that limits set on exports in bilateral treaties must increase by at least 6% per year. The growth in restraints ensures that trade can develop and expand. The only exception to the 6% growth rate is when the situation of market disruption will clearly recur if the 6% rate is implemented. In that case, a lower but still positive growth rate may be decided on after consultation with the exporting country.

The other articles of the MFA provide for the monitoring of textile and apparel trade, an arbitration body, and further definition of the situations of market disruption.

The actual limits for trade are established in bilatral treaties, negotiated between individual member nations. These limits take the form of quota values, and can be enforced at the discretion of each member nation.

The basic provisions of the MFA have remained intact throughout all four versions of the agreement. However, the world market for textiles and apparel has changed radically in the last decade, and the MFA has attempted to adapt to these changes. One of the changes, the development of ramie, and the adaptation to this new development are discussed in the following sections.

INNOVATION FOR A LOOPHOLE

Since 1981, the main producers of non-MFA fiber garments have been Hong Kong, China, and Taiwain. The trend of using linen, jute, and especially ramie in apparel production to circumvent quotas first became noticeable in 1981.

With the exception of cotton, ramie is the primary vegetable fiber used in apparel production. Often known as China grass, it is one of the oldest known sources of fiber, and has been cultivated in eastern Asia since prehistoric times. The ramie plant, *Boehmeria nivea,* is a native of China, Japan, and Malaysia. In 1855, it was brought to the United States, where it was experimentally grown in Florida and other southern states.

The plant is a perennial, producing multiple stalks which average between six and eight feet tall. The plants usually grow best in rich, well drained, sandy soil, in a warm, moist climate. The crops are usually propagated with cuttings from underground stems. Rootstocks continually produce new stems, so as many as four crops may be harvested annually.

Ramie fibers are removed by decortication, a hand or mechanical process in which the bark and the adhering fiber are separated from the stalk and soaked in water allowing the fiber to be scraped from the bark. Spinning is difficult because of the ramie fiber's brittle quality and low elasticity, although it can be done on silk machines,[1] which is one possible reason for the Asian comparative advantage in processing ramie.

After the processing, ramie fiber is pure white in color, smooth, and moisture absorbent. Fabric made from ramie fiber gets stronger when wet, and does not lose its shape. In addition to apparel, ramie is used to make such products as fishing nets, filter cloth, and paper.

Because of the large labor requirements and the processing difficulties, western textile producers have not developed the ramie fiber as a substitute for cotton. The primary advantage to the use of such a fiber was its ability to circumvent the MFA quota guidelines. However, this was not an advantage to western producers, who did not have quotas to contend with.

The original Multifibre Arrangement placed limits on those textile poroducts where the majority of a product's value is made of cotton, wool, or man-made fibers. The purpose of these limits was to protect the domestic firms involved in the production of cotton, wool, and man-made fiber products. Article 12 of the document specifically states that

> for the purposes of the Arrangement, the expression "textiles" is limited to tops, yarns, piece goods, made-up articles, garments, and other textile manufactured products of cotton, wool, man-made fibers, or blends thereof, in which any or all of those fibers represent either the chief value of the fibers or 50% or more by weight of the product.

This article left a loophole through which a large amount of goods could be exported. Alert producers realized that if the majority of the value of the product was made of a "non-MFA" fiber such as ramie, jute, or linen, it could be exported without quota limitations.

Therefore, certain vegetable fibers, such as ramie, jute, and linen, which had seen little previous use were developed to slip through the loophole. Much of the development was done by the large Asian producers. They would blend the vegetable fibers to produce such textile products as sweaters, blouses, jackets, trousers, and luggage.

Table 1. U.S. Imports of Other Non-MFA Apparel (Figures in millions SYE*)

	1982	*1983*	*1984*	*1985*	*1986***
World	22.852	41.278	189.699	370.950	128.571
Hong Kong	15.225	25.486	19.306	176.332	29.508
Korea	4.685	9.200	27.964	90.798	39.564
China	1.862	4.451	29.946	47.657	42.656
Taiwan	1.079	2.142	24.317	34.682	8.355

Notes: * SYE = square yards equivalent.
** Data available through November 1986 only.
Source: U.S. Department of Commerce (January 1986).

Table 2. Market Share of Non-MFA Fiber Apparel

	1982	*1983*	*1984*	*1985*	*1986*
World	100.00	100.00	100.00	100.0	100.0
Hong Kong	62.37	58.62	48.13	46.82	22.95
Korea	12.49	13.77	14.74	25.80	30.77
China	8.79	11.80	15.79	12.98	33.18
Taiwan	3.58	3.99	12.82	9.20	6.50

Source: U.S. Department of Commerce (January 1986).

For example, they found that a "cotton" sweater could be made of a blend of 55% ramie and 45% cotton. Because ramie, an unregulatged fiber, made up the majority of the garment's value and weight, the sweater could be imported into the United States without being subject to any quota limitations. Unlimited amounts of these sweaters could be exported, and have been, in increasing numbers since 1981. This technique was applied to other types of apparel. Therefore, other goods whose chief value was not contributed by cotton, wool, or man-made fibers could be exported without limit as well.

In Table 1, data are presented which record the increasing amount of non-MFA apparel exports through 1986. The general pattern of non-MFA fiber exports shows a large overall increase in the export of such goods over the period 1982 through 1985. In 1986, however, Hong Kong, Korea, and Taiwan show a significant decrease in the level of their exports. The reason for this decrease will be discussed in the concluding section.

Table 2 displays the export patterns found in the non-MFA fiber apparel. From 1982 until 1985, Hong Kong was the largest exporter of these garments, as it garnered an average of 54% of the non-MFA fiber apparel market. Korea, China, and Taiwan lagged far behind in 1982, capturing 12.5, 8.8, and 3.6%

Table 3. ONMFA* Fiber Apparel Relative to MFA Fiber Apparel

	*MFA***	*ONMFA***	*ONMFA as Percentage of Total*
Hong Kong	824.886	176.332	21.38
Korea	672.251	90.798	13.51
China	421.741	47.657	11.30
Taiwan	958.554	34.682	3.62

Notes: * ONMFA = non-MFA other than silk.
** In millions of square yards equivalent (SYE).
Source: U.S. Department of Commerce (1986).

of the market, respectively. This ranking remained fairly constant until 1986. The only change was a gradual erosion of Hong Kong's market share, which was captured by the other three countries, led by Korea. In 1985, Hong Kong still maintained its market superiority with nearly half of the "non-MFA" fiber exports, while Korea had 25.8% of the market, China caputred nearly 13%, and Taiwain's share had grown to 9% of the market.

An examination of market statements, prepared by the Department of Commerce, provides more specific information on import penetration levels. These market statements are required to support contentions that exports have reached a significant level and are disrupting the domestic market. A specific example discusses the amount of ONMFA (non-MFA other than silk).

An analysis of Chinese exports showed that U.S. imports of category 845/846 from China were 511,631 dozen during the first half of 1986, compared to 287,132 dozen imported during the first half of 1985, a 78% increase. The ratio of imports to production in Category 345/445/446/645/646, cotton, wool and man-made fiber sweaters increased to 236% at the end of 1985. The share of this market, held by domestic manufacturers, dropped to 30% in 1985. The market statement also noted that at least 85% of the imports in category 845/846 entered the United States at landed duty paid values below the U.S. producers' prices for comparable sweaters in the first half of 1986 (U.S. Committee for the Implementation of Textile Agreements 1986).

The market statement for China and other data sources shows that garments made of non-MFA fiber blends comprise a significant portion of all apparel exported by the Asian countries. In Table 3, ratios of vegetable fiber apparel, excluding those made of silk blends, compared to those made of cotton, wool, and man-made fiber have been calculated. This table shows that many producers in Hong Kong, Korea, China, and Taiwan have been producing a significant level of garments not regulated by MFA quota guidelines, relative to their production of regulated apparel.

Another analysis of the non-MFA fiber apparel data shows that certain categories have even more significant levels of ONMFA exports than the

Table 4. ONMFA* Sweater Exports Relative to Total Sweater Exports

	Exports				*To Total Exports*	
	Cotton	*Wool*	*MMF*	*Total*	*ONMFA*	*Ratio of ONMFA*
Hong Kong	15.253	19.671	50.444	85.368	135.166	158.33
Korea	3.421	0.999	123.080	127.500	81.602	64.00
China	3.712	2.879	23.510	30.101	25.264	83.93
Taiwan	3.886	0.869	151.200	155.955	28.671	18.38

Note: * ONMFA = non-MFA other than silk.
Source: U.S. Department of Commerce (1986).

aggregate data would indicate. An example of this is found in the sweater categories.

Table 4 shows the number of cotton, wool and man-made fiber sweaters exported by the four primary producers, relative to those sweater exports made of non-MFA fibers such as ramie. From this table, one can see that a large amount of the sweaters exported to the United States in 1985 were produced using unregulated vegetable fiber blends. Hong Kong has concentrated on the production of such sweaters, to such a degree that it produces one-and-a-half times the amount of non-MFA fiber sweaters as cotton, wool, and man-made fiber sweaters combined. In Korea and China, vegetable blend sweaters constitute a large part of the sweaters produced and exported. Taiwan is the only major Asian exporter whose non-MFA fiber sweaters from only a small percentage of tis total sweater output.

While this is only one example of ramie and other vetable fiber blend exports, the data show that the growth of the exports of these garments was significant. This, added to the overall rising level of apparel and textile imports, greatly disturbed U.S. textile and apparel producers. Therefore, the renewal of a stronger MFA was of prime importance to them.

REACTION

During the most recent round of MFA renewal negotiations, the United States called for the restriction of ramie, jute, and linen to protect its domestic markets from increased levels of imports. American negotiators felt that the imports of the blended-fiber clothing disrupted the domestic market in cotton, wool, and man-made fibers in the same way that unrestricted imports made solely of cotton, wool, and man-made fibers would have. They argued that the primary purpose of fibers such as ramie was to compete with cotton apparel and circumvent the guidelines of the MFA. And so, the August 1986 version of the MFA (MFA IV) included an annex which limited the exports of

Table 5. Percentage of Sweater Quotas Filled (1983)

Country	*Percentage of Sweater Quotas Filled*
China	99
Hong Kong	114
Korea	98
Macau	131
Taiwan	97

Source: Stern (1985, p. 67).

vegetable fiber apparel which was in direct competition with those garments previously protected by the MFA.

The Multifibre Arrangement does not provide for negotiations when the domestic market is disrupted by "factors such as technological changes or changes in consumer preference which are instrumental in switches to directly competitive products made by the same industry or similar factors" (U.S. Committee for the Implementation of Textile Agreements 1986). However, world textile and apparel producers accepted the idea that the increased use of ramie did not priamrily happen because of a change in technology or because of an increase in consumer demand for ramie. Therefore, something had to be done to limit exports.

The most important change in the fourth MFA was an extension of the quota restriction to those goods which compete with cotton, wool, or man-made fibers. MFA IV specifically named vegetable fibers such as ramie, jute, and linen as fibers which compete with cotton. It further closed the loophole through which these products had been exported by extending limits on other fibers which might be developed in the future. If other fibers are developed to compete with cotton, wool, and man-made fibers, and subsequently make significant inroads on previously established markets, they will also be subject to the quota guidelines. In other words, textile and apparel exporting countries will no longer have the incentive to develop new fibers expressly to circumvent quota guidelines.

The new provisions found in the fourth MFA allowed further limitation of textile and apparel exports. Consequently, when new bilateral treaties on textiles were negotiated between the United States and Hong Kong, Korea, and Taiwan, quotas were placed on their exports of non-MFA fiber garments. At the end of 1986, the result of these quotas was clear—decreased exports of ramie, linen, and jute apparel (see Table 2).

In 1986, the effects of the newly-established limits on silk blends and other vegetable fiber products are seen. The limits established by the Bilateral Textile

Table 6. Restraints on Korean Apparel Exports

Category	Four-Month Restraint Limit (September 1-December 31, 1986)		
831-844 and 847-859	Aggregate Limit	=	7,173,833 SYE
835	9,000 Dozen or		371,700 SYE
836	24,667 Dozen or		1,117,451 SYE
840	38,333 Dozen or		555,828 SYE
845	769,375 Dozen or		28,313,000 SYE
846	284,047 Dozen or		10,452,929 SYE

Source: U.S. Committee for the Implementation of Textile Agreements (1987, p. 1520).

Agreement of November 21 and December 4, 1986 between the governments of the United States and the Republic of Korea for these fibers are listed in Table 6.

The limits on Group I and Group II categories—those categories regulated by the third MFA—were established for the 12-month period from January 1, 1986 through December 31, 1986. Limits were also established for those categories regulated by the fourth MFA, generally labeled as Group III and IV categories. However, these limits were prorated and only limited these categories from September 1, 1986 until December 31, 1986.

In order to gain some perspective on these restraints, one can compare these restraints to the previous year's unrestricted exports. In 1985, the exports in categories 845 and 846 totalled 81.602 million Square Yards Equivalent (SYE), as compared to the limit of 38.766 million SYE established for the final four months of 1986.

If the 4-month limit on these categories were extended over the full 1986 12-month period, the limit on these categories would be 116.297 million. In other words, the effect of the restraints seemed to be perceived rather than actual. Korea could have even increased its exports of non-MFA fiber sweaters by nearly 40% and still have been below the limit set by the new bilateral treaty.

To implement the quota guidelines of the fourth MFA, the bilateral agreement between the United States and Taiwan was amended to restrain exports of the non-MFA fiber garments. The agreement between the two countries set limits on silk blends and vegetable fiber blend apparel, categories 831-844 and 845-859, as a group, and individual limits on categories 845 and 970, produced in Taiwan and exported between January 1, 1987 and December 31, 1987.

It is interesting to note that the restraints negotiated by Taiwan in all categories are somewhat higher than those negotiated by Korea in corresponding categories. Historically, Korea has had a much higher level of

Table 7. Restraints on Taiwanese Apparel Exports

Category	*Twelve-Month Restraint Limit (January 1-December 31, 1987)*		
831-844 and 846-859	Aggregate Limit	=	9,155,087
845	845,120 Dozen	or	31,100,416
870	5,234,877 Pounds		

Source: U.S. Committee for the Implementation of Textile Agreements (1987, p. 1523).

exports than Taiwan, yet growth rates accorded to Taiwan are considerably higher than those allowed to Korea. It is conceivable that Taiwan could surpass Korea in terms of non-MFA fiber exports, a result contrary to the pattern established over the past several years.

In 1986, there was also a large change in the market pattern. Hong Kong was no longer the top producer of non-MFA fiber garments. Its share had fallen to 25% of the market. This decrease occurred because of the newly negotiated limits on ramie and other vegetable-fiber blend garments. Hong Kong, Korea, and Taiwan's newly negotiated treaties held ONMFA exports down. The holes in the market left by the newly negotiated textile treaties were filled by Chinese production. In 1986, China's market share nearly tripled from the 1985 figure of 12.98%.

The extended coverage of the fourth MFA has already helped to control the size of this loophole. However, by the time that guidelines were established, the level of exports of vegetable blend garments was already significant for the large Asian producers. The MFA requires that new quotas be based on a category's exports of the previous 12 months. Consequently, the quotas for vegetable fiber-blend apparel after August 1986 were not able totally to cut off the flow of these garments. However, the new quotas could regulate the *growth* of this type of export. Therefore, the fourth MFA cannot be said to have closed a loophole, merely to have controlled it.

Over the next several years, a more quantitative measure of the effect of the increased coverage by the Multifibre Arrangement can be developed and used. The International Trade Commission has studied the effect of restraints on the level of clothing and textile imports. It related that

> by analyzing the degree to which restraint limits on a certain product have been filled and the volume of imports of the product that were not subject to restraints ... it is possible to illustrate whether MFA restraints were the major factor in controlling imports of a particular product.

Table 8. Selected Imports and Percentage of Quota Filled by Category

	*Total Imports (1,000 Doz.)**		*Percentage of Quota Filled*	
Category	*1980*	*1983*	*1980*	*1983*
Cotton broadwoven fabric	713,896	1,067,200	43.5	50.9
Man-made broadwoven fabric	306,929	603,834	36.1	84.7
Undergarments	12,665	13,063	67.2	70.6
Women's coats**	4,005	5,444	60.8	73.6
Gloves	15,596	19,476	63.8	75.2
Sweaters	12,554	14,564	89.8	65.3
Women's knit shirts	22,066	26,456	56.0	57.4
Women's woven shirts	10,661	15,175	86.1	90.3

Notes: * Cotton and man-made fabric is listed as 1,000 square yards; Gloves are listed as 1,000 pairs.
** Women's coats include infant's and girl's coats.

Source: Stern (1985, pp. 57-71).

Therefore, if quotas were filled, one can assume that more trade would have taken place in the absence of restrictions. Also, if the percentage used of the quota category has increased, while the amount of imports allowed under those quotas has also increased, one can assume that trade is increasing and might increase more if there were no restrictions.

An example of this type of analysis is shown in Table 8. It presents the amount of imports under MFA II (1980) and those under MFA III (1983). It also shows how much of each quota category has been used under MFA II and III.

Tables 5 and 8 show that quotas probably restrained imports in the past. Even though quota limits were increased in the third MFA, there is also an increase in the amount of quota categories filled from 1980 to 1983. This would indicate that textile and apparel trade has been restricted by the MFA. A similar type of analysis could be done on the levels of ramie exports, and the relevant quotas that were utilized by Asian producers. This would help to show how successful the new restraints were in limiting this type of export, and thus closing the loophole. It would also show whether there was still an incentive for the use of these vegetable-fiber blend apparel.

If success means the closing of the ramie loophole, in order to remove a source of competition for the cotton, wool, and man-made fiber apparel markets, then these provisions have not achieved their goal. The import of this type of garment is still allowed under the new provisions. In fact, the limits placed on these garments are even higher than the previous year's imports. Under the conditions of the MFA, these limits must increase by 6% per year. Therefore, the amount of vegetable fiber imports could legally increase over the significant 1985 levels.

However, if the definition of success involves controlling the growth of these imports, then the new guidelines have been successful. There was a substantial decrease in the level of imports of the vegetable-fiber blend apparel after the new provision was included in the fourth MFA. Therefore, one can say that the size of the ramie loophole of the MFA has been controlled but not closed.

NOTE

1. For more information on ramie, see *Encyclopedia Britannica* (1985 ed.), s.v. "Ramie" and *Encyclopedia Americana* (1985 ed.), s.v. "Ramie."

REFERENCES

American Textile Manufacturers Institute. (1986). *Textile and Apparel Imports: A National Concern.* Washington, DC: American Textile Manufacturers Institute.

Brockman, B.A. (1987). "Ramie: An Opening and Controlling of a Loophole in the Multifiber Arrangement." Master's Thesis, Rutgers University.

Curzon, G. et al. (1981). *MFA Forever? The Future of the Arrangement for Trade in Textiles.* Thames Essay no. 23. London: Trade Policy Research Center.

Gray, H.P. (1985). *Free Trade or Protection?* New York: St. Martin's Press.

Howell, T. et al. (1986). *The Textile and Apparel Trade Crisis.* Washington, DC: The Fiber, Fabric and Apparel Coalition for Trade.

Stern, P., Chairwoman, International Trade Commission. (1985). *The Multifiber Arrangement–Report on Investigation No. 332-189 of the Tariff Act of 1930.* USITC Publication no. 1693. Washington, DC: U.S. International Trade Commission.

U.S. Committee for the Implementation of Textile Agreements. (1986). "Requesting Public Comment on Bilateral Textile Consultations with the Government of the People's Republic of China to Review Trade in Category 845/846." *Federal Register* 51, no. 193 (October 6), p. 35547.

———. (1987). "Establishment of Import Restraint Limits for Certain Cotton, Wool and Man-made Fiber, Silk Blends and Other Vegetable Fiber Textiles and Textile Products from the Republic of Korea." *Federal Register* 52, no. 9 (January 14), p. 1520.

U.S. Department of Commerce, International Trade Administration, Office of Textiles. (1986). *Major Shippers of Cotton, Wool and Man-made Fibers, Textiles and Apparel* (January).

U.S. Department of State. (1974). "Arrangement Regarding International Trade in Textiles." *United States Treaties and Other International Agreements* (January 1), p. 1018.